Film Adaptation

Rutgers Depth of Field Series

Richard Abel, ed., Silent Film

John Belton, ed., Movies and Mass Culture

Matthew Bernstein, ed., Controlling Hollywood: Censorship and Regulation in the Studio Era

John Thornton Caldwell, ed., Electronic Media and Technoculture

Peter Lehman, ed., Defining Cinema

James Naremore, ed., Film Adaptation

Valerie Smith, ed., Representing Blackness: Issues in Film and Video

Janet Staiger, ed., The Studio System

Linda Williams, ed., Viewing Positions: Ways of Seeing Film

Edited and with an introduction by
James Naremore

Film Adaptation

Rutgers
University
Press

New Brunswick,
New Jersey

Library of Congress Cataloging-in-Publication Data

Naremore, James.
    Film adaptation / edited and with an introduction by James Naremore.
      p.   cm. — (Rutgers depth of field series)
    Includes bibliographical references and index.
    ISBN 0-8135-2813-5 (cloth : alk. paper) — ISBN 0-8135-2814-3 (pbk. : alk. paper)
    1. Film adaptations.   2. Motion pictures and literature.   I. Title.   II. Series.
PN1997.85 .N27 2000
791.43′6 21—dc21   99-045923
                                                        CIP

British Cataloging-in-Publication Data for this book is available from the British Library

Manufactured in the United States of America.

For James L. Naremore, Amy Rubin, and their sons, Alexander and Patrick

Acknowledgments

For their helpful suggestions I thank Christopher Anderson, Dudley Andrew, Anton Kaes, Barbara Klinger, Kathleen McHugh, and Phillip Rosen. For their patience and editorial guidance I am grateful to Charles and Mirella Affron, Robert Lyons, and Leslie Mitchner. Anne Hegeman and Cyd Westmoreland provided expert help with production of this volume.

Contents

Film Adaptation

James Naremore

Introduction: Film and the Reign of Adaptation

The title of my introduction alludes to a relatively little-known essay by French film theorist André Bazin—"Adaptation, or the Cinema as Digest"—which was written in 1948 but translated into English only a few years ago for Burt Cardullo's useful anthology, *Bazin at Work*. This essay is reprinted as the first chapter of the following collection, and I especially recommend it to American readers, who tend to think of Bazin almost exclusively as an eloquent proponent of a certain kind of humanist realism in the cinema. Without denying the importance of Bazin's writings on the phenomenology of the photographic image and the realistic uses of the camera, we need to remember that an entire volume of the French edition of his posthumously collected criticism, published in four volumes under the single title *What Is Cinema?*, was devoted to the relationship between film and the other media. The essay on adaptation is one of his most intriguing statements on behalf of what he called "mixed cinema," and it enables us to see him in a new light, as someone who has a good deal to contribute to contemporary cultural studies.

I shall return to Bazin at the end of my introduction, but first I want to comment on some of the reasons why his essay on adaptation may have been neglected, and why the very subject of adaptation has constituted one of the most jejune areas of scholarly writing about the cinema. One of the major reasons, as Robert B. Ray suggests in this volume, is institutional: a great many film programs in the academy are attached to literature departments, where the theme of adaptation is often used as a way of teaching celebrated literature by another means. Thus we immediately think of the film *Mrs. Dalloway* (1998) or even of the more freely derivative *Orlando* (1993) as adaptations, but not of *The Set Up* (1949, based on a narrative poem), *Batman* (1989, based on a comic book), *His Girl Friday* (1940, based on a play), *Mission Impossible* (1996, based on a television series), or *Twelve Monkeys* (1995, based on an art film). Even within the realm of the novel, the range of things usually discussed under the rubric of adaptation is quite narrow. Twentieth-Century Fox's 1940 production of *The Grapes of Wrath* is always seen in relation to John Steinbeck, but the same studio's 1944 production of *Laura* is almost never viewed as an adaptation of Vera Casparay (even though the film's main title reads *"Laura*, by Vera Casparay")—probably because Casparay's postproletarian, protofeminist thriller has long been out of print and has barely been read by English teachers.

Unfortunately, most discussions of adaptation in film can be summarized by a *New Yorker* cartoon that Alfred Hitchcock once described to François Truffaut: two goats are eating a pile of film cans, and one goat says to the other, "Personally, I liked the book better." Even when academic writing on the topic is not directly concerned with a given film's artistic adequacy or fidelity to a beloved source, it tends to be narrow in range, inherently respectful of the "precursor text," and constitutive of a series of binary oppositions that poststructuralist theory has taught us to deconstruct: literature versus cinema, high culture versus mass culture, original versus copy. Such oppositions are themselves the products of the submerged common sense of the average English department, which is composed of a mixture of Kantian aesthetics and Arnoldian ideas about society.

When I use the term *Arnoldian* I am chiefly referring to Matthew Arnold's *Culture and Anarchy* (1869), which argues that culture is synonymous with great works of art and that the inherited cultural tradition of the Judeo-Christian world, embodied in "the best that has been thought and said," can have a civilizing influence, transcending class tensions and leading to a more humane society. The study of English literature in American universities owes its very existence to this argument, which was more subtly elaborated by such later figures as T. S. Eliot and F. R. Leavis; as a result, English professors have traditionally been suspicious of mass-produced narratives from Hollywood, which seem to threaten or debase the values of both "organic" popular culture and high literary culture. When I use the term *Kantian* I am speaking of a slightly older, more complex, mode of idealist philosophy that emerged toward the end of the eighteenth century in Europe and that we commonly associate not only with Immanuel Kant, but also with Georg Hegel, Johann von Schiller, and Samuel Taylor Coleridge. Beginning in the mid–nineteenth century and continuing throughout the period of high literary modernism, all art in the European world was theorized under what might be roughly described as a Kantian set of assumptions; that is, both the making and the appreciation of art were conceived as specialized, autonomous, and transcendent activities having chiefly to do with media-specific form.[1] A locus classicus of such reasoning (perhaps even a parody of it) is the fifth chapter of James Joyce's *Portrait of the Artist as a Young Man* (1914), in which Stephen Dedalus tells us that art differs from pornography because it does not elicit desire, from propaganda because it does not teach or move to political action, and from market goods because it has no entertainment value or practical utility. The proper effect of art, Dedalus says, is the "luminous silent stasis of aesthetic pleasure," which can be achieved only through the contemplation of formal or part-to-whole relationships.

Never mind that Joyce's own novel problematized such ideas and that his next novel, *Ulysses*, pushed aestheticism far beyond its sustainable limits. Some variation of aesthetic formalism has nonetheless continued to underpin every modern discipline that claims to be dealing with art. Consider, for example, David Bordwell and Kristin Thompson's excellent college textbook, *Film Art*, which has long been used in introductory film study courses throughout the United States. Bordwell and Thompson are quite different from the literary dandies and philosophical idealists of the late nineteenth or early twentieth century; their approach is practical and undogmatic, grounded in empirical evidence from an exceptionally wide range of films, and their chief theoretical influences are contemporary narratology and the quasi-scientific work of the Russian formalists. Even so, they devote themselves to teaching us how to recognize cinema-specific codes and how to appreciate part-whole relationships within individual movies.

I hasten to confess that I myself am something of an aesthete, and I strongly believe that no proper criticism of art can ignore questions of form. I am also a former English major, and I do not think that we can simply dismiss Matthew Arnold or that we should stop reading the Great Books and seeing films based on them. It is nevertheless important to understand that both the Arnoldian defense of high culture and the Kantian aesthetic movement were historically situated ideologies, generated largely in response to industrial capitalism and mechanical reproduction. Their culminating or extreme instance, and in one sense their crisis, was the period immediately before and after World War II, when Hollywood was fully rationalized by the studio system, when New Criticism was in the ascendancy in American universities, and when modernist intellectuals, including such otherwise quite different theorists as Theodor Adorno and Clement Greenberg, enunciated an idea of "authentic" art in defense against the culture industries. Greenberg's famous essay "Avant- Garde and Kitsch," for example, describes the essential project of modernism as follows: "Content is to be dissolved so completely into form that the work of art or literature cannot be reduced in whole or in part to anything not itself."[2]

Greenberg was writing in 1939, at a moment of trauma for Popular-Front intellectuals; when Fascism had overtaken Europe; when modern art, which had already been assimilated into bourgeois culture, was being assailed from both the left and the right for its decadence and elitism; and when aestheticism seemed caught in a struggle to survive the two reigning forms of materialist utopia—capitalism and Stalinism.

For Greenberg, the only refuge of "authentic" art lay in the realm of the "merely artistic," or in the radically formal exploration of artistic media. The artistic imitation of the natural or social world, he argued, needed to be replaced by the study of "the disciplines and processes of art and literature themselves" (p. 23). As Juan A. Suarez has recently observed in a fine commentary on Greenberg, the result of this policy was "an exacerbation of formalism and a sort of art in exile from the values of audiences; that is, an art which seeks to remain untainted by reigning mercantilism and instrumental rationality."[3]

The capitalist movie industry, especially in Hollywood, has always operated by a dialectically opposite logic. It recognized from the beginning that it could gain a sort of legitimacy among middle-class viewers by reproducing facsimiles of more respectable art or by adapting literature to another medium. Film scholars William Uricchio and Roberta E. Peterson have demonstrated that as early as 1908, at the height of the nickelodeon boom and partly in response to the Reform Movement in American politics, the Vitagraph film company in New York engaged in an aggressive, concentrated effort to appeal to the middle class by making one-reel adaptations of Shakespeare and Dante.[4] At virtually the same moment, Parisian financiers established the *Societé de Film d'Art*, which made quite profitable feature-length films based on the dramas of Rostand and Sardou, as well as silent versions of Dickens's *Oliver Twist* and Goethe's *The Sorrows of Young Werther*. (Quite similar versions of art cinema sprang up elsewhere—for example, in Brazil, where the works of novelist José de Alencar were adapted into numerous short films.) Historian David Cook remarks, "For a while it seemed as if everything written, sung, or danced (for photographed ballet and opera formed a large part of the film d'art corpus) in Western Europe between 1900 and the Renaissance, and Greek tragedy as well, found its way into one of these stage-bound and pretentious productions."[5]

Uncinematic as the *films d'art* may seem today, they were among the first feature films, and their drive for respectability pointed toward the development of the star system, the picture palace, and in one sense Hollywood itself. Equally important were the hugely successful Italian historical pictures of the same period, especially Enrico Guazzoni's *Quo Vadis* (1912), a nine-reel spectacular based on a novel by Nobel laureate Henryk Sienkiewicz, which established the market for "blockbuster" movies such as *Birth of a Nation* (also an adaptation).

The advent of the talkies and the Fordist organization of the major film studios produced a great appetite for literature among Hollywood moguls, who provided a source of major income, if not artistic satisfaction, for every important playwright and author in the United States, including Eugene O'Neill, Scott Fitzgerald, John Dos Passos, and William Faulkner. But here we encounter a significant historical irony. At the same time that the movies, the legitimate theater, and the book-publishing industry were growing closer together, sophisticated art in general was in active rebellion against bourgeois culture and was intentionally producing work that could not be easily assimilated into the mainstream. Modernism was not only willfully difficult and formally "experimental"; it was also sexually scandalous, critical of progress, and offensive to the Babbitts and the Bovarys who supposedly made up the viewing audience. Thus, in the heyday of the classic studio system, when Hollywood was absorbing every kind of artistic talent and establishing itself as the very emblem of modernity, the Production Code Administration began to engage in what Richard Maltby, another writer represented in this book, calls "a conscious ideological project" aimed at preventing what one of its leaders described as "the prevalent type of book and play" from becoming "the prevalent type of movie." This did not mean that literature was no longer adapted. Classic Hollywood still wanted to acquire every sort of cultural capital (in the 1940s, Twentieth-Century Fox even proposed John Ford as the possible director of an adaptation of *Ulysses*), but it was especially interested in source material that could easily be transformed into an aesthetically and morally conservative form of entertainment. Even after the qualified relaxation of censorship restrictions in the 1950s, the most adaptable sources for movies were the "readerly" texts of the nineteenth century rather than the "writerly" texts of high modernism, which were explicitly designed to resist being "reduced" to anything not themselves.

Meanwhile, in still another historical irony, film was being regarded in some quarters as the quintessentially modernist medium. Some of the most talented movie directors in the first half of the century approached the problem of literary adaptation in a spirit of intense aestheticism, as did Stroheim in his version of *Greed* or Eisenstein in his abortive attempt to film *An American Tragedy*. Along similar lines, high modernist fiction and the international art cinema strongly influenced one another—as can be seen in John Dos Passos's *USA* trilogy, which Dos Passos began shortly after meeting Eisenstein and reading the Soviet theories of montage. Eventually the cinema was theorized as the dominant "way of seeing" in the modern world and as a condition toward which most of the visual and literary arts aspired. Cultural critic Arnold Hauser once placed the whole of twentieth-century art, including such things as Cubist paintings and poems like *The Waste Land*, under the evocative rubric of "the film age." In an influential book written in the 1950s, French critic Claude-Edmonde Magny proposed that the period between the two world wars had been "the age of the American novel" and that the leading American writers, especially Hemingway and Faulkner, had been guided by a "film aesthetic."[6] More recently, American critics Alan Spiegel and Keith Cohen have each written books arguing that modernist literature as a whole—especially the writings of Flaubert,

Proust, James, Conrad, Joyce, and Woolf—is fundamentally "cinematic" in its form.[7]

It was not until 1957, however, that the movies seemed to have "matured" enough to inspire the first full-scale academic analysis of film adaptation in America: George Bluestone's *Novels into Film: The Metamorphosis of Fiction into Cinema* (Johns Hopkins University Press). In this book Bluestone argues that certain movies (his examples are all from Hollywood, including *The Informer, Wuthering Heights,* and *The Grapes of Wrath*) do not debase their literary sources; instead, they "metamorphose" novels into another medium that has its own formal or narratological possibilities. Such an argument seems hardly likely to provoke controversy; its difficulty, at least insofar as Bluestone's general aim of giving movies artistic respectability is concerned, is not so much that it leads to the wrong conclusions, but that it takes place on the grounds of high modernist aestheticism. Given the modernist ideology of art, film cannot acquire true cultural capital unless it first theorizes a media-specific form. Bluestone recognizes this fact, and as a result he bases his entire book on the notion that "the end products of novel and film represent different aesthetic genera, as different from each other as ballet is from architecture" (p. 5). At the same time, his subject matter and entire approach tend to confirm the intellectual priority and formal superiority of canonical novels, which provide the films he discusses with their sources and with a standard of value against which their success or failure is measured.

Bluestone does not seem to realize that when we start from the modernist position, the only way to avoid making film seem belated, middlebrow, or culturally inferior is to devalue straightforward, high-cultural adaptation altogether. And indeed, that is exactly what happened in Europe at the very moment when Bluestone's book was published. The central importance of the French New Wave in the history of worldwide taste and opinion was that it was able to break with traditional movie criticism and establish a truly modernist (as well as somewhat Arnoldian) film criticism by launching an attack on what Truffaut called a "Tradition of Quality," made up of respectable literary adaptations. One of the best-kept secrets of the New Wave filmmakers was that many of their own films were based on books; the sources they chose, however, were often lowbrow, and when they adapted "serious" works or wrote essays about film adaptations (such as Bazin's famous essay on *Diary of a Country Priest*), they made sure that the auteur would seem more important than the author.

The French auteurists never treated filmmaking as a "seventh art" or as a separate but equal member of the cultural pantheon. Instead they adopted Alexandre Astruc's idea of the "camera stylo" and spoke of film as a language and the film director as a kind of writer, motivated by a desire for personal expression, wielding a lens instead of a pen. They elevated the cinematic mise-en-scène (the director's treatment of camera movement, space, decor, and acting) to a greater importance than the scenario; and, partly as a result of the critical revolution they helped to inspire, it is now commonplace for film historians to speak of directorial masterpieces or canonical works of cinema—even from Hollywood—that revise and far surpass their relatively minor written sources. (My own personal list of such pictures would include Murnau's *Sunrise*, Welles's *The Magnificent Ambersons*, Ophuls's *Letter from an Unknown Woman*, Ford's *The Man Who Shot Liberty Valance*, and Hitchcock's *Psycho*.) By the same token, we can easily speak of Hollywood adaptations that, despite their great intrinsic interest, do not and probably could not achieve the importance of their literary forebears (Huston's *The Maltese Falcon*, Minnelli's *Madame Bovary*, Kubrick's *Lolita*) or of Hollywood "originals" that could never be so perfect as plays or novels (Keaton's *Sherlock, Jr.*, Lubitsch and Raphaelson's *Trouble in Paradise*, Welles and Mankiewicz's *Citizen Kane*, Peckinpah's *The Wild Bunch*, Polanski and Towne's *Chinatown*, and many others).

It is also commonplace to observe that some of the best movie directors deliberately avoid adaptations of great literature in order to foreground their own artistry. The practice is enshrined during Hitchcock's interview with Truffaut, in which Hitchcock claims that the approach he usually takes to sources is to "read a story only once, and if I like the basic idea, I just forget about the book and start to create cinema."[8] He says that he would never adapt *Crime and Punishment*, in part because he thinks that feature films are more like short stories than like novels, and in part because "in Dostoyevsky's novel there are many, many words and all of them have a function" (p. 72). Truffaut quickly agrees, voicing one of the axioms of modernist aesthetics: "That's right. Theoretically, a masterpiece is something that has already found its perfection of form, its definitive form" (p. 72). Hitchcock's credits lend support to these conclusions, although it should be noted that there are exceptions to the rule: *The 39 Steps* (based on a novel by John Buchan), *Sabotage* (based on a novel by Joseph Conrad), and *The Birds* (based on a short story by Daphne DuMaurier) are quite free adaptations, but the half-hour television film, "Lamb to the Slaughter," which is one of Hitchcock's most perfect achievements, is a literal adaptation of a Roald Dahl short story, scripted by Dahl himself.

Since the 1960s, academic writing on adaptation has gained considerable sophistication by making use of important theoretical writings on both literature and film, including the structuralist and poststructuralist poetics of Roland Barthes, the narratology of Gérard Genette, and the neoformalism of Bordwell and Thompson.[9] In general, however, it continues to waver back and forth between the two approaches exemplified by Bluestone and the auteurists. The Bluestone approach relies on an implicit metaphor of translation, which governs all investigations of how codes move across sign systems. Writing in this category usually deals with the concept of literary versus cinematic form, and it pays close attention to the problem of textual fidelity in order to identify the specific formal capabilities of the media. By contrast, the auteurist approach relies on a metaphor of performance. It, too, involves questions of textual fidelity, but it emphasizes difference rather than similarity, individual styles rather than formal systems. The two approaches are mirrored in the practice of certain filmmakers, as can be seen in Jonathan Rosenbaum's discussion of two quite different forms of literary adaptation later in this volume; and both give valid answers to the kinds of questions they ask, although I myself have always preferred the approach of the auteurists because they are less reverent toward literature and more apt to consider such things as audiences, historical situations, and cultural politics.

The problem with most writing about adaptation as translation is that it tends to valorize the literary canon and essentialize the nature of cinema. Consider Seymour Chatman's "What Novels Can Do That Film Can't (and Vice Versa)," first published in *Critical Inquiry* in 1981, a theoretically informed essay that offers an intelligent discussion of Jean Renoir's 1936 adaptation of Guy de Maupassant's *Une Partie de campagne*, showing how the same narrative is represented in different media.[10] Chatman is ostensibly unconcerned with questions of value, but his argument is nevertheless based on a highly regarded literary text. He makes some interesting observations about the ways description and point of view are treated respectively in realist fiction and narrative cinema, but he also makes dubious generalizations about the nature of film. (In the last analysis, film is best defined in material terms, as nothing more nor less than a recording instrument, capable of representing virtually the whole range of signifying practices.) Ultimately, he demonstrates less about what conventional novels can do that narrative films cannot than we could learn by reading certain books and by broadening the textual milieu we examine. For example, Charles Willeford's *Pick-up*, a pulp fiction paperback of the 1950s, would present more difficulty for a filmmaker than Joyce's *Finnegans Wake* (which has, in fact, been turned into a movie), for the simple reason that a crucially important word describing the central character does not appear until the final sentence. I refrain from quoting the word here and simply recommend this intriguing book to my readers.

Notice, furthermore, that most writing on adaptation as translation, even when it assumes a tone of quasi-scientific objectivity, betrays certain unexamined ideological concerns because it deals of necessity with sexually charged materials and cannot avoid a gendered language associated with the notion of "fidelity." George Bluestone tries to defend certain movies against the accusation that they "violate" their sources. Seymour Chatman spends almost half of his essay on the two versions of *Une Partie de campagne* analyzing the way Renoir adapts a description of a flirtatious young woman on a swing. ("She was a pretty girl of about eighteen," Maupaussant writes, and Chatman comments at length on the problem of how to convey the tone of "about eighteen" in cinematic imagery.) In a *New York Times* essay that is far less systematic and more judgmental than Chatman's, "What Only Words, Not Film, Can Portray," literary critic Cynthia Ozick derides Jane Campion's 1997 adaptation of *A Portrait of a Lady*, saying it "perverts" Henry James, replacing his "gossamer vibrations of the interior life" and "philosophy of the soul" with "crudity," "self-oriented eroticism," and "voluptuous gazing."[11] Ozick's commentary is especially intriguing because it reverses the standard imagery of modernist aestheticism, so that mass culture seems less like an ignorant shop girl and more like a crude or lascivious male, bent on despoiling a loved object. I am reminded of the first sentence of Fredric Jameson's *Signatures of the Visible*, a book about movies by the most distinguished contemporary proponent of the modernist tradition: "The visual is *essentially* pornographic," Jameson declares, as if the very act of translating words into photographic images involves a move toward something bodily and nasty.[12]

The most recent book on adaptation as translation, Brian McFarlaine's *Novel to Film* (1996), shows an awareness of at least some of the problems I have been describing. It begins with an attack on "fidelity criticism" and devotes a chapter each to MGM's *Random Harvest*, which is based on a best-seller, and Martin Scorsese's remake of *Cape Fear*, which is based at least secondhand on a pulp novel. It also contains some brief but useful discussion of what McFarlaine describes as "extra-novelistic influences" and "other elements of intertextuality." And yet McFarlaine himself is obsessively concerned with problems of textual fidelity—and necessarily so, because the major purpose of his book is to demonstrate how the "cardinal features" of narrative, most of them exemplified by canonical, nineteenth-century novels from British and American authors, can be transposed intact to movies. As he puts it, he wants to set up "procedures for distinguishing between that which can be transferred from one medium to another (essentially, narrative) and that which, being dependent on different signifying systems, cannot be transferred (essentially, enunciation)."[13] Here as elsewhere, the study of adaptation stops at the water's edge, as if it were hesitant to move beyond literary formalism and ask more interesting questions.

Writing about adaptation ought to provide a more flexible, animating discourse in film studies, if only because it can address such a wide variety of things. As Dudley Andrew pointed out in 1984 in a seminal essay that is reprinted in this volume, every representational film (and, I would add, every representational artifact) can be regarded as an adaptation—hence the very word *representation*. Andrew estimates that more than half of all commercial movies derive from novels. In his chapter in this volume, Robert B. Ray points out that Andrew's figure may be high, but it is not wildly exaggerated; in fact, in 1985 *The New York Times* said that one in fifty novels published in this country were optioned by Hollywood.[14] If we extend the idea of adaptation beyond novels, the number of "derivative" films is quite large. *Variety* recently published statistics indicating that 20 percent of the movies produced in 1997 had books as their sources. (The list of authors is intriguing; it includes John Grisham, Stephen King, Michael Crichton, Howard Stern, James Ellroy, and Leo Tolstoy.) Another 20 percent were derived from plays, sequels, remakes, television shows, and magazine or newspaper articles. This means that only about half of the pictures seen by the public that year originated from scripts.[15]

Academics have limited the issues at stake, not only by focusing largely on novels, but also by insisting on what Andrew calls the "cultural status" of a prior model. "In the case of those texts explicitly termed 'adaptations,'" Andrew writes, "the cultural model which the cinema represents is already treasured as a representation in another sign system." One could hardly expect to find a better definition of what adaptation means to most of the scholars who have published books and essays on the topic. But as long as we continue to accept this definition, as Andrew himself does, we need to ask: Treasured by whom? The question would reveal that adaptation study in the limited academic sense is only partly about enunciative techniques or the "cardinal features" of narrative; it is also about the interpretation of canonical literature in more or less traditional fashion. In other words, it is a system of critical writing that tends to reproduce a bourgeois mode of reception.

To his credit, Andrew argues, "It is time for adaptation stud[y] to take a sociological turn." And yet, because he remains committed to the notion of the "already treasured," the kind of things he recommends for us to discuss remain conventionally literary—for example, the changing history of naturalism in Zola, Gorky, and Renoir. I would suggest that what we need instead is a broader definition of adaptation and a sociology that takes into account the commercial apparatus, the audience, and the academic culture industry. In selecting the essays that form the chapters of this anthology, therefore, I have tried to move the discussion of adaptation slightly away from the Great-Novels-Into-Great-Films theme, and I've selected writings that give somewhat less attention to formal than to economic, cultural, and political issues. Although I have chosen to reprint some unusually significant essays on these topics, most of the contributions appear here for the first time, and their authors attempt to chart relatively new territory.

The volume is divided into two parts, the first dealing with the theory of adaptation and the second with case studies. The theorists in the first section have in common a discontent with or skepticism about the usual writings on adaptation, and in different ways they suggest how a moribund field might be brought to life. The critics in the second section provide informative illustrations of how to write about specific adaptations, in the process raising theoretical issues of their own. Most of the writers in this section are interested in movies based on novels, and in some cases they deal with the usual Anglo-American literary suspects, including Austen and Dickens; the question of cinema-specific form, however, is not one of their major concerns, and as a group they discuss a fairly broad range of possible sources. Thus, in addition to the pieces on film versions of canonical novels, the reader will find chapters about Shakespearian films, about a Japanese adaptation of a novel by Ed McBain, about an adaptation of William Burrough's unclassifiable *Naked Lunch*, and about a Brazilian movie derived from a sixteenth-century German travel narrative.

Given enough space, I would have extended the discussion even more broadly. I especially regret the absence of any writings about made-for-television adaptations or about the relation between television and theatrical film. For the past twenty-five years, Mobil's *Masterpiece Theater* has been the major producer of filmed adaptations of "respectable" literature in America, reaching audiences as large as Hollywood in its heyday and probably helping to identify a niche market for the successful Merchant-Ivory adaptations of E. M. Forster novels that have played in movie theaters. Public television is not alone in producing such material. The Arts and Entertainment cable network recently aired a miniseries based on C. S. Forester's *Horatio Hornblower*, the USA network has produced *Moby-Dick*, and Bravo has aired *The Count of Monte Cristo*. Turner Network Television has announced that during the 1999–2000 season it will produce adaptations of *Animal Farm*, *A Christmas Carol*, *David Copperfield*, and *Don Quixote*. "We're taking a big risk," network president Brad Siegel told a reporter; but he seemed optimistic because, as he said, "the audience we're trying to attract is looking for that kind of quality programming."[16] (As the list of programs suggests, nineteenth-century classics have always been the best sources for "prestige" movies on television, just as they have always been for the movies.)

Whatever the limitations of its scope, I hope this book will at least indicate the kind of work that might be done with regard to film adaptation in its most general sense. In my view, the anthology as a whole can be regarded as a call for further research and writing on several topics. For example, we need to ask why certain canonical books have been of interest to Hollywood in specific periods, and we need more elaborate investigations into the historical relation between movies and book publishing. We also need to ask what conditions of the marketplace govern the desire for textual fidelity. (An audience survey conducted by David Selznick in the 1940s determined that very few people had read

Jane Eyre and that the movie based on the novel did not need to be especially faithful to the novel; on the other hand, Selznick was a fanatic about maintaining textual fidelity in *Gone With the Wind* and *Rebecca,* because he knew that a substantial part of the audience had read Margaret Mitchell's and Daphne DuMaurier's best-selling books.[17]) In addition, we need more writing about adaptation of "low" or pop-cultural texts, and we need to think about how certain texts are adapted cross-culturally—as Matthew Bernstein has done for his chapter in this volume on the adaptation of an Ed McBain novel in Japan. Equally important, we need writings that address the uses of canonical literature by specific filmmakers. Some directors have been intent on faithfully illustrating their sources, whereas others have been motivated by a desire to interrogate or "read" the prior text. A good example of the latter tendency was Rainer Werner Fassbinder, who once argued, "Cinematic transformation of a literary work should never assume that its purpose is simply the maximal realization of the images that literature evokes in the minds of its readers." Such an assumption is "preposterous," Fassbinder wrote, because there are so many different readers with different fantasies. His own aim, as he described it in relation to adaptations such as *Berlin Alexanderplatz, Effi Brest,* and *Querelle,* was to avoid a "composite fantasy" and to engage in what he called "an unequivocal and single-minded questioning of the piece of literature and its language."[18] Along similar lines, many directors have used canonical literature for politically or culturally resistant purposes, sometimes filming it more or less faithfully, and sometimes radically changing it. For a striking case in point, see Darlene J. Sadlier's commentary on Nelson Pereira dos Santos in the second part of this anthology.

In addition to expanding the kinds of texts we take into account, we need to augment the metaphors of translation and performance with the metaphor of intertextuality, or with what M. M. Bakhtin called "dialogics." This approach is adumbrated by several of the writers collected here—especially by Guerric DeBona and Gilberto Perez, who remind us that literary adaptations also draw on visual and theatrical sources, and by Darlene J. Sadlier, who shows us how a single film can weave together multiple prior texts. The specifically Bakhtinian notion of dialogics, however, is elaborated by Robert Stam, who emphasizes "the infinite and open-ended possibilities generated by all the discursive practices of a culture" and the "entire matrix of communicative utterances within which the artistic text is situated." Stam takes us beyond formalism and beyond simple attempts to compare "originals" with "transformations." If we followed his advice, adaptation study would be brought more into line with both contemporary theory and contemporary filmmaking.

We now live in a media-saturated environment dense with cross-references and filled with borrowings from movies, books, and every other form of representation. Books can become movies, but movies themselves can also become novels, published screenplays, Broadway musicals, television shows, remakes, and so on.[19] As one minor example of a recent film that reflects this protean and highly allusive environment, consider Richard Kwieniowski's *Love and Death on Long Island* (1998), which tells the story of a sheltered British novelist who goes to see an E. M. Forster adaptation at the local cineplex and wanders by mistake into *Hot Pants College II*. The novelist develops a crush on a young actor he sees on the screen, who reminds him of Henry Wallis's painting of the death of Chatterton in the Tate Gallery. I shall not describe the plot any further, except to note that Kwieniowski's film is based on a novel by Gilbert Adair and that the novel is itself a rewriting of Mann's *Death in Venice* and Nabokov's *Lolita*. The film complicates things still more by introducing full-scale parodies of Hollywood B movies and television sitcoms. It brings high culture and low culture, the "literary" and the "cinematic," into ludic juxtaposition, reminding its audience that every text is already intersected with multiple other texts.

Significantly, *Hot Pants College II*, the film that stimulates the lonely novelist's desire, is a sequel; and, on a theoretical level, the problem of sequels and remakes, like the even broader problem of parody and pastiche, is quite similar to the problem of adaptation.[20] (In her chapter in this volume, Lesley Stern posits that *Clueless* is a "remake" rather than an adaptation, but in so doing she helps to call our attention to the fundamental affinities between the two terms.) All these forms can be subsumed under the more general theory of artistic imitation, in the restricted sense of works of art that imitate other works of art. Notice, moreover, that all the "imitative" types of film are in danger of being assigned a low status, or even of eliciting critical opprobrium, because they are copies of "culturally treasured" originals. By way of demonstration, we need only compare the critical discourse surrounding Hitchcock's *Psycho* (itself an adaptation that some American critics once regarded as a tasteless horror movie, but that nearly everyone now acknowledges as a masterpiece) with the discourse surrounding both its sequels and prequel and its 1998 remake, which encountered nearly universal derision.

Viewed from the larger perspective of cultural anthropology and Bakhtinian dialogics, every movie can be seen to problematize originality, autonomy, and the bourgeois mode of reception. Walter Benjamin was aware of this phenomenon in his famous essay on mechanical reproduction, where he quoted Abel Gance's enthusiastic 1927 pronouncement, "'Shakespeare, Rembrandt, Beethoven will make films.'" "Presumably without intending it," Benjamin remarks, Gance was issuing "a far-reaching liquidation."[21] What we may not realize is that André Bazin was aware of much the same issues in his 1948 essay on adaptation, to which I alluded at the beginning of this introduction. In this remarkable essay Bazin asks us to think of film adaptation in relation to commercialism, industrial modernity, and democracy, and to compare it with an engraving or digest that makes the so-called original "readily accessible to all." Most discussion of such films, he notes, has been conducted on the level of formalist aesthetics, which is preoccupied with the nature of the "cinematic." But "one must first know," he writes, "to what end the adaptation is designed: for the cinema or its audience. One must also realize that most adaptors care far more about the latter than about the former."

Bazin attacks the "clichéd bias according to which culture is inseparable from intellectual effort," and the "classical modes of cultural communication, which are at once a defense of culture and a secreting of it behind high walls." He also observes that adaptation has a number of important social functions, one of which is directly pedagogical, taking the form of everything from nineteenth-century "abridged" classics to more recent things Bazin does not mention, such as *Classics Illustrated* comics, *Reader's Digest* condensed books, and plot summaries in *Cliff Notes*. (Where the notion of the "digest" is concerned, an interesting study could be written about the long and complex relationship between educational institutions and Hollywood. In his chapter for this volume, Guerric DeBona points out that David Selznick's 1935 adaptation of *David Copperfield* was marketed to high school English teachers by means of a free illustrated monograph on the art of cinematic adaptation, complete with study questions for students.) Still another function of adaptation, Bazin suggests, is the creation of national or cultural mythology. How many of us have actually read *Moby-Dick*, and how many of us have seen one of the comic book, theatrical, television, or film adaptations that give it folkloric significance? The most highly "adaptable" authors—Twain and Shakespeare are preeminent examples in the Anglo-American world—have been especially important to the formation of national myths or to what the Marxist theorist Antonio Gramsci described as the ideology of the "national-popular." But this mythic or ideological dimension of adaptation (indirectly addressed by Michael Anderegg in his chapter in this volume) is often overlooked because of what Bazin refers to as "a rather modern notion for which the critics are in large part responsible: that of the untouchability of a work of art." The nineteenth century, he says, "firmly established an idolatry of form, mainly literary, that is still with us." And the idolatry of form blinds us to the fact that all great novels—even the ones by Flaubert or Joyce— create characters that can be appropriated for many uses.

At this juncture and many others in his essay, Bazin sounds like what today we call a poststructuralist or postmodernist. "The ferocious defense of literary works," he says, "is, to a certain extent, aesthetically justified; but we must also be aware that it rests on a rather recent, individualistic conception of the 'author' and of the 'work,' a conception that was far from being ethically rigorous in the seventeenth century and that started to become legally defined only at the end of the eighteenth. . . . All things considered, it is possible to imagine that we are moving toward a reign of adaptation in which the notion of the unity of the work of art, if not the very notion of the author himself, will be destroyed." Some would say we have already arrived at that point. In any case, it is high time that writers on adaptation, however they might label their methodology, recognize what Bazin saw in 1948. The study of adaptation needs to be joined with the study of recycling, remaking, and every other form of retelling in the age of mechanical reproduction and electronic communication. By this means, adaptation will become part of a general theory of repetition, and adaptation study will move from the margins to the center of contemporary media studies.

NOTES

1. For a cogent discussion of both Matthew Arnold and the Kantian philosophy of aesthetics see Terry Eagleton, "The Rise of English," in *Literary Theory: An Introduction* (Minneapolis: University of Minnesota Press, 1983), pp. 17–53.

2. Clement Greenberg, "Avant-Garde and Kitsch," in *Pollack and After* (New York: Harper and Row, 1985), p. 25.

3. Juan A. Suarez, *Bike Boys, Drag Queens, and Superstars: Avant-Garde, Mass Culture, and Gay Identities in 1960s Underground Cinema* (Bloomington: Indiana University Press, 1996), pp. 6–7.

4. William Uricchio and Roberta E. Peterson, *Reframing Culture* (Princeton, N.J.: Princeton University Press, 1993).

5. David A. Cook, *A History of Narrative Film* (New York: W. W. Norton and Company, 1996), p. 53.

6. Claude-Edmonde Magny, *The Age of the American Novel: The Film Aesthetic of Fiction between the Two Wars*, trans. Eleanor Hochman (New York: Ungar, 1972).

7. Alan Spiegel, *Fiction and the Camera Eye: Visual Consciousness in Film and the Modern Novel* (Charlottesville: University Press of Virginia, 1976); Keith Cohen, *Film and Fiction: The Dynamics of Exchange* (New Haven, Conn.: Yale University Press, 1979). See also the concluding chapter, "Point of View in Narrative," in Robert Scholes and Robert Kellogg, *The Nature of Narrative* (New York: Oxford University Press, 1966), pp. 240–82. The "cinematic" techniques usually attributed to modernist fiction include experiments with focalization or point of view, a marked preference for "showing" rather than "telling," and a tendency to organize the text in the form of a montage.

8. François Truffaut, *Hitchcock*, revised edition (New York: Simon and Schuster, 1985), p. 71.

9. For influential writings on narrative, see Roland Barthes, *A Barthes Reader*, ed. Susan Sontag (New York: Hill and Wang, 1982); Gérard Genette, *Narrative Discourse: An Essay in Method*, trans. Jane E. Lewin (Ithaca, N.Y.: Cornell University Press, 1980); David Bordwell, *Narration in the Fiction Film* (Madison: University of Wisconsin Press, 1985); and Kristin Thompson, *Breaking the Glass Armor: Neoformalist Film Analysis* (Princeton, N.J.: Princeton University Press, 1988).

10. Seymour Chatman, "What Novels Can Do That Films Can't (and Vice Versa)," in *On Narrative*, ed. W. J. T. Mitchell (Chicago: University of Chicago Press), pp. 117–36.

11. Cynthia Ozick, "What Only Words, Not Film, Can Portray," *The New York Times* (5 January 1997), Arts and Leisure section, p. 1.

12. Fredric Jameson, *Signatures of the Visible* (New York: Routledge, 1990), p. 1.

13. Brian McFarlaine, *Novel to Film: An Introduction to the Theory of Adaptation* (Oxford: Clarendon Press, 1996).

14. Edwin McDowell, "Hollywood and the Novelist—It's a Fickle Romance, at Best," *The New York Times* (14 July 1985), section 2, p. 1.

15. Dan Cox, "H'wood Hunts 'The Great Idea,'" *Variety* (28 February 1998), p. 1.

16. Quoted in Jim McConville, "TNT Movies Join Cable's Book Club," *Electronic Media* (7 April 1999), p. 57.

17. See Jeffrey Sconce, "Narrative Authority and Social Narrativity: The Cinematic Reconstitution of Brontë's *Jane Eyre*," in *The Studio System*, ed. Janet Staiger (New Brunswick, N.J.: Rutgers University Press, 1995), pp. 140–62.

18. Rainer Werner Fassbinder, "Preliminary Remarks on *Querelle*," in *The Anarchy of the Imagination*, ed. Michael Toteberg and Leo A. Lensing, trans. Krishna Winston (Baltimore, M: The Johns Hopkins University Press, 1992), p. 168.

19. For a discussion of marketing strategies and the economic relationship between the various contemporary media, see Justin Wyatt, *High Concept: Movies and Marketing in Contemporary Hollywood* (Austin: University of Texas Press, 1985).

20. See Andrew Horton and Stuart Y. McDougal, eds., *Play It Again, Sam: Retakes on Remakes* (Berkeley: University of California Press, 1998).

21. Walter Benjamin, "The Work of Art in the Age of Mechanical Reproduction," in *Illuminations* (New York: Schocken Books, 1969), p. 151.

Adaptation in Theory

André Bazin

Adaptation, or the Cinema as Digest

The problem of digests and adaptations is usually posed within the framework of literature. Yet literature only partakes of a phenomenon whose amplitude is much larger. Take painting, for instance. One might even consider an art museum as a digest, for we find collected there a selection of paintings that were intended to exist in a completely different architectural and decorative context. Nonetheless, these works of art are still original. But now take the imaginary museum proposed by Malraux. It refracts the original painting into millions of facets thanks to photographic reproduction, and it substitutes for that original images of different dimensions and colors that are readily accessible to all. And, by the way, photography for its part is only a modern substitute for engraving, which previously had been the only approximate "adaptation" available to art connoisseurs.[1] One must not forget that the adaptation and summary of original works of art have become so customary and so frequent that it would be next to impossible to question their existence today. For the sake of argument, I shall take my examples from the cinema.

More than one writer, more than one critic, more than one filmmaker, even, has challenged the aesthetic justification for the adaptation of novels to the screen; however, there are few examples of those who take actual exception to this practice, of artists who refuse to sell their books, or to adapt other people's books, or to direct such adaptations when producers come along with the right blandishments. So their theoretical argument does not seem altogether justified. In general, they make claims about the specificity or distinctness of every authentic literary work. A novel is a unique synthesis whose molecular equilibrium is automatically affected when you tamper with its form. Essentially, no detail of the narrative can be considered secondary; all syntactic characteristics, then, are in fact expressions of the psychological, moral, or

Translated by Alain Piette and Bert Cardullo. Copyright © 1997. From *Bazin at Work* by Bert Cardullo. Reproduced by permission of Routledge, Inc.

metaphysical content of the work. André Gide's simple pasts[2] are, in a way, inseparable from the events of *The Pastoral Symphony* (1919), just as Camus's present perfects are inherent in the metaphysical drama of *The Stranger* (1942).

Even when it is posed in such complex terms, however, the problem of cinematic adaptation is not absolutely insolvable, and the history of the cinema already proves that this problem has often been solved in various ways. I shall cite only incontestable examples here: Malraux's *Man's Hope* (*Espoir*, a.k.a. *Sierra de Teruel*, 1939), Jean Renoir's *A Day in the Country* (1936), after Maupassant, and the recent *Grapes of Wrath* (1940; directed by John Ford), from Steinbeck. I find it easy to defend even a qualified success such as *The Pastoral Symphony* (1949; directed by Jean Delannoy). It is true that not everything in the film is a success, but this is certainly not due to what some consider the ineffable aspect of the original. I do not care much for Pierre Blanchar's acting, but I do think that Michèle Morgan's beautiful eyes—which are able to communicate the blind Gertrude's innermost thoughts—and the omnipresent motif of the ironically serene snow are acceptable substitutes for Gide's simple pasts. All it takes is for the filmmakers to have enough visual imagination to create the cinematic equivalent of the style of the original, and for the critic to have the eyes to see it.

To be sure, this theory of adaptation comes with the following warning: that one not confuse prose style with grammatical idiosyncrasies or, more generally still, with formal constants. Such confusion is widespread—and, unfortunately, not merely among French teachers. "Form" is at most a sign, a visible manifestation, of style, which is absolutely inseparable from the narrative content, of which it is, in a manner of speaking and according to Sartre's use of the word, the metaphysics. Under these circumstances, faithfulness to a form, literary or otherwise, is illusory: what matters is the *equivalence in meaning of the forms*.[3] The *style* of Malraux's film is completely identical to that of his book, even though we are dealing here with two different artistic forms, cinema on the one hand and literature on the other. The case of *A Day in the Country* is subtler: it is faithful to the spirit of Maupassant's short story at the same time that it benefits from the full extent of Renoir's genius. This is the refraction of one work in another creator's consciousness. And there is not a person who will deny the beauty of the result. It took somebody like Maupassant, but also someone like Renoir (both of them, Jean and Auguste), to achieve it.

The hard-liners will respond that the above-mentioned examples prove only that it is perhaps not metaphysically impossible to make a cinematic work inspired by a literary one, with sufficient faithfulness to the spirit of the original and with an aesthetic intelligence that permits us to consider the film the equal of the book; but they will also say that this is no longer the kind of "adaptation" I was talking about at the beginning of this chapter. They will say that *A Day in the Country* on screen is a different work from the novel and is equal or superior to its model because Jean Renoir is, in his own right, an artist of the same rank as Maupassant, and because he has of course benefited from the work of the writer, which is anterior to his own. They will claim that, if we examine the countless American and European novels that are adapted to the screen every month, we will see that the films are something completely different from the novels, that they are the condensed versions, summaries, film "digests" of which I spoke earlier. For instance, take aesthetically indefensible films such as *The Idiot* (1946; directed by Georges Lampin) and *For Whom the Bell Tolls* (1943; directed by Sam Wood), or those never-ending "adaptations" of Balzac, which seem to have more than amply demonstrated that the author of *The Human Comedy*[4] is the least "cinematic" of all novelists. To be sure, one must first know to what end the adaptation is designed: for the cinema or for its audience. One must also realize that most adapters care far more about the latter than about the former.

The problem of adaptation for the audience is much more evident in the case of radio. Indeed, radio is not quite an art like the cinema: it is first and foremost a means of reproduction and transmission. The digest phenomenon resides not so much in the actual condensing or simplification of works as in the way they are consumed by the listening public. The cultural interest of radio—precisely the aspect of it that scares Georges Duhamel[5]—is that it allows modern man to live in an environment of sound comparable to the warm atmosphere created by central heating. As for me, although I have had a radio set for barely a year now, I feel the need to turn it on as soon as I get home; often I even write and work with the radio on as my companion. Right now, as I write this article, I am listening to Jean Vittold's[6] excellent daily morning broadcast on the great musicians. Earlier today, while I was shaving, Jean Rostand,[7] juggling with chromosomes, told me why only female cats (or was it male cats?) can be of three colors simultaneously, and I do not remember who explained to me while I was having breakfast how, through simple scraping with sand, the Aztecs carved extraordinary masks of polished quartz that one can see at the Musée de l'Homme.[8] Jules Romains's[9] appalling hoax on extraocular vision was itself seriously adapted for radio.

Radio has created an atmospheric culture that is as omnipresent as humidity in the air. For those who think that culture can be achieved only through hard work, the ease of physical access that radio allows to works of art is at least as antagonistic to the nature of these works as any tampering with their form. Even if it is well rendered or integrally performed on radio, the Fifth Symphony is no longer Beethoven's work when you listen to it while in your bathtub; music must be accompanied by the ritual of attending a concert, by the sacrament of contemplation.

However, one can also see in radio the spreading of culture to everyone—the physical spread of culture, which is the first step toward its spiritual ascendance. Radio comfortably provides, like one more modern convenience, "culture for everyone." It represents a gain of time and a reduction of effort, which is the very mark of our era. After all, even M. Duhamel will take a cab or the metro to get to the concert hall.

The clichéd bias according to which culture is inseparable from intellectual effort springs from a bourgeois, intellectualist reflex. It is the equivalent in a rationalistic society of the initiatory rites in primitive civilizations. Esoterism is obviously one of the grand cultural traditions, and I am not pretending that we should completely banish it from our civilization. But we could simply put it back in its place, which should in no way be absolute. There is a definite pleasure in cracking or conquering the hermeticism of a work of art, which then refines our relationship to that work of art. So much the better. But mountain climbing has not yet replaced walking on level ground. In place of the classical modes of cultural communication, which are at once a defense of culture and a secreting of it behind high walls, modern technology and modern life now more and more offer up an extended culture reduced to the lowest common denominator of the masses. To the defensive, intellectual motto of "No culture without mental effort," which is in fact unconsciously elitist, the up-and-coming civilization now responds with, "Let's grab whatever we can." This is progress—that is, if there really is such a thing as progress.

As far as the cinema is concerned, my intention is not to defend the indefensible. Indeed, most of the films that are based on novels merely usurp their titles, even though a good lawyer could probably prove that these movies have an indirect value, since it has been shown that the sale of a book always increases after it has been adapted to the screen. And the original work can only profit from such an exposure. Although *The Idiot*, for example, is very frustrating on the screen, it is undeniable that many potential readers of Dostoyevsky have found in the film's oversimplified psychology and action a kind of preliminary trimming that has given them easier access to an otherwise difficult novel. The process is somewhat similar to that of M. de Vogüe, the author of "abridged" classics for schools in the nineteenth century. These are despicable in the eyes of devotees of the Russian novel (but they have hardly anything to lose by this process, and neither does Dostoyevsky), yet extremely useful to those who are not yet familiar with the Russian novel and who thus can benefit from an introduction to it. In any event, I shall not comment further on this, for it has more to do with pedagogy than with art. I would much prefer to deal with a rather modern notion for which the critics are in large part responsible: that of the untouchability of a work of art.

The nineteenth century, more than any other, firmly established an idolatry of form, mainly literary, that is still with us and that has made us relegate what has in fact always been essential for narrative composition to the back of our critical consciousness: the invention of character and situation. I grant that the protagonists and events of a novel achieve their aesthetic existence only through the form that expresses them and that somehow brings them to life in our minds. But this precedence is as vain as that which is regularly conveyed to college students when they are asked to write an essay on the precedence of language over thought. It is interesting to note that the novelists who so fiercely defend the stylistic or formal integrity of their texts are also the ones who sooner or later overwhelm us with confessions about the tyrannical demands of their characters. According to these writers, their protagonists are *enfants terribles* who completely escape from their control once they have been conceived. The novelist is totally subjected to their whims; he is the instrument of their wills. I am not doubting this for a minute, but then writers must recognize that the true aesthetic reality of a psychological or social novel lies in the characters or their environment rather than in what they call its style. The style is in the service of the narrative: it is a reflection of it, so to speak, the body but not the soul. And it is not impossible for the artistic soul to manifest itself through another incarnation. This assumption, that the style is in the service of the narrative, appears vain and sacrilegious only if one refuses to see the many examples of it that the history of the arts gives to us, and if one therefore indulges in the biased condemnation of cinematic adaptation. With time, we do see the ghosts of famous characters rise far above the great novels from which they emanate. Don Quixote and Gargantua dwell in the consciousness of millions of people who have never had any direct or complete contact with the works of Cervantès and Rabelais. I would like to be sure that all those who conjure up the spirit of Fabrice and Madame Bovary have read (or reread, for good measure) Stendhal and Flaubert, but I am not so sure. Insofar as the style of the original has managed to create a character and impose him on the public consciousness, that character acquires a greater autonomy, which might in certain cases lead as far as quasi-transcendence of the work. Novels, as we all know, are mythmakers.

The ferocious defense of literary works is, to a certain extent, aesthetically justified; but we must also be aware that it rests on a rather recent, individualistic conception of the "author" and of the "work," a conception that was far from being ethically rigorous in the seventeenth century and that started to become legally defined only at the end of the eighteenth. In the Middle Ages there were only a few themes, and they were common to all the arts. That of Adam and Eve, for instance, is to be found in the mystery plays, painting, sculpture, and stained-glass windows, none of which were ever challenged for transferring this theme from one art form to another. And when the subject of the Rome Prize for Painting is "the love of Daphnis and Chloë,"[10] what else is it but an adaptation? Yet nobody is claiming that copyright has been violated. In justification of the artistic multiplication of works with biblical and Christian themes during the Middle Ages, it would be wrong to say that they were part of a common fund, a kind of public domain of Christian civilization: the copiers or imitators had no more respect for the *chansons de gestes*, the Old French epic poems, than they did for religious literature. The reason is that the work of art was not an end in itself; the only important criteria were its content and the effectiveness of its message. But the balance between the public's needs and the requirements for creation was such in those days that all the conditions existed to guarantee the excellence of the arts. You may perhaps observe that those days are over and that it would be aesthetic nonsense to want to anachronistically reverse the evolution of the relationship among the creator, the public, and the work of art. To this I would respond that, on the contrary, it is possible that artists and critics remain blind to the birth of the new, aesthetic Middle Ages, whose origin is to be found in the accession of the masses to power (or at least their participation in it) and in the emergence of an artistic form to complement that accession: the cinema.

But even if this thesis is a rather risky one that would require additional arguments in its support, it remains true that the relatively new art of cinema is obliged to retrace the entire evolution of art on its own, at an extraordinarily quickened pace, just as a fetus somehow retraces the evolution of mankind in a few months. The only difference is that the paradoxical evolution of cinema is contemporaneous with the deep-seated decadence of literature, which today seems designed for an audience of individualist elites. The aesthetic Middle Ages of the cinema finds its fictions wherever it can: close at hand, in the literatures of the nineteenth and twentieth centuries. It can also create its own fictions, and has not failed to do so, particularly in comic films, from the first French ones to the American comedies of, say, Mack Sennett and above all Charlie Chaplin. The defenders of seriousnessness in the cinema will name instead examples such as the Western epics and those of the Russian revolution, or such unforgettable pictures as *Broken Blossoms* (1919; directed by D. W. Griffith) and *Scarface* (1932; directed by Howard Hawks). But there is nothing that can be done to bring back the halcyon past. Youth is transient, and grandeur with it; another grandeur will take its place, if perhaps a bit more slowly. In the meantime, the cinema borrows from fiction a certain number of well-wrought, well-rounded, or well-developed characters, all of whom have been polished by twenty centuries of literary culture. It adopts them and brings them into play; according to the talents of the screenwriter and the director, the characters are integrated as much as possible into their new aesthetic context. If they are not so integrated, we naturally get these mediocre films that one is right to condemn, provided one does not confuse this mediocrity with the very principle of cinematic adaptation, whose aim is to simplify and condense a work from which it basically wishes to retain only the main characters and situations. If the novelist is not happy with the adaptation of his work, I, of course, grant him the right to defend the original (although he sold it, and thus is guilty of an act of prostitution that deprives him of many of his privileges as the creator of the work). I grant him this right only because no one has yet found anyone better than parents to defend the rights of children until they come of age. One should not identify this natural right with an a priori infallibility, however.

Instead of Kafka's *Trial,* which was adapted to the stage by André Gide (1947) from a translation by André Vialatte, I shall take the more appropriate example of *The Brothers Karamazov,* adapted by Jacques Copeau (*Les Frères Karamazov,* 1911), in my defense of the condensed adaptation. The only thing Copeau has done—but he did it more skillfully than did M. Spaak[11] in *The Idiot*—is to extract the characters from Dostoyevsky's novel and condense the main events of their story into a few dramatic scenes. There is something slightly different about these theatrical examples, however: the fact that today's theater-going public is educated enough to have read the novel. But Copeau's work would remain artistically viable even if this were not the case.

To take another example, I suffered when I saw *Devil in the Flesh* (1947; directed by Claude Autant-Lara), because I know Raymond Radiguet's book; the spirit and "style" of that book had somehow been betrayed. But it remains true that this adaptation is the best one that could be made from the novel and that, artistically, it is absolutely justified. Jean Vigo would probably have been more faithful to the original, but it is reasonable to conclude that the resulting film would have been impossible to show to the public because the reality of the book would have ignited the screen. The work of the screenwriters Aurenche and Bost consisted, so to speak, in "transforming" (in the sense that an electric transformer does) the voltage of the novel. The aesthetic energy is almost all there, but it is distributed—or, perhaps better, dissipated— differently according to the demands of the camera lens. And yet, although Aurenche and Bost have succeeded in transforming the absolute amoralism of the original into an almost too decipherable moral code, the public has been reluctant to accept the film.

In summary, adaptation is aesthetically justified, independent of its pedagogical and social value, because the adapted work to a certain extent exists apart from what is wrongly called its "style," in a confusion of this term with the word *form.* Furthermore, the standard differentiation among the arts in the nineteenth century and the relatively recent subjectivist notion that an author as identified with a work no longer fit in with an aesthetic sociology of the masses in which the cinema runs a relay race with drama and the novel and does not eliminate them, but rather reinforces them. The true aesthetic differentiations, in fact, are to be made not among the arts, but within genres themselves: between the psychological novel and the novel of manners, for example, rather than between the psychological novel and the film that one would make from it. Of course, adaptation for the public is inseparable from adaptation for the cinema, insofar as the cinema is more "public" than the novel.

The very word *digest*, which sounds at first contemptible, can have a positive meaning. "As the word indicates," Jean-Paul Sartre writes, "it is a literature that has been previously digested, a literary chyle." But one could also understand it as a literature that has been made more accessible through cinematic adaptation, not so much because of the oversimplification that such adaptation entails (in *The Pastoral Symphony*, the narrative on screen is even more complex than the one in the novel), but rather because of the mode of expression itself, as if the aesthetic fat, differently emulsified, were better tolerated by the consumer's mind. As far as I am concerned, the difficulty of audience assimilation is not an a priori criterion for cultural value.

All things considered, it is possible to imagine that we are moving toward a reign of the adaptation in which the notion of the unity of the work of art, if not the very notion of the author himself, will be destroyed. If the film that was made of Steinbeck's *Of Mice and Men* (1940; directed by Lewis Milestone) had been successful (it could have been so, and far more easily than the adaptation of the same author's *Grapes of Wrath*), the (literary?) critic of the year 2050 would find not a novel out of which a play and a film had been "made," but rather a single work reflected through three art forms, an artistic pyramid with three sides, all equal in the eyes of the critic. The "work" would then be only an ideal point at the top of this figure, which itself is an ideal construct. The chronological precedence of one part over another would not be an aesthetic criterion any more than the chronological precedence of one twin over the other is a genealogical one. Malraux made his film of *Man's Hope* before he wrote the novel of the same title, but he was carrying the work inside himself all along.

NOTES

This essay was first published in French in *Esprit* 16:146 (July 1948), pp. 32–40.

1. Bazin's note: In a recent radio broadcast of *French Cancan*, during which Messieurs Pierre Benoit (1886–1962; French novelist, member of the Académie Française, author of *Koenigsmark* and *L'Atlantide*), Labarthe (obscure French literary figure of Bazin's time, coauthor with Marcel Brion, Jean Cocteau, Fred Bérence, Emmanuel Berl, Danielle Hunebelle, Robert Lebel, Jean-Lucas Dubreton, and Jean-Jaques Salomon of a volume entitled *Léonard de Vinci* [1959]), and several others exchanged a great number of utter platitudes, we heard Curzio Malaparte (1898–1957; Italian novelist, celebrated author of *Kaputt* and many other works, who contributed one film to Italian cinema, *Il Cristo Proibito* [*Forbidden Christ*, 1950], which he wrote, directed, and scored and was released

in the United States in 1953) ask the speaker what he would think of a "condensed version" of the Parthenon, for example. In his mind, this was supposed to be the ultimate argument against the "digest." Nobody was there to respond that such a condensed version had been realized a long time ago in the casts that were made of the Parthenon's friezes, and above all in the photo albums of the Acropolis that anybody can buy at a reasonable price in a gift shop.

2. Translator's note: Bazin is here using the term *passé simple* in French. This tense does not exist in English. It is a form of the simple past, which itself is called *imparfait* in French. *Imparfait* tends to be used more often in everyday language, whereas *passé simple* is a more literary term for the same tense.

3. Bazin's note: There are types of stylistic transfer that are indeed reliable, however, such as those "simple pasts" of André Gide that unfortunately were not built into the actual cutting of *The Pastoral Symphony* (i.e., its filmic syntax), but did show up in the eyes of an actress and in the symbolism of the snow.

4. Translator's note: This was the title given by Honoré de Balzac to his collected stories and novels, thus casting his copious fictions as a single, secular reply to Dante's *Divine Comedy*. *La Comédie Humaine* was published in sixteen volumes by Furne, Paulin, Dubochet, and Hetzel between 1842 and 1846; a seventeenth supplementary volume appeared in 1847.

5. Translator's note: Georges Duhamel (1884–1966), now a largely forgotten figure, achieved fame before World War II, being elected to the Académie Française in 1935. He is remembered for two cycles of novels: *Vie et Aventures de Salavin* (1920–32) and the popular *Chronique des Pasquier* (1933–45). Writing with warmth and humor, Duhamel used the saga of the Pasquier family to attack materialism and defend the rights of the individual against the collective forces of society.

6. Translator's note: Vittold was a famous French musicologist.

7. Translator's note: Rostand was a well-known French biologist who did much to popularize the study of science.

8. Translator's note: Famous anthropological museum in Paris.

9. Translator's note: Jules Romains (pseudonym of Louis Farigoule, 1885–1972) was a French novelist, dramatist, poet, and essayist, elected to the Académie Française in 1946. *La Vie Unanime*, a collection of poems published in 1908, and much of his later verse and prose were influenced by Unanimist theories of social groups and collective psychology. Before the outbreak of war in 1914 he published more collections of poetry, a verse play, *L'Armée dans la Ville* (1911), and two novels, *Mort de Quelqu'un* (1911) and the farcical *Les Copains* (1913).

The farcical comedies *Knock, ou le Triomphe de la Médecine* (1923), *M. Le Troubadec Saisi par la Débauche* (1923), and *Le Mariage de M. Le Troubadec* (1925) earned him much popularity after the war. Interesting collections of essays include *Hommes, Médecins, Machines* (1959) and *Lettre Ouverte contre une Vaste Conspiration* (1966), with its strictures on modern cultural attitudes and standards.

10. Translator's note: Daphnis and Chloë were two lovers in an old Greek pastoral romance of the same name, attributed to Longus (of the third century A.D. [?]). Daphnis himself was a Sicilian shepherd renowned in Greek myth as the inventor of pastoral poetry.

11. Charles Spaak was a Belgian screenwriter whose credits include *Carnival in Flanders* (1935) and *La Grande Illusion* (1937).

Dudley Andrew

Adaptation

The Sources of Films

Frequently the most narrow and provincial area of film theory, discourse about adaptation, is potentially as far-reaching as you like. Its distinctive feature, the matching of the cinematic sign system to prior achievements in some other system, can be shown to be distinctive of all representational cinema.

Let us begin with an example, *A Day in the Country*. Jean Renoir set himself the task of putting his knowledge, his troupe, and his artistry at the service of a tale by Guy de Maupassant. No matter how we judge the process or the success of the film, its "being" owes something to the tale that was its inspiration and potentially its measure. That tale, "A Country Excursion," bears a transcendent relation to any and all films that adapt it, for it is itself an artistic sign with a given shape and value, if not a finished meaning. A new artistic sign will then feature this original sign as either its signified or its referent. Adaptations claiming fidelity bear the original as a signified, whereas those inspired by or derived from an earlier text stand in a relation of referring to the original.

The notion of a transcendent order to which the system of the cinema is beholden in its practice goes well beyond this limited case of adaptation.[1] What is a city symphony, for example, if not an adaptation of a concept by the cinema?[2] A definite notion of Berlin preexisted Walter Ruttman's 1927 treatment of that city. What is any documentary, for that matter, except the signification by the cinema of some prior whole, some concept of person, place, event, or situation? If we take seriously the arguments of Marxist and other social theorists that our consciousness is not open to the world, but filters the world according to the shape of its ideology, then every cinematic rendering will exist in relation to some prior whole lodged unquestioned in the personal or public system of experience. In other words, no filmmaker and no film (at least in the representational mode) responds immediately to reality itself or to its own inner vision. Every representational film adapts a prior conception. Indeed, the very term *representation* suggests the existence of a model. Adaptation delimits representation by insisting on the cultural status of the model, on its existence in the mode of the text or the already textualized. In the case of those texts explicitly termed adaptations, the cultural model that the cinema represents is already treasured as a representation in another sign system.

The broader notion of the process of adaptation has much in common with interpretation theory, for in a strong sense adaptation is the appropriation of a meaning from a prior text. The hermeneutic circle, central to interpretation theory, preaches that an explication of a text occurs only after a prior understanding of it, yet that prior understanding is justified by the careful explication it allows.[3] In other words, before we can go about discussing and analyzing a text we must have a global conception of its meaning. Adaptation is similarly both a leap and a process. It can put into play the intricate mechanism of its signifiers only in response to a general understanding of the signified it aspires to have constructed at the end of its process. Although all representational films function this way (as interpretations of a person, place, situation, event, and so forth), we reserve a special place for those films which foreground this relation by announcing themselves as versions of some standard whole. A standard whole can only be a text. A version of it is an adaptation in the narrow sense.

Although these speculations may encourage a hopelessly broad view of adaptation, there is no question that the restricted view of adaptation from known texts in other art forms offers a privileged locus for analysis. I do not say that such texts are themselves privileged. Indeed, the thrust of my earlier remarks suggests quite the opposite. Nevertheless, the explicit, foregrounded relation of a cinematic text to a well-constructed original text from which it derives and which in some sense it strives to reconstruct provides the analyst with a clear and useful "laboratory" condition that should not be neglected.

The making of film out of an earlier text is virtually as old as the machinery of cinema itself. Well over half of all commercial films have come from literary originals—though by no means all of these originals are revered or respected. If we confine ourselves to those cases where the adaptation process is foregrounded—that is, where the original is held up as a worthy source or goal—there are still several possible modes of relation between the film and the text. These modes can, for convenience, be reduced to three: borrowing, intersection, and fidelity of transformation.

Borrowing, Intersecting, and
Transforming Sources

In the history of the arts, surely "borrowing" is the most frequently used mode of adaptation. Here the artist employs, more or less extensively, the material, idea, or form of an earlier, generally successful, text. Medieval paintings featuring biblical iconography, and miracle plays based on Bible stories drew on an exceptional text whose power they borrowed. In a later, secular age the artworks of an earlier generation might be used as sacred in their own right. The many types of adaptations from Shakespeare come readily to mind. Doubtless in these cases, the adapter hopes to win an audience for the adaptation by the prestige of its borrowed title or subject. But at the same time, it seeks to gain a certain respectability, if not aesthetic value, as a dividend in the transaction. Adaptations from literature to music, opera, or paintings are of this nature. There is no question of the replication of the original in Strauss's *Don Quixote.* Instead the audience is expected to enjoy basking in a certain preestablished presence and to call up new or especially powerful aspects of a cherished work.

To study this mode of adaptation the analyst needs to probe the source of power in the original by examining the use made of it in adaptation. Here the main concern is the generality of the original, its potential for wide and varied appeal—in short, its existence as a continuing form or archetype in culture. This is especially true of that adapted material which, because of its frequent reappearance, claims the status of myth: *Tristan and Isolde,* for certain, and *A Midsummer Night's Dream,* possibly. The success of adaptations of this sort rests on the issue of their fertility, not their fidelity. Frank McConnell's ingenious *Storytelling and Mythmaking* catalogues the garden of culture by examining borrowing as the history of grafting and transplantation in the fashion of Northrop Frye or even Carl Jung.[4] This direction of study will always elevate film by demonstrating its participation in a cultural enterprise whose value is outside film and, for Jung and others, outside texts altogether. Adaptation is the name of this cultural venture at its most explicit, though McConnell, Frye, and Jung would all immediately want to extend their theories of artistic fertility to "original" texts that upon inspection show their dependence on the great fructifying symbols and mythic patterns of civilization.

This vast and airy mode of borrowing finds its opposite in that attitude toward adaptation I choose to call intersecting. Here the uniqueness of the original text is preserved to such an extent that it is intentionally left unassimilated in adaptation. The cinema, as a separate mechanism, records its confrontation with an ultimately intransigent text. Undoubtedly the key film exhibiting this relation is Robert Bresson's *Diary of a Country Priest.* André Bazin, championing this film and this mode,[5] claimed that in this instance we are presented not with an adaptation so much as a refraction of the original. Because Bresson featured the writing of the diary and because he went out of his way to avoid "opening up" or in any other way cinematizing the original, Bazin claims that the film *is* the novel as seen by cinema. To extend one of his most elaborate metaphors,[6] the original artwork can be likened to a crystal chandelier whose formal beauty is a product of its intricate but fully artificial arrangement of parts, whereas the cinema would be a crude flashlight interesting not for its own shape or the quality of its light, but for what it makes appear in this or that dark corner. The intersection of Bresson's flashlight and the chandelier of Bernanos's novel produces an experience of the original modulated by the peculiar beam of the cinema. Naturally a great deal of Bernanos fails to be lit up, but what is lit up is only Bernanos, Bernanos however as seen by the cinema.

The modern cinema is increasingly interested in just this sort of intersecting. Bresson, naturally, has given us his Joan of Arc from court records and his *Mouchette* once again from Bernanos. Straub has filmed Corneille's *Othon* and *The Chronicle of Anna Magdalena Bach.* Pasolini audaciously confronted Matthew's gospel, with many later texts (musical, pictorial, and cinematic) that it inspired. His later *Medea, Canturbury Tales,* and *Decameron* are also adaptational events in the intersecting mode. All such works fear or refuse to adapt. Instead they present the otherness and distinctiveness of the original text, initiating a dialectical interplay between the aesthetic forms of one period and the cinematic forms of our own period. In direct contrast to the manner in which scholars have treated the mode of "borrowing," such intersecting insists that the analyst attend to the specificity of the original within the specificity of the cinema. An original is allowed its life, its own life, in the cinema. The consequences of this method, despite its apparent forthrightness, are neither innocent nor simple. The disjunct experience such intersecting promotes is consonant with the aesthetics of modernism in all the arts. This mode refutes the commonplace that adaptations support only a conservative film aesthetics.

Unquestionably the most frequent and most tiresome discussion of adaptation (and of film and literature relations as well) concerns fidelity and transformation. Here it is assumed that the task of adaptation is the reproduction in cinema of something essential about an original text. Here we have a clear-cut case of film's trying to measure up to a literary work or of an audience's expecting to make such a comparison. Fidelity of adaptation is conventionally treated in relation to the "letter" and to the "spirit" of a text, as though adaptation were the rendering of an interpretation of a legal precedent. The letter would appear to be within the reach of cinema, for it can be emulated in mechanical fashion. It includes aspects of fiction generally elaborated in any film script: the characters and their interrelation; the geographical, sociological, and cultural information providing the fiction's context; and the basic narrational aspects that determine the point of view of the narrator (tense, degree of participation and knowledge of the storyteller, and so on). Ultimately— and this was Bazin's complaint about faithful transformations—a literary work can readily become a scenario written in typical scenario form. The skeleton of the original can, more or less thoroughly, become the skeleton of a film.

More difficult is fidelity to the spirit, to the original's tone, values, imagery, and rhythm, since finding stylistic equivalents in film for these intangible aspects is the opposite of a mechanical process. The cinéaste presumably must intuit and reproduce the feeling of the original. It has been argued variously that this is frankly impossible, that it involves the systematic replacement of verbal signifiers by cinematic signifiers, or that it is the product of artistic intuition, as when Bazin found the pervasive snowy decor in *Symphonie Pastorale* (1946) to reproduce adequately the simple past tense that all of Gide's verbs bear in that tale.[7]

It is at this point that the specificity of these two signifying systems is at stake. Generally film is found to work from perception toward signification, from external facts to interior motivations and consequences, from the givenness of a world to the meaning of a story cut out of that world. Literary fiction works oppositely. It begins with signs (graphemes and words), building to propositions that attempt to develop perception. As a product of human language it naturally treats human motivation and values, seeking to throw them out onto the external world, elaborating a world out of a story.

George Bluestone, Jean Mitry, and a host of others find this opposition most graphic in adaptations.[8] Therefore, they take pleasure in scrutinizing this practice even while ultimately condemning it to the realm of the impossible. Since signs name the inviolate relation of signifier to signified, how is translation of poetic texts conceivable from one language to another (where signifiers belong to different systems), and how is it possible to transform the signifiers of one material (verbal) to signifiers of another material (images and sounds)? It would appear that one must presume that the global signified of the original is separable from its text if one believes it can be approximated by other sign clusters. Can we attempt to reproduce the meaning of the *Mona Lisa* in a poem, or of a poem in a musical phrase, or even of a musical phrase in an aroma? If one accepts this possibility, at the very least one is forced to discount the primary articulations of the relevant language systems. One would have to hold that although the material of literature (graphemes, words, and sentences) may be of a different nature from the materials of cinema (projected light and shadows, identifiable sounds and forms, and represented actions), both systems may construct in their own way, and at higher levels, scenes and narratives that are indeed commensurable.

The strident and often futile arguments over these issues can be made sharper and more consequential in the language of E. H. Gombrich or the even more systematic language of semiotics. Gombrich finds that all discussion of adaptation introduces the category of "matching."[9] First of all, like Bazin he feels one cannot dismiss adaptation, since it is a fact of human practice. We can and do correctly match items from different systems all the time: a tuba sound is more like a rock than like a piece of string; it is more like a bear than like a bird; more like a Romanesque church than a Baroque one. We are able to make these distinctions and insist on their public character because we are matching equivalents. In the system of musical instruments the tuba occupies an equivalent position to that enjoyed by the Romanesque in its system of architectural styles. Nelson Goodman has treated this issue at length in *The Language of Art*, pointing to the equivalence not of elements but of the position elements occupy vis-à-vis their different domains.[10] Names of properties of colors may thus metaphorically, but correctly, describe aspects of the world of sound (a blue note, a somber or bright tone). Adaptation would then become a matter of searching two systems of communication for elements of equivalent position in the systems capable of eliciting a signified at a given level of pertinence, for example, the description of a narrative action. For Gombrich adaptation is possible, though never perfect, because every artwork is a construct of elements built out of a traditional use of a system. Since humans have the general capacity to adapt to new systems with different traditions in achieving similar goals or constructs, artistic adaptation poses no insurmountable obstacles. Nevertheless, attention to such "proportional consistencies" demands that the study of adaptation include the study of both art forms in their proper *historic* context.

Gombrich and Goodman anticipated the more fashionable vocabulary of semiotics in their clarification of these issues. In *Film and Fiction, The Dynamics of Exchange* Keith Cohen tries to justify this new, nearly scientific approach to questions of relations between these arts; he writes, citing Metz:

A basic assumption I make is that both words and images are sets of signs that belong to systems and that, at a certain level of abstraction, these systems bear resemblances to one another. More specifically, within each such system there are many different codes (perceptual, referential, symbolic). What makes possible, then, a study of the relation between two separate sign systems, like novel and film, is the fact that the same codes may reappear in more than one system. . . . The very mechanisms of language systems can thus be seen to carry on diverse and complex interrelations: "one function, among others, of language is to name the units segmented by vision (but also to help segment them), and . . . one function, among others, of vision is to inspire semantic configurations (but also to be inspired by them)."[11]

Cohen, like Metz before him, suggests that despite their very different material character, despite even the different ways we process them at the primary level, verbal and cinematic signs share a common fate: that of being condemned to connotation. This is especially true in their fictional use, where every signifier identifies a signified, but also elicits a chain reaction of other relations that permits the elaboration of the fictional world. Thus, for example, imagery functions equivalently in films and novels. This mechanism of implication among signs leads Cohen to conclude that "narrativity is the most solid median link between novel and cinema, the most pervasive tendency of both verbal and visual languages. In both novel and cinema, groups of signs, be they literary or visual signs, are apprehended consecutively through time; and this consecutiveness gives rise to an unfolding structure, the diegetic whole that is never fully *present* in any one group yet always *implied* in each such group."[12]

Narrative codes, then, always function at the level of implication or connotation. Hence they are potentially comparable in a novel and a film. The story can be the same if the narrative units (characters, events, motivations, consequences, context, viewpoint, imagery, and so on) are produced equally in two works. Now this production is, by definition, a process of connotation and implication. The analysis of adaptation, then, must point to the achievement of equivalent narrative units in the absolutely different semiotic systems of film and language. Narrative itself is a semiotic system available to both and derivable from both. If a novel's story is judged in some way comparable to its filmic adaptation, the strictly separate but equivalent processes of implication that produced the narrative units of that story through words and audiovisual signs, respectively, must be studied. Here semiotics coincides with Gombrich's intuition: such a study is not comparative between the arts, but is instead intensive within each art. And since the implicative power of literary language and of cinematic signs is a function of its use as well as of its system, adaptation analysis ultimately leads to an investigation of film styles and periods in relation to the literary styles of different periods.

We have come round the other side of the argument now to find once more that the study of adaptation is logically tantamount to the study of the cinema as a whole. The system by which film involves us in fictions and the history of that system are ultimately the questions we face even when starting with the simple observation of an equivalent tale told by novel and film. This is not to my mind a discouraging arrival, for it drops adaptation and all studies of film and literation out of the realm of eternal principle and airy generalization and onto the uneven but solid ground of artistic history, practice, and discourse.

The Sociology and Aesthetics of Adaptation

It is time for adaptation studies to take a sociological turn. How does adaptation serve the cinema? What conditions exist in film style and film culture to warrant or demand the use of literary prototypes? Although the volume of adaptation may be calculated as relatively constant in the history of cinema, its particular function at any moment is far from constant. The choices of the mode of adaptation and of prototypes suggest a great deal about the cinema's sense of its role and aspirations from decade to decade. Moreover, the stylistic strategies developed to achieve the proportional equivalences necessary to construct matching stories not only are symptomatic of a period's style, but may crucially alter that style.

Bazin pointed to an important instance of this in the immediate postwar era when adaptations from the stage by Cocteau, Welles, Olivier, Wyler, and others not only developed new ways for the cinema to be adequate to serious theater, but also developed a kind of discipline in mise-en-scène whose consequences go far beyond the production of *Macbeth*, *Les Parents Terribles*, *The Little Foxes*, and *Henry V*.[13] Cocteau's film, to take one example, derives its style from Welles's use of interior shooting in *Citizen Kane* and *The Ambersons*, thus responding to a new conception of dramatic space, but at the same time his film helped solidify a shooting style that would leave its mark on Alexandre Astruc and André Michel, among others. Furthermore, his particular cinematic *écriture* would allow Truffaut to set him against the cinema of quality in the famous 1954 diatribe.[14] It is instructive to note that although Truffaut railed against the status quo for its literariness and especially for its method of adaptation, the directors he praised were also working with literary originals: Bresson adapting Bernanos, Ophuls adapting Maupassant and Schnitzler, and Cocteau adapting his own theater pieces. Like Bazin, Truffaut looked upon adaptation not as a monolithic practice to be avoided, but as an instructive barometer for the age. The cinema *d'auteur* that he advocated was not to be pitted against a cinema of adaptation; rather one method of adaptation was to be pitted against another. In this instance adaptation was the battleground even though it prepared the way for a stylistic revolution, the New Wave, which would for the most part avoid famous literary sources.

To take another sort of example, particular literary fashions have at times exercised enormous power over the cinema and, consequently, over the general direction of its stylistic evolution. The Romantic fiction of Hugo, Dickens, Dumas, and countless lesser figures originally set the stylistic requirements of American and mainstream French cinema at the end of the silent era. Similarly, Zola and Maupassant, always of interest to French cinéastes, helped Jean Renoir muscularly reorient the style of world cinema in the 1930s. Not only that; through Luchino Visconti this naturalist impulse directly developed one strain of neorealism in his adaptations of Giovanni Verga (*La Terra Trema*) and James M. Cain (*Ossessione*).

This latter case forces us to recall that the "dynamics of exchange," as Cohen calls them, go both ways between film and fiction. Naturalist fiction helped cinema develop its interest in squalid subjects and a hardhitting style. This, in turn, affected American hard-boiled novelists like Cain and Hammett, eventually returning to Europe in the film style of Visconti, Carné, Clouzot, and others. This general trading between film and literature in the currency of naturalism had some remarkable individual incidents associated with it. Renoir's adaptation of *The Lower Depths* can serve as an example. In 1881 Zola had cried out for a naturalist theater[15] and had described twenty years before its creation precisely the sort of drama Gorki would write in *The Lower Depths:* a collection of real types thrown together without a domineering plot, the drama driven by the natural rhythms of little incidents and facts exposing the general quality of life in an era. Naturalism here coincided with a political need, with Gorki's play preceeding the great uprisings in Russia by only a few years.

In another era and in response to a different political need, Renoir leapt at the chance to adapt the Gorki work. This was 1935, the year of the ascendancy of the Popular Front, and Renoir's treatment of the original is clearly marked by the pressures and aspirations of that moment. The film negotiates the mixture of classes that the play only hints at. Louis Jouvet as the Baron dominates the film, descending into the social depths and helping organize a collective undoing of Kastylylov, the capitalist landlord. Despite the gloomy theme, the murder, a jailing, and deaths by sickness and suicide, Renoir's version overflows with a general warmth evident in the airy setting by the Marne and the relaxed direction of actors who breathe languidly between their lines.

Did Gorki mind such an interpretation? We can never know, since he died a few months before its premier. But he did give Renoir his imprimatur and looked forward to seeing the completed version, despite the fact that in 1932 he declared that the play was useless, out of date, and unperformable in socialist Russia. Perhaps these statements were the insincere self-criticism which that important year elicited from many Russian artists. I prefer, however, to take Gorki at his word. More farsighted than most theorists, let alone most authors, he realized that *The Lower Depths* in 1932 Russia was by no means the same artwork as *The Lower Depths* in the France of the Popular Front. This is why he put no strictures on Renoir, assuming that the cinéaste would deal with his play as he felt necessary. Necessity is, among other things, a product of the specific place and epoch of the adaptation, both historically and stylistically. The naturalist attitude of 1902, fleshing out the original plans of Zola, gave way to a new historic and stylistic moment and fed the style that Renoir had begun elaborating ever since *La Chienne* in 1931 and that, despite its alleged looseness and airiness in comparison to that of Gorki, would help lead European cinema onto the naturalistic path.

This sketch of a few examples from the sociology of adaptation has rapidly taken us into the complex interchange between eras, styles, nations, and subjects. This is as it should be, for adaptation, although a tantalizing keyhole for theorists, nevertheless partakes of the universal situation of film practice, dependent as it is on the aesthetic system of the cinema in a particular era and on that era's cultural needs and pressures. Filmmaking, in other words, is always an event in which a system is used and altered in discourse. Adaptation is a peculiar form of discourse, but not an unthinkable one. Let us use it not to fight battles over the essence of the media or the inviolability of individual artworks. Let us use it as we use all cultural practices, to understand the world from which it comes and the one toward which it points. The elaboration of these worlds will demand, therefore, historical labor and critical acumen. The job of theory in all this is to keep the questions clear and in order. It will no longer do to let theorists settle things with a priori arguments. We need to study the films themselves as acts of discourse. We need to be sensitive to that discourse and to the forces that motivate it.

NOTES

1. For this idea I am indebted to a paper written by Dana Benelli in a class at the University of Iowa, autumn term 1979.

2. The "city symphony" is a genre of the 1920s that includes up to fifteen films all built on formal or abstract principles, yet dedicated to the presentation of a single city, be it Berlin, Paris, Nice, Moscow, or the like.

3. In the theory of interpretation this is generally attributed to Wilhelm Dilthey, although Martin Heidegger has made much of it in our century.

4. Frank McConnell, *Storytelling and Mythmaking* (New York: Oxford University Press, 1979).

5. André Bazin, *What Is Cinema?* (Berkeley: University of California Press, 1968), p. 142.

6. Bazin, p. 107.

7. Bazin, p. 67.

8. George Bluestone, *Novels into Film* (Berkeley: University of California Press, 1957), and Jean Mitry, "Remarks on the Problem of Cinematic Adaptation," *Bulletin of the Midwest Modern Language Association* 4:1 (Spring 1971), pp. 1–9.

9. E. H. Gombrich, *Art and Illusion* (Princeton: Princeton University Press, 1961), p. 370.

10. Nelson Goodman, *Languages of Art* (Indianapolis: Hackett, 1976), especially pp. 143–48.

11. Keith Cohen, *Film and Literature: The Dynamics of Exchange* (New Haven: Yale University Press, 1979), p. 4.

12. Cohen, p. 92.

13. Bazin, *What Is Cinema?*, p. 76.

14. François Truffaut, "A Certain Tendency in French Cinema," in *Movies and Methods*, ed. Bill Nichols (Berkeley: University of California Press, 1976), pp. 224–36.

15. Emile Zola, "Naturalism and the Theater," in *The Experimental Novel and Other Essays*, trans. Belle Sherman (New York: Haskell House, 1964).

Robert B. Ray

The Field of "Literature and Film"

When you talk about the media today, one question constantly recurs: Do the new media wipe out the old?
Walter J. Ong

When you get right down to it, the most fantastic thing you could film is people reading.
Jean-Luc Godard

Although few people writing on the subject of film and literature have acknowledged it, a single question haunts this area of media studies: Why has this topic, obviously central to humanities-based film education, prompted so little distinguished work? In 1975 Louis D. Giannetti did manage to propose an answer: "The overwhelming bulk of what's been written about the relationship of film and literature is open to serious question."[1] Twenty-five years later, however, even that judgment seems generous, with its implication that books like George Bluestone's *Novels into Film* and Robert Richardson's *Literature and Film* would demand (and ultimately receive) a series of vigorous responses.[2] Instead, contemporary film study has simply ignored these books, dismissing them as completely as modern scientists have pre-Newtonian physics. And indeed, if a practicing physicist perforce regards as irrelevant to his own work Aristotle's theory of motion, what must a film semiotician or poststructuralist make of Richardson's chapter-length analysis of Eliot's *The Waste Land* and Fellini's *La Dolce Vita* as modern reworkings of *Ecclesiastes'* theme, "the emptiness of life"?[3] Thus, throughout much of the 1980s and 1990s, "Film and Literature" fell into thorough disrepute, as if the sensed inadequacies of the field's principal books, journal, and textbooks had somehow discredited the subject itself.[4] How did this situation arise? Answering that question should tell us something not only about film and literature, but also about the apparatuses[5] under which both have been taught.

Like the historical formation of any field of study, the formation of the field of film and literature is overdetermined. In other words, if we want to know why it took the direction it did, we need to look at the factors that influenced its development, in particular, from the most general to the most immediate: (1) the nature of narrative, (2) the norm of cinema, (3) the methods of academic literary and film study, and (4) the exigencies of the academic profession. Each of these factors has shaped the writing and teaching that have gone under the rubric "Film and Literature."

The Nature of Narrative

If from the early days of film criticism the cinema invited comparisons with literature (rather than with music, sculpture, architecture, or painting), the reason was obvious: both were narrative in format. (In fact, "film and literature" has always meant film and the novel or film and drama, never film and poetry, unless the poetry under consideration tells a story.) Theoretical work in "narratology," the study of narrative wherever it may be found, legitimized that comparison, demonstrating that as a means of organizing information, narrative is not specific to any one medium.[6] Since literature departments were traditionally charged with the responsibility for narrative, they inevitably appropriated for study this powerful new means of actualizing it—the movies. In doing so, however, these departments neglected to ask two questions that now seem crucial: first, do popular narratives differ in some fundamental way from "artistic," "high art" ones; and second, why had the cinema committed itself almost exclusively to storytelling? These questions went unaddressed as critics contented themselves with interminable analyses of individual cases, comparisons between novels and their filmed versions. In retrospect, the two questions overlooked seem to hold the key to the comparison between film and literature, and the failure to take them up almost certainly accounts for the dead end at which the field quickly found itself.

Of all academics, scholars of film and literature should have been the best situated to spot the first question's significance. With the whole enterprise of the Film and Literature founded on the hypothesis of narrative transmutability, they might have seen that stories (and popular stories in particular) depend for their legibility on codes, conventions, connotations, topoi, and tropes that similarly migrate from medium to medium—in short, on an intertextuality that includes not only film and literature, but all the other media as well. As Roland Barthes described this process, "The cultural codes [deployed by any single story] . . . will emigrate to other texts; there is no lack of hosts."[7]

Take, for example, the scene in *Casablanca* that introduces Rick Blaine (Humphrey Bogart). After a close-up of Rick's hand boldly authorizing a check, the camera pulls back to reveal Bogart, seated in a white dinner jacket, smoking a cigarette, playing with a chess set placed next to a half-empty champagne glass. As Hollywood knew perfectly well, the immediate, efficient, shorthand characterization telegraphed by this image (a sophisticated, jaded, clever man, simultaneously proud and melancholy) derived from the objects (tuxedo, champagne glass, and chess set), whose meaning had become coded through repeated similar uses in other movies, popular fiction, advertising, and comic strips and was also revealed by "common sense." At its most extreme, the Hollywood system sought to codify even its leading actors, turning them into predictably signifying objects, not only through consistent cinematic use (typecasting), but also through extracinematic, semiliterary forms of publicity (press releases, fan magazine articles, bios, interviews, and news plants).[8] Long before its critics, in other words, Hollywood recognized the perpetual interchange between film and writing and its role in creating (or controlling) meaning.

Film and literature scholars might have spotted this interchange, too, had they noticed how popular narratives differ from the avant-garde in relying heavily on codes that are never medium-specific.[9] Their specialized literary training, however, predisposed these critics to attend only to how a work functioned within its own medium's tradition: if *Madame Bovary* could best be explained by studying Flaubert's use of the novel form, then so could a movie. But although even (especially?) avant-garde texts deploy general codes (in the process Bakhtin called "heteroglossia"[10]), they typically display a preoccupation with their own medium that popular works, aimed at nonspecialist audiences, cannot afford. Further, as Barthes demonstrates in *S/Z*, avant-garde ("writerly") texts criticize, ironize, and parody the conventions on which popular ("readerly") works depend. Indeed, far from contesting their signifiers' received connotations, popular narratives such as *Casablanca* ratify them. To the extent that the sum of such connotations equals a culture's ideology, such ratification amounts to a political act affirming the status quo, and one no less important for taking place at the level of signs.

Their failure to spot popular narratives' distinctive, radical intertextuality caused film and literature scholars to miss an insight that was right before their eyes: if narrative was not specific to any medium, neither was ideology. Indeed, the instant accessibility of popular stories, especially those told by the movies, depends on a signifier's connotation remaining consistent as it migrates from form to form: if a champagne glass meant one thing in an ad and another in a film, *Casablanca*'s audience might not be so readily able to decipher Rick Blaine's character.

The histories of semiotic, reader-response, and structuralist accounts of the reading process (our negotiation with signs) converged in ideological criticism, a theoretical practice that the movies, a thoroughly commercial practice utterly exposed to the whims of the marketplace, have always demanded. Barthes made the connection between semiotics and ideology at least as early as *Mythologies* (1957; English version, 1972), his now-classic analysis of the behavior, events, and culture of everyday life. His 1964 dissection of a French pasta ad ("The Rhetoric of the Image")[11] made this point more explicit: immediate intelligibility requires signifiers whose connotations are predictable within a culture (e.g., a champagne glass, as opposed to a beer bottle, must always be used to suggest sophistication); the sum of these stock connotations equals a culture's ideology, its elaborate lexicon of representations. Understanding even a single ad, in short, requires that a reader participate (however ironically) in that lexicon whose signifiers he or she has necessarily encountered elsewhere.

Serious investigations of narrative intertextuality (and the ideological disposition it entails) began only with Barthes's *S/Z* (1970; English version, 1974). By subjecting a single Balzac novella to what he called "a slow motion reading" and by contrasting its "readerly" acceptance of convention with the ambivalence of *Bouvard and Pecuchet*, Barthes demonstrated that popular narratives not only follow the route of received ideology; they also propagate it. Such ideology is intertextual ("there is no lack of hosts"), but film and literature are especially visible sites of its traces.

Presumably familiar with both written and filmed narratives, film and literature scholars might have been among the first to recognize both the conventional ideological grounding of popular storytelling and its thoroughgoing intertextuality. Most, however, treated all narratives alike, simply transposing methods developed for the study of "high art" literature. Nevertheless, the few who immediately followed Barthes's lead often came from literature departments.[12] As a group, they distinguished themselves by appearing more interested in ideology and theory than in either literature or film per se. But their training in the latter two enabled them to detect the elaborate intertextual, ideological scaffolding that sustained popular fictions. Therefore, although the non-literature-based film program at Wisconsin became famous for distinguished aesthetic, formalist analyses, several of Indiana's film students from a comparative literature department went on to found *Jump Cut*, a Marxist journal that monitors the indiscriminate wanderings of ideology among the various narrative media, which now include music video.

The Norm of Cinema

The basic interest of the field of film and literature in how stories travel from medium to medium might have allowed the field to anticipate contemporary theory's linked concerns with narrative, intertextuality, and ideology. Sensing the importance of the second question—Why had the cinema committed itself almost exclusively to storytelling?—would have been more difficult. In fact, the overwhelmingly dominant filmmaking enterprise, Hollywood, has always worked as hard as possible to keep that question from occurring to anyone. Taking that effort into account, we can rephrase the question: Why was commercial filmmaking so eager to make the feature-length fictional narrative seem the inherent definition of *the cinema?* Significantly, the answer to that question involves narrative literature and, in particular, its favored status among a certain filmgoing population.

As early as 1964, Marshall McLuhan suggested an answer to the question of why movies tell stories: the content of a new medium, he wrote in *Understanding Media,* is always an old medium.[13] Therefore, written narratives appropriate oral tales just as the movies borrow from books and television from film. When we remember that more than half of all commercial movies derive from literature,[14] that television's basic genres (news, situation comedy, the detective story, melodrama, the western, etc.) descend from Hollywood, and that television devotes an enormous percentage of its programming to literally replaying old movies, we may think that McLuhan cleared up the problem.[15] But McLuhan articulated as a metaphysical principle what in fact was a historical development. There is no inherent definition of *the cinema.* For specific, albeit multiple reasons, our films have been almost exclusively fictional narratives. Under different circumstances, however, they might have become primarily lyric expressions, theoretical essays, scientific investigations, vaudeville reviews, or all these things and others besides. That they did not, of course, has everything to do with money.

Although the cinema has most often been compared with literature, it really has far more in common with architecture. Both forms are public, collaborative, and above all, expensive. In both arts, economic constraints have always dictated the shape of the work produced. By comparison, literature (especially "serious" literature) seems almost a priestly calling: novelists and poets, at least since Romanticism, have (for better or worse) been largely able to write whatever pleased them, without regard for audience or expense. At its origins, the cinema attested to divergent concerns, some similarly disinterested. Although Méliès intended his films as entertainments, the Lumière brothers, as Noël Burch has argued, regarded theirs as part of the scientific, research tradition of photographers Eadweard Muybridge and Albert Londe.[16] Although that tradition has survived in the documentary, both it and the stunts of Méliès quickly gave way, under commercial pressure, to what became the movies' principal form: narrative fiction.

In a series of important essays, Burch has maintained that although primitive cinema's *presentational* mode appealed to a proletarian audience accustomed to vaudeville, melodrama, circus, puppet shows, conjuring, and street entertainment, it did not satisfy the bourgeoisie's taste for the *representational*. The movies could do so only by adopting the bourgeoisie's preferred arts, the nineteenth-century realistic novel and drama, reactualized in cinema by means of what Burch calls "the Institutional Mode of Representation," his term for what is more commonly called "continuity" or "the invisible style."[17] In brief, the film industry spent the twentieth century's first two decades developing the cinematic equivalent of that seamless "writing degree zero" that Barthes saw as the essence of realist prose fiction.[18] The resulting system, largely in place by the early 1920s, and requiring for its perfection only the final cement of synchronous sound, turned on detailed protocols regarding shot-to-shot matching and mise-en-scène centering. The result was a rhetoric so naturalized that its traces disappeared: what appeared on the screen seemed the work of no maker's hand. More important, the single form that the movies had become now appeared the inevitable definition of *the cinema,* whose other possibilities were quickly forgotten.[19] This naturalized norm served another immediate purpose. As George Mitchell described, the major film producers' tacit decision to define *the movie* as a feature-length fiction employing stars and elaborate sets created a drastically effective barrier to entry that rapidly destroyed most independent production and established the oligopolistic industry we still know today.[20]

The whole enterprise of continuity rested on film's rapprochement with literature, especially with narrative prose fiction, whose enigmas, forward momentum, and psychological coherence motivate, and thereby conceal, all rhetorical machinery.[21] More urgently, literature provided a young, voracious, financially vulnerable industry with an apparently limitless supply of proved raw material. With "embourgeoisement" and consolidation achieved, Hollywood needed to concentrate on maintaining a hold over its recently acquired audience. Significantly, it often sought to do so, especially during box office downturns, by increasing its reliance on presold product: an already successful novel, story, Broadway play, or classic—in short, on literature.

Hollywood made its appropriation of literature's narrative mode seem inevitable. Nevertheless, in Ian Watt's 1957 *The Rise of the Novel,* film and literature scholars had a powerful precedent for regarding any aesthetic form as the product of historical (particularly economic) circumstances.[22] Their failure to make this connection had to do with the prevailing paradigm of English and with the concrete demands of the academic profession.

The Methods of Academic Study
of Film and Literature

Contemporary critical theory, perhaps emulating the Frankfurt School's productive merger of Freud and Marx, has typically worked synthetically. Film critics especially seized on the discovery that the apparently natural norm of realist narrative in fact rested on an ideologically sustained network of stock intertextual connotations. This position, in turn, led to the by now well-developed critique of realism as an inherently repressive mode.[23] Although their field might have given them a privileged viewpoint on these developments, film and literature scholars, as we have seen, did not anticipate Barthes's suggestive analyses of ideology's intertextual migrations and did not follow up on Watt's treatment of the novel as a historical formation. What did film and literature scholars do? Adaptation studies.

A look at Jeffrey Egan Welch's *Literature and Film: An Annotated Bibliography, 1909–1977*[24] will suggest the dominance of this one approach. Of 1,235 entries, the vast majority come equipped with titles such as the following:

> "Hemingway on the Screen: His Universal Themes Fared Better than His Topical Ones"
>
> "*Macbeth:* The Making of the Film"
>
> "Reconciliation: *Slaughterhouse-Five*—The Film and the Novel"
>
> "Sirk's *The Tarnished Angels: Pylon* Recreated"
>
> "Henry James into Film"
>
> "Films and Edith Wharton"
>
> "*Blow-up* from Cortazar to Antonioni"
>
> "*The Bridge on the River Kwai:* From the Novel to the Movie"
>
> "*The Fox:* The Film and the Novel"
>
> "Three Filmed *Hamlets*"

The sheer number of these articles, their dogged resort to the individual case study, the lack of any evidence of cumulative knowledge development or heuristic potential—all these factors suggest that, as a discipline, film and literature largely remained in what Thomas Kuhn called a "preparadigmatic state."[25] Without benefit of a presiding poetics, film and literature scholars could only persist in asking about individual movies the same unproductive layman's question (How does the film compare with the book?), getting the same unproductive answer (The book is better). Each article seemed isolated from all the others; its insights apparently stopped at the borders of the specific film or novel selected for analysis.

Strictly speaking, however, the field of film and literature was not without paradigm; for a field growing in the 1960s out of literature departments, it simply inherited the assumptions of the dominant New Criticism. But despite its paraphernalia of manifestos and scientistic vocabulary, the New Criticism proved ultimately antitheoretical. Its grounding in the individual critical sensibility (exemplified by T. S. Eliot's statement, "There is no method except to be very intelligent"[26]) and a reified notion of the text (which was to be appreciated for its "integrity," "relevance," "unity," "function," "maturity," "subtlety," and "adequacy"[27]) authorized only close readings of particular cases, not a more sweeping, explanatory poetics. Further, New Criticism's veneration of "art" and its famous hostility to translation ("the Heresy of Paraphrase"[28]) sponsored the obsessive refrain of the film and literature field that cinematic versions of literary classics failed to live up to their sources. Indeed, most of the articles written could have used a variation of the words in the title "But Compared to the Original . . . ."[29]

The inadequacy of this objection has become apparent. Philosophically, it rests on a hierarchy or opposition of *original* and *copy* that Jacques Derrida has repeatedly deconstructed. Practically, it rests on a notion that the "aura" of an original is dissipated by what Walter Benjamin first described as modernity's rapidly accumulating tools for mechanical reproduction.[30] In Derrida's terms, any criticism that denounces the copy in the name of the original works in vain to arrest the inevitable volatility of signs:

> And this is the possibility on which I want to insist: the possibility of disengagement and citational graft which belongs to the structure of every mark, spoken or written. . . . every sign, linguistic or non-linguistic, spoken or written . . . in small or large unit, can be *cited*, put between quotation marks; and in doing so it can break with every given context, engendering an infinity of new contexts in a manner which is absolutely illimitable.[31]

The film adaptation, in Derridean language, is not simply a faded imitation of a superior authentic original: it is a "citation" grafted into a new context, and thereby inevitably refunctioned. Therefore, far from destroying the literary source's meaning, adaptation "disseminates" it in a process that Benjamin found democratizing:

> Technical reproduction can put the copy of the original into situations which would be out of reach for the original itself. Above all, it enables the original to meet the beholder halfway, be it in the form of a photograph or a phonograph record. The cathedral leaves its locale to be received in the studio of a lover of art; the choral production, performed in an auditorium or in the open air, resounds in the drawing room. . . .
>
> One might generalize by saying: the technique of reproduction detaches the reproduced object from the domain of tradition. By making many reproductions it substitutes a plurality of copies for a unique

existence. And in permitting the reproduction to meet the beholder or listener in his own particular situation, it reactivates the object reproduced. These two processes lead to a tremendous shattering of tradition. . . .

Instead of being based on ritual, it [art] begins to be based on another practice—politics.[32]

Many film and literature scholars, however, resisted the process that Benjamin celebrated as inescapable. Fearful of seeing literature's narrative role usurped by the movies, and under the sway of New Criticism's religious reverence for "serious art," these critics typically used adaptation study to shore up literature's crumbling walls.

New Criticism's attempts to define the essence of poetry, the novel, and literature also encouraged film and literature scholars to use articles on adaptation as vehicles for speculating about, in the words of an article by Seymour Chatman, "What Novels Can Do That Films Can't (and Vice Versa)."[33] Such articles normally advised readers of the cinema's limitations: it had, for example, no tenses, no means of maintaining strict points of view, no descriptions, and no way of revealing "interior consciousness." Most of this criticism was useless, based as it was on the severely curtailed definition of *the movies* that Hollywood had successfully naturalized. Even in its reverse formulation—Eisenstein-sponsored discoveries of literary "anticipations" of cinematic devices such as montage—this whole project rested on notions of unchanging, idealist objects ("Literature" and "Cinema") now thoroughly discredited.

In sum, film and literature scholars wrote adaptation studies because New Criticism had trained them to do so. For some reason, they did not see that the cinema's very different determinations (commercial exposure, collaborative production, and public consumption) made irrelevant the methods of analysis developed for "serious literature."[34] That reason has much to do with the immediate demands of the academic profession.

The Exigencies of the Academic Profession

In Spring 1971 the Midwest Modern Language Association (MMLA) devoted its entire *Bulletin* to two topics: film and literature and the growing crisis in the academic job market.[35] Although the MMLA obviously regarded these two subjects as discrete, hindsight has exposed their connection. The sociology of knowledge has repeatedly demonstrated that basic academic structures, normally taken for granted (having been naturalized as thoroughly as Hollywood's continuity style), materially affect such things as canon formation, choice of methodologies, and definitions of literacy.[36] In specific, Jonathan Culler has observed how professional obligations have reinforced scholars' preference for isolated close readings:

> Our tenure system creates a need for theories and methods that gener-
> ate numerous small projects which can be completed in less than six
> years and listed on curriculum [sic] vitae. Since interpretation can gen-
> erate an endless series of twenty-page articles, it suits our system much
> better than theories whose projects would take years to complete. . . . It
> would be interesting to investigate whether in countries with different
> academic reward systems many fewer interpretations are published and
> writing about literature takes more varied forms.[37]

"An endless series of twenty-page articles" amounts to a reason-able description of what has been produced under the rubric of film and literature. In seeking why that situation came about, we should first remember that academic film study began its rise precisely at the moment when the job market for Ph.D.s in literature first fell apart—in the late 1960s and early 1970s. Obviously the admission of film study into literature departments was itself motivated by an attempt to main-tain declining enrollments in the humanities. For the individual job can-didate, untenured assistant professor, or ambitious tenured faculty mem-ber, the rapidly escalating requirements for employment, tenure, and promotion conspired to encourage rapid and frequent publication. Re-stricted in scope, demanding neither sustained research into nor histori-cal study about the two media, the typical adaptation study had things in common with that undergraduate staple, the comparison–contrast paper—it was easy to turn out, it satisfied the requirements, and it could be done over and over again. Surely it is no accident that the principal journal for such articles, *Literature/Film Quarterly,* began in 1973 as the job market worsened. Significantly (and admirably), that journal has always reserved most of its space for articles by graduate students, jun-ior faculty, and teachers at small, relatively unprestigious colleges and universities—all obviously groups needing to publish.[38]

Coda: Possibilities for Future Work

> *Inevitably, all writing will return to the pictogram. It's*
> *been foretold down the century as words turned into*
> *objects, stories fell apart, and the medium became the*
> *message.*
>
> C. Carr[39]

Twenty years ago, one of American film studies' most prominent fig-ures, Dudley Andrew, called for a moratorium on the kind of film and lit-erature article I have been describing—what Andrew referred to as "the discourse of fidelity," "unquestionably the most frequent and most tiresome discussion of adaptation." Nevertheless, Andrew summoned E. H. Gombrich and André Bazin as supporters for the argument that "one cannot dismiss adaptation since it is a fact of human practice." In his article, reprinted in this volume, he wrote:

> We can and do correctly match items from different systems all the time: a tuba sound is more like a rock than a piece of string; it is more like a bear than a bird; more like a Romanesque church than a Baroque one. . . . Adaptation then becomes a matter of searching two systems of communication for elements of equivalent position in the system capable of eliciting a signified at a given level of pertinence, for example, the description of a narrative action.[40]

Speculating about possibilities for future research in film and literature requires that we ask the question: What do we need to know? Elsewhere in his article, Andrew proposed that adaptation studies might continue fruitfully were film and literature brought "out of the realm of eternal principle and airy generalization, and onto the uneven but solid ground of artistic history, practice, and discourse" (p. 14)—an indisputable suggestion, but one that might simply foster more rigorous investigations of the transactions between classic literature and serious filmmaking. I think we more urgently need to know something else.

If, in Gombrich's terms, knowledge about adaptation simply entails the ability to isolate systematic equivalences capable of generating the same signified, then the commercial media, never fussy about mixing forms, have long since beaten academics to the punch. Confronted by our century's distinctive feature—a media industry whose shared (and oppressive) representations converge from every side to structure even our unconscious lives—we have no idea how to fight back. Academic life and its resulting pedagogy are still bound to the word; the more supple tools that impinge upon us—images and sounds combined with language—we have not yet learned to use.

As a movement in the arts, sciences, and critical theory, postmodernism teaches that things repressed (objects, groups, signs, questions) return in displaced form. Ignored soup labels return as Warhol's avant-garde paintings, women's studies becomes feminist theory, and photographs of Vietnam appear on punk rock album covers. Similarly, film and literature, repressed as a topic by film studies' leading institutions and scholars, has for some time been reappearing as explorations into transactions between word and image. Prominent precedents have long existed: Freud's positing of the unconscious (and the dream) as a rebus, Eisenstein's and Pound's fascination with the Chinese ideogram, Barthes's semiotic inquiries into the relationships between photograph and caption, Godard's experiments with language remotivating imagery, Eikhenbaum's thesis that filmwatching depends on the viewer's accompanying the images viewed with his or her own "inner speech," Francis Yates's description of Renaissance memory systems founded on mentally stored images, Derrida's research into the vestigial hieroglyphic elements of our writing, and Alexandre Astruc's famous demand that we use the camera to *write*.[41] Why as students and teachers should we care about the relationship of word and image? The answer is already contained in the writings I've just mentioned, which ought to provoke future work in a transformed field of film and literature.

In a provocative series of essays analyzing the decisive shift from orality to writing in Ancient Greece, Eric A. Havelock demonstrated that every facet of a culture's life is influenced by its presiding means of communication.[42] Nearly fifty years ago, Arnold Hauser labeled the twentieth century "The Film Age."[43] Although film and television, and now computers, have steadily supplanted the book as our presiding means of communication, we continue to live in a period of transition, with the two forms, word and image, existing side by side. Commercial interests have long since learned *one* way of using the communications resources whose richness no other historical period can equal. The task facing all of us, especially film and literature scholars, involves rethinking the media's fait accompli, imagining new ways in which words and images can be adapted or combined, as well as new purposes for those combinations.

NOTES

1. Louis D. Giannetti, *Godard and Others: Essays on Film Form* (Rutherford, N.J.: Fairleigh Dickinson University Press, 1975), p. 89.

2. George Bluestone, *Novels into Film: The Metamorphosis of Fiction into Cinema* (Berkeley: University of California Press, 1968); Robert Richardson, *Literature and Film* (Bloomington: Indiana University Press, 1969).

3. Richardson, *Literature and Film*, pp. 194–218. This chapter is discussed (critically) by James Goodwin in "Literature and Film: A Review of Criticism," *Quarterly Review of Film Studies*, 4:2 (Spring 1974), pp. 227–46 (see especially pp. 229–30). Goodwin's survey article provides the best early introduction to the field of film and literature. By far the best recent survey is Timothy Corrigan's *Film and Literature: An Introduction and Reader* (Upper Saddle River, N.J.: Prentice-Hall, 1999).

4. The subject's main journal is *Literature/Film Quarterly*, begun in 1973 at Salisbury State College. Of the earlier books, Seymour Chatman's *Story and Discourse: Narrative Structure in Fiction and Film* (Ithaca, N.Y.: Cornell University Press, 1978) and Dudley Andrew's chapter "Adaptation," in *Concepts in Film Theory* (New York: Oxford University Press, 1984), seem the most abidingly useful.

5. I am using the word *apparatus* in Brecht's sense to mean the conditions under which information is produced, distributed, and consumed. As Brecht pointed out, in a justifiably famous remark, "Great apparati like the opera, the stage, the press, etc., impose their views as it were incognito." *Brecht on Theatre*, ed. John Willett (New York: Hill and Wang, 1964), p. 34.

6. For an excellent discussion of this point, see Seymour Chatman's "What Novels Can Do That Films Can't (and Vice Versa)," *Critical Inquiry*, 7:1 (Autumn 1980),

Robert B. Ray

pp. 121–22. Robert Scholes makes the same point in *Semiotics and Interpretation* (New Haven: Yale University Press, 1982), p. 57.

7. Roland Barthes, *S/Z*, trans. Richard Miller (New York: Hill and Wang, 1974), p. 205.

8. For two excellent discussions of how the apparently extratextual material (e.g., publicity, distribution, even rumor) inflects the readings of a particular text, see Tony Bennett, "Text and Social Process: The Case of James Bond," *Screen Education* 41 (Winter–Spring 1982), pp. 3–14, and Annette Kuhn, *Women's Pictures: Feminism and the Cinema* (London: Routledge and Kegan Paul, 1982), pp. 3–18, 125–26, and 178–96.

9. I recognize that this point is debatable. A counterargument might invoke Barthes's *S/Z* as evidence of the radical intertextuality of all texts. But we often forget that *S/Z*'s point is based on an analysis of a popular text, Balzac's *Sarrasine*.

10. M. M. Bakhtin, *The Dialogic Imagination*, trans. Caryl Emerson and Michael Holquist (Austin: University of Texas, 1981), pp. 263, 428.

11. In Roland Barthes, *Image Music Text*, trans. Stephen Heath (New York: Hill and Wang, 1977), pp. 32–51.

12. Judith Mayne, for example, superbly outlined *S/Z*'s importance to the subject of film and literature in "Introduction: Film/Narrative/The Novel," *Ciné-Tracts* 13 (1981), not paginated. I am also thinking here of Julia Lesage, who quickly saw *S/Z*'s relevance to film study. See her "*S/Z* and Film Criticism" and "*S/Z* and *Rules of the Game*," *Jump Cut* 12–13 (1976), pp. 41–51, and "Teaching the Comparative Analysis of Novels and Films," *Style* 9 (1975), pp. 453–68. Lesage studied in Indiana University's Comparative Literature department and cofounded *Jump Cut*.

13. Marshall McLuhan, *Understanding Media: The Extensions of Man* (New York: McGraw-Hill, 1964), p. vii.

14. Dudley Andrew, "The Well-Worn Muse: Adaptation in Film History and Theory," in *Narrative Strategies: Original Essays in Film and Prose Fiction*, ed. Syndy M. Conger and Janice R. Welsch (Macomb: Western Illinois University Press, 1980), p. 10. This estimate may be high. In "The Literary Adaptation," *Screen* 23:1 (May–June 1982), p. 3, John Ellis says: "About 30 percent of all narrative films made in Hollywood's classic period were adapted from novels and short stories." Even working from the other direction, the percentages still startle: in "Hollywood and the Novelist: It's a Fickle Romance, at Best," *The New York Times* (14 July 1985), section 2, p. 1, Edwin McDowell once estimated that one in fifty novels gets optioned for the movies.

15. Between 1952 and 1955 all the major Hollywood studios except MGM sold most of their pre-1948 films to distributors who promptly sold them to local television stations. See Erik Barnouw, *Tube of Plenty: The Evolution of American Television* (New York: Oxford University Press, 1975), pp. 197–98. By 1968, apart from its non-prime-time showings, television had an *ABC Sunday Night Movie*, an *NBC Monday Night Movie*, an *NBC Tuesday Night Movie*, an *ABC Wednesday Night Movie*, a *CBS Thursday Night Movie*, a *CBS Friday Night Movie*, and to complete the week, an *NBC Saturday Night Movie*. For listings of the annual prime-time schedules, see Tim Brooks and Earle Marsh, *The Complete Directory to Prime Time Network and Cable TV Shows 1946–Present* (New York: Ballantine, 1995).

16. Noël Burch, "Charles Baudelaire versus Doctor Frankenstein," *Afterimage* (London) 8–9 (Spring 1981), pp 4–21.

17. For portions of Burch's argumentative archaeology of the cinema, see the following: "Porter, or Ambivalence," *Screen* 19:4 (Winter 1978–79), pp. 91–105; "Film's Institutional Mode of Representation and the Soviet Response," *October* 11 (Winter 1979), pp. 77–96; "A Parenthesis on Film History," in Burch's *To the Distant Observer: Form and Meaning in the Japanese Cinema* (Berkeley: University of California Press, 1979), pp. 61–66; "How We Got into Pictures: Notes Accompanying Correction Please," *Afterimage* (London) 8–9 (Spring 1981), pp. 22–38. Burch summarized this argument in his book *Life to Those Shadows*, trans. Ben Brewster (Berkeley: University of California Press, 1990).

The book, however, proved less interestingly provocative than the articles from which it was derived. Burch based part of his argument about the "embourgeoisement" of the cinema on Russell Merritt's landmark article, "Nickelodeon Theaters, 1905–1914: Building an Audience for the Movies," in *The American Film Industry*, ed. Tino Balio (Madison: University of Wisconsin Press, 1985), pp. 83–102. Another excellent article in this tradition is Margaret Morse's "Paradoxes of Realism: The Rise of Film in the Train of the Novel," *Ciné-Tracts* 13 (Spring 1981), pp. 27–37.

18. Roland Barthes, *Writing Degree Zero*, trans. Annette Lavers and Colin Smith (New York: Hill and Wang, 1968).

19. Readers interested in a brief description of classic Hollywood's stylistic protocols may wish to consult my book *A Certain Tendency of the Hollywood Cinema, 1930–1980* (Princeton, N.J.: Princeton University Press, 1985), pp. 32–55.

20. George Mitchell, "The Consolidation of the American Film Industry 1915–1920," *Ciné-Tracts* 6 (Spring 1979), pp. 28–36, and *Ciné-Tracts* 7–8 (Fall 1979), pp. 63–70.

21. In *S/Z* Barthes wittily observes (p. 127) that often a narrative's sheer speed keeps a reader from asking questions.

22. Another precedent was Arnold Hauser's monumental four-volume *The Social History of Art* (New York: Vintage), which first appeared in the United States in 1951.

23. The leading book in this "constructivist" tradition is, of course, *S/Z*. A useful summary of this position appears in Tony Stevens, "Reading the Realist Film," *Screen Education* 26 (Spring 1978), pp. 13–35. Other important discussions in this vein include Colin MacCabe, "Realism and the Cinema: Notes on Some Brechtian Theses," *Screen* 15:2 (Summer 1974), pp. 7–27; Terry Lovell, *Pictures of Reality: Aesthetics, Politics and Pleasure* (London: British Film Institute, 1980); Sylvia Harvey, *May '68 and Film Culture* (London: British Film Institute, 1978); and Catherine Belsey, *Critical Practice* (London: Methuen, 1980).

24. Jeffrey Egan Welch, *Literature and Film: An Annotated Bibliography, 1909–1977* (New York: Garland, 1981).

25. Thomas Kuhn, *The Structure of Scientific Revolutions* (Chicago: University of Chicago Press, 1970), pp. 10–22, 43–51.

26. Quoted by Terence Hawkes in *Structuralism and Semiotics* (Berkeley: University of California Press, 1977), p. 152. Hawkes's book contains a useful summary of New Criticism's assumptions (pp. 151–56).

27. These words come from one of New Criticism's manifestos, W. K. Wimsatt and Monroe Beardsley's "The Intentional Fallacy," in Wimsatt's *The Verbal Icon: Studies in the Meaning of Poetry* (Lexington: University of Kentucky Press, 1954).

28. The title of Cleanth Brooks's famous essay, found in his book *The Well-Wrought Urn: Studies in the Structure of Poetry* (New York: Harcourt, Brace and World, 1947), pp. 192–214.

29. An actual title of an article by William Fadiman, who, in fact, criticized the tendency I am describing. See *Films and Filming* 11:5 (1965), pp. 21–23.

30. For film students, a convenient place to find Walter Benjamin's famous essay "The Work of Art in the Age of Mechanical Reproduction" is in *Film Theory and Criticism*, eds. Leo Braudy and Marshall Cohen (New York: Oxford University Press, 1999), pp. 731–51. It also appears, differently translated, in Benjamin's *Illuminations* (New York: Schocken, 1969).

31. Jacques Derrida, "Signature Event Context," *Glyph* 1 (1977), p. 185.

32. Braudy and Cohen, *Film Theory and Criticism*, pp. 733–34, 736.

33. Seymour Chatman, "What Novels Can Do That Films Can't (and Vice Versa)," *Critical Inquiry* 7:1 (Autumn 1980), pp. 121–40.

34. Not surprisingly, initial work on television made the same mistake by simply carrying over a series of questions from film study that may or may not obtain in this different medium. When scholars trained in New Criticism's methods of close reading first

approached the cinema, they inevitably gravitated to apparently complex, ambiguous "art" films such as Bergman's, and rightly so, because Hollywood films, although even more complex with their concealed reliance on intertextual networks, seemed slight by comparison. Making sense of how these popular movies worked required a whole new set of questions—those having to do with ideology, semiotics, the experiences of reading, and identification. Those issues may or may not apply to basic television genres. So far, the best work on television takes into account television viewers' far more casual attention to images and sounds that have become, for many people, almost part of the household furniture.

35. *The Bulletin of the Midwest Modern Language Association* 4:1 (Spring 1971).

36. See, for example, Brian McCrea's argument that English professors' need for apparently complex texts has resulted in the banishment from the curriculum of the relatively straightforward Addison and Steele in *Addison and Steele Are Dead: The English Department, Its Canon, and the Professionalization of Literary Criticism* (Newark: University of Delaware Press, 1990). The most comprehensive discussion of how academic structures affect assumed notions about "literature" and teaching appears in Gerald Graff's *Professing Literature: An Institutional History* (Chicago: University of Chicago Press, 1987). Also useful is Robert Scholes's *The Rise and Fall of English* (New Haven: Yale University Press, 1998).

37. Jonathan Culler, "The Critical Assumption," in *SCE Reports* 6 (Fall 1979) (The Society for Critical Exchange), p. 83.

38. I have written elsewhere about the job market's pernicious effect on the kinds of film study work that gets published. See my book *The Avant-Garde Finds Andy Hardy* (Cambridge: Harvard University Press, 1995), pp. 5–10.

39. C. Carr, "M. Kasper's Glyph Hangers," *The Village Voice Literary Supplement* (March 1985), p. 19.

40. Dudley Andrew, "The Well-Worn Muse: Adaptation in Film History and Theory," in *Narrative Strategies: Original Essays in Film and Prose Fiction*, note 19, pp. 12–13, quoted as edited for this volume. For an excellent discussion of "the discourse of fidelity," see Christopher Orr, "The Discourse on Adaptation," *Wide Angle* 6:2 (1984), pp. 72–76.

41. On Freud's analogy of the unconscious and the dream to the rebus, see *The Interpretation of Dreams*, trans. A. A. Brill (New York: Modern Library, 1950). On the ideogram, see Sergei Eisenstein, "The Cinematographic Principle and the Ideogram," in his *Film Form*, trans. Jay Leyda (New York: Harcourt, 1949), pp. 28–44, and Ernest Fenollosa, *The Chinese Written Character as a Medium for Poetry*, ed. Ezra Pound (San Francisco: City Lights Books, 1936). For Barthes's semiotic investigations, see "The Photographic Message" and "Rhetoric of the Image" in his *Image Music Text*, trans. Stephen Heath (New York: Hill and Wang, 1977), pp. 7–31.

Almost all Godard's films explore the relationship between word and image (he calls his own production company Sonimage). I am thinking in particular of two scenes: the first, in *Masculin-Féminin* (1966), in which the image of the pretty "Mademoiselle 19 Ans" competes with the tendentious caption ("Dialogue with a Consumer Product") that introduces her; the second, in *2 ou 3 choses que je sais d'elle* (1966), in which consecutive voice-overs introduce the same woman as first actress and then fictional character.

The best article on Eikhenbaum's "inner speech" is Paul Willemen's "Cinematic Discourse: The Problem of Inner Speech," in his *Looks and Frictions: Essays in Cultural Studies and Film Theory* (Bloomington: Indiana University Press/British Film Institute, 1994), pp. 27–55. See also my book *The Avant-Garde Finds Andy Hardy* (Cambridge: Harvard University Press, 1995), chapter 2. On Renaissance memory systems, see Frances Yates, *The Art of Memory* (Chicago: University of Chicago Press, 1966). For a fascinating historical extrapolation from Yates's work, see Jonathan D. Spence, *The Memory Palace of Matteo Ricci* (New York: Viking, 1984). The best study of Derrida's interest in hieroglyphics is Gregory L. Ulmer's *Applied Grammatology: Post(e)-Pedagogy from Jacques Derrida to Joseph Beuys* (Baltimore: Johns Hopkins University Press, 1985). On the *caméra-stylo,* see Alexandre Astruc, *"Le caméra-stylo,"* in *The New Wave,* ed. Peter Graham (Garden City, N.J.: Doubleday, 1968), pp. 17–24.

42. See Eric A. Havelock, *Preface to Plato* (Cambridge: Harvard University Press, 1963) and *The Literate Revolution in Greece and Its Cultural Consequences* (Princeton: Princeton University Press, 1982).

43. Hauser, *The Social History of Art,* vol. 4 (New York: Vintage, 1951), pp. 226–59.

Robert Stam

Beyond Fidelity:
The Dialogics of Adaptation

The language of criticism dealing with the film adaptation of novels has often been profoundly moralistic, awash in terms such as *infidelity, betrayal, deformation, violation, vulgarization,* and *desecration,* each accusation carrying its specific charge of outraged negativity. *Infidelity* resonates with overtones of Victorian prudishness; *betrayal* evokes ethical perfidy; *deformation* implies aesthetic disgust; *violation* calls to mind sexual violence; *vulgarization* conjures up class degradation; and *desecration* intimates a kind of religious sacrilege toward the "sacred word." In this chapter I would like to move beyond a moralistic approach to propose specific strategies for the analysis of adaptations. Rather than develop a full-blown narratological theory of novel and film, my agenda is modest and practical. But first I need to deal with the issue of "fidelity."

The Chimera of Fidelity

Let me begin by acknowledging that the notion of the fidelity of an adaptation to its source novel does contain its grain of truth. When we say an adaptation has been "unfaithful" to the original, the term gives expression to the disappointment we feel when a film adaptation fails to capture what we see as the fundamental narrative, thematic, and aesthetic features of its literary source. The notion of fidelity gains its persuasive force from our sense that some adaptations are indeed better than others and that some adaptations fail to "realize" or substantiate that which we most appreciated in the source novels. Words such as *infidelity* and *betrayal* in this sense translate our feeling, when we have loved a book, that an adaptation has not been worthy of that love. We read a novel through our introjected desires, hopes, and utopias, and as we read we fashion our own imaginary mise-en-scène of the novel on the private stages of our minds. When we are confronted with someone else's phantasy, as Christian Metz pointed out long ago, we feel the loss of our own phantasmatic relation to the novel, with the result that the adaptation itself becomes a kind of "bad object."[1] To paraphrase the Georges Perec lines borrowed by Godard in *Masculin Feminin*, "We left the theatre sad. It was not the adaptation of which we had dreamed. . . . It wasn't the film we would have liked to make. Or, more secretly, that we would have liked to live."[2]

But the partial persuasiveness of "fidelity" should not lead us to endorse it as an exclusive methodological principle. The notion of fidelity is highly problematic for a number of reasons. First, it is questionable whether strict fidelity is even possible. A counter-view would insist that an adaptation is automatically different and original due to the change of medium. Here we can take as our own Fritz Lang's response (in *Contempt*) to the producer Prokosch's accusation of infidelity to the script: "Yes, Jerry, in the script it's written, in a film it's images and sounds . . . a motion picture it's called." The words of a novel, as countless commentators have pointed out, have a virtual, symbolic meaning; we as readers, or as directors, have to fill in their paradigmatic indeterminances. A novelist's portrayal of a character as "beautiful" induces us to imagine the person's features in our minds. Flaubert never even tells us the exact color of Emma Bovary's eyes, but we color them nonetheless. A film, by contrast, must choose a specific performer. Instead of a virtual, verbally constructed Madame Bovary open to our imaginative reconstruction, we are faced with a specific actress, encumbered with nationality and accent, a Jennifer Jones or an Isabelle Huppert.

This "automatic difference" between film and novel becomes evident even in fairly straightforward adaptations of specific novelistic passages. Take, for example, the passage from Steinbeck's *The Grapes of Wrath* in which Ma Joad contemplates her memorabilia just before leaving her Oklahoma home for California:

> She sat down and opened the box. Inside were letters, clippings, photographs, a pair of earrings, a little gold signet ring, and a watch chain braided of hair and tipped with gold swivels. She touched the letters with her fingers, touched them lightly, and she smoothed a newspaper clipping on which there was an account of Tom's trial. (*The Grapes of Wrath*, London: Penguin, 1976, p. 118)

In this case a realist director (John Ford) adapted a realist novel just a few months after the novel's publication, attempting a "faithful" rendition of the specific passage. In the film we see Ma Joad sit down, open the box, and look at letters, clippings, photographs, and so forth. But even here the "cinematization" generates an inevitable supplement. Where Steinbeck wrote "photographs," Ford had to choose specific photographs. The mention of "earrings" in the novel does not dictate Ford's choice of having Ma Joad try them on. The newspaper account of Tom's trial requires the choice of a specific newspaper, specific headlines, specific illustrations, and specific fonts, none of which is spelled out in the original. But beyond such details of mise-en-scène, the very processes of filming—the fact that the shots have to be composed, lit, and edited in a certain way—generates an automatic difference. Nothing in the novel prepares us for the idea that Ma Joad will look at the memorabilia by the light of a fire or that the fire's reflection will flicker over her face. Nothing dictates the point-of-view cutting that alternates close shots of Ma Joad's face with what she is looking at, the contemplative rhythm of shot and reverse shot, or the interplay of on-screen and off-screen space, all of which is arguably in the spirit of the novel but not literally in the written text. Nor does the Steinbeck passage mention music, yet the Ford version features a melancholy accordion version of a song ("Red River Valley"). And even if the text had mentioned "Red River Valley," that would still be quite different from our actually hearing it performed. And even if the passage had mentioned both the music and the firelight and the light's flickering over Ma Joad's face, that would still not be anything like our seeing her face (or Jane Darwell's) and hearing the music at the same time.

The shift from a single-track, uniquely verbal medium such as the novel, which "has only words to play with," to a multitrack medium such as film, which can play not only with words (written and spoken), but also with theatrical performance, music, sound effects, and moving photographic images, explains the unlikelihood—and I would suggest even the undesirability—of literal fidelity. Because novels do not usually feature soundtracks, for example, should the filmmaker deprive him or herself of music as an expressive resource?[3] But quite apart from this change in signifying materials, other contingencies also render fidelity in adaptation virtually impossible. The demand for fidelity ignores the actual processes of making films—for example, the differences in cost and in modes of production. A novel is usually produced by a single individual; the film is almost always a collaborative project, mobilizing at minimum a crew of four or five people and at maximum a cast and crew and support staff of hundreds. Although novels are relatively unaffected by questions of budget, films are deeply immersed in material and financial contingencies. Therefore, grand panoramic novels such as *War and Peace* might be difficult to film on a low budget, whereas interiorized novellas such as *Notes from Underground* seem more manageable. With a novel, questions of material infrastructure enter only at the point of distribution, whereas in the cinema they enter at the phase of production of the text itself. Although a novel can be written on napkins in prison, a film assumes a complex material infrastructure—camera, film stock, laboratories—simply in order to exist. Although it costs almost nothing for a novelist to write "The Marquis left Versailles palace at 5:00 P.M. on a cold and wintry day in January 1763," the filmmaker requires substantial funding in order to stage a simulacral Paris (or to shoot on location), to dress the actors in period costume, and so forth.

The notion of "fidelity" is essentialist in relation to both media involved. First, it assumes that a novel "contains" an extractable "essence," a kind of "heart of the artichoke" hidden "underneath" the surface details of style. Hidden within *War and Peace*, it is assumed, there is an originary core, a kernel of meaning or nucleus of events that can be "delivered" by an adapation. But in fact there is no such transferable core: a single novelistic text comprises a series of verbal signals that can generate a plethora of possible readings, including even readings of the narrative itself. The literary text is not a closed, but an open structure (or, better, structuration, as the later Barthes would have it) to be reworked by a boundless context. The text feeds on and is fed into an infinitely permutating intertext, which is seen through ever-shifting grids of interpretation.

This process is further complicated by the passage of time and by change of place. The verbal signals are not always communicated in the same way in a changed context. References obvious to eighteenth-century readers of *Robinson Crusoe* are not necessarily obvious to twentieth-century readers. References clear to English readers of the novel are not necessarily clear to French readers. At the same time, certain features of Defoe's hero, such as his misogyny and latent homoeroticism, might be *more* visible to present-day than to eighteenth-century readers precisely because contemporary critical discourses have made feminist and homosexual readings available. The greater the lapse in time, the less reverence toward the source text and the more likely the reinterpretation through the values of the present. Thus Jack Gold's adaptation of *Robinson Crusoe, Man Friday*, "sees" the Defoe novel through the contemporary values of the counter-culture—spontaneity, sexual freedom, antiracism.

The question of fidelity ignores the wider question: Fidelity to what? Is the filmmaker to be faithful to the plot in its every detail? That might mean a thirty-hour version of *War and Peace*. Virtually all filmmakers condense the events of the novels being adapted, if only to conform to the norms of conventional theatrical release. Should one be faithful to the physical descriptions of characters? Perhaps so, but what if the actor who happens to fit the description of Nabokov's Humbert also happens to be a mediocre actor? Or is one to be faithful to the author's intentions? But what might they be, and how are they to be inferred? Authors often mask their intentions for personal or psychoanalytic reasons or for external or censorious ones. An author's expressed intentions are not necessarily relevant, since literary critics warn us away from the "intentional fallacy," urging us to "trust the tale not the teller." The author, Proust taught us, is not necessarily a purposeful, self-present individual, but rather "un autre moi." Authors are sometimes not even aware of their own deepest intentions. How, then, can filmmakers be faithful to them? And to what authorial instance is one to be faithful? To the biographical author? To the textual implied author? To the narrator? Or is the adapter-filmmaker to be true to the style of a work? To its narrative point of view? Or to its artistic devices?[4]

Much of the discussion of film adaptation quietly reinscribes the axiomatic superiority of literary art to film, an assumption derived from a number of superimposed prejudices: *seniority,* the assumption that older arts are necessarily better arts; *iconophobia,* the culturally rooted prejudice (traceable to the Judaic-Muslim-Protestant prohibitions on "graven images" and to the Platonic and Neoplatonic depreciation of the world of phenomenal appearance) that visual arts are necessarily inferior to the verbal arts; and *logophilia,* the converse valorization, characteristic of the "religions of the book," of the "sacred word" of holy texts.

Structuralist and poststructuralist theoretical developments, meanwhile, indirectly undermine some of these prejudices in ways that have implications for our discussion of adaptation. The structuralist semiotics of the 1960s and 1970s treated all signifying practices as productive of "texts" worthy of the same close attention as literary texts. The Bakhtinian "translinguistic" conception of the author as the orchestrator of preexisting discourses, meanwhile, along with Foucault's downgrading of the author in favor of a pervasive anonymity of discourse, opened the way to a "discursive" and nonoriginary approach to all arts. With poststructuralism the figure of the author, rather like the Robin Williams character in *Deconstructing Harry,* loses focus and firmness. Derridean deconstruction, meanwhile, by dismantling the hierarchy of "original"and "copy," suggests that both are caught up in the infinite play of dissemination. A film adaptation seen as a "copy," by analogy, would not necessarily be inferior to the novel as the "original." And if authors are fissured, fragmented, multidiscursive, hardly "present" even to themselves, how can an adaptation communicate the "self-presence" of authorial intention? In the same vein, Roland Barthes's provocative leveling of the hierarchy between literary criticism and literature tends, by analogy, to rescue the film adaptation as a form of criticism or "reading" of the novel, one not necessarily subordinate to the source novel.

From Essence to Specificity

A variation on the theme of fidelity suggests that an adaptation should be faithful not so much to the source text, but rather to the essence of the medium of expression. This "medium-specificity" approach assumes that every medium is inherently "good at" certain things and "bad at" others.[5] A cinematic essence is posited as favoring certain aesthetic possibilities and foreclosing others, as if a specific aesthetic were inscribed on the celluloid itself. Here is film critic Pauline Kael (in *Deeper into Movies*) on the subject of the "natural" propensities of the film medium:

> Movies are good at action; they're not good at reflective thought or conceptual thinking. They're good at immediate stimulus, but they're not a good means of involving people in the other arts or in learning about a subject. The film techniques themselves seem to stand in the way of the development of curiosity.

Kael seems to be saying that films cannot be intelligent or reflective—and this is from someone who claims to be a "fan" of the movies. Despite her self-proclaimed populism, Kael shares with certain literary elitists the assumption that the cinema inevitably lacks the depth and dignity of literature. But apart from her factitious hierarchizing of the arts, Kael makes suspect generalizations about the cinema. Are films good at portraying only action and not subjective states? What about surrealism and expressionism, not to mention music and video or the work of Alfred Hitchcock? Should film not be "theatrical"? Should all the films inspired by Brecht in their dramaturgy or by Stanislavsky in their acting be dismissed as "uncinematic"? Notions of filmic and literary essence, in this sense, impose an oppressive straitjacket on an open-ended and "non-finalized" set of practices.

A more satisfying formulation would emphasize not ontological essence, but rather diacritical specificity. Each medium has its own specificity deriving from its respective materials of expression. The novel has a single material of expression, the written word, whereas the film has at least five tracks: moving photographic image, phonetic sound, music, noises, and written materials. In this sense, the cinema has not lesser, but rather greater resources for expression than the novel, and this is independent of what actual filmmakers have done with these resources. (I am arguing not superiority of talent, but only complexity of resources. Indeed, one could credit literary fictioners with doing a lot with little, whereas filmmakers could be censured for doing so little with so much.) In a suggestive passage, Nabokov's Humbert Humbert laments the prodding deliberateness of prose fiction, with its subordination to linear consecution, its congenital incapacity to seize the moment in its multifaceted simultaneity. Gleefully reporting his wife Charlotte's providential death by car crash, he deplores having to put "the impact of an instantaneous vision into a sequence of words." The "physical accumulation on the page," he complains, "impairs the actual flash, the sharp unity of impression" (*Lolita* [New York: Berkley Medallion, 1977], p. 91). By contrast, the same crash as staged by Kubrick's *Lolita* offers precisely this simultaneity of impression: we see the crash as we hear it, along with the commentative music that conveys a specific attitude toward the events presented. Yet I am in no way arguing the superiority of the

Kubrick rendition. Nabokov, paradoxically, conveys more sense of discontinuity (for example, between the tragic theme of untimely death on the one hand and Humbert's flip, cynical, self-regarding style of presentation on the other) than does Kubrick, despite the discontinuous multiplicity of the film tracks.

Although Humbert Humbert lusts after the cinema's "fantastic simultaneousness," he might also envy its potential for nonsimultaneity, its capacity for mingling apparently contradictory times and temporalities. Each of the filmic tracks can potentially develop an autonomous temporality entering into complex relations with the other tracks. Film's multitrack nature makes it possible to stage contradiction between music and image—for example, Kubrick's underscoring of the opening shot of nuclear bombers, in *Dr. Strangelove*, with the instrumental version of "Try a Little Tenderness." A quoted piece of music, with its own rhythm and continuity, can "accompany" an image track characterized by a different rhythm and continuity. Thus the cinema offers possibilities of disunity and disjunction not immediately available to the novel. The possible contradictions between tracks become an aesthetic resource, opening the way to a multitemporal, polyrhythmic cinema.

The novelistic character also potentially undergoes a kind of fissure or fragmentation within the film adaptation. Although the novelistic character is a verbal artifact, constructed quite literally out of words, the cinematic character is a uncanny amalgam of photogenie, body movement, acting style, and grain of voice, all amplifed and molded by lighting, mise-en-scène, and music. And although novels have only character, film adaptations have both character (actantial function) and performer, allowing for possibilities of interplay and contradiction denied a purely verbal medium. In the cinema a single actor can play many roles: Peter Sellers played three roles in *Dr. Strangelove*, Eddie Murphy five roles in *The Nutty Professor*. Conversely, multiple performers can play a single role: different actors portrayed the four incarnations of Christ in Rocha's *Age of the Earth*, and two actresses (Angela Molina and Carole Bouquet) played Conchita in Buñuel's adaptation of *The Woman and the Puppet* (*That Obscure Object of Desire*).

In the cinema the performer also brings along a kind of baggage, a thespian intertext formed by the totality of antecedent roles. Thus Lawrence Olivier brings with him the intertextual memory of his Shakespeare performances, just as Madonna brings the memory of the various personae of her music videos. By casting Jack Palance as the hated film producer Prokosch in *Contempt*, the auteurist Godard brilliantly exploited the sinister memory of Palance's previous roles as a barbarian (in *The Barbarians*, 1959), and as Atilla the Hun (in *Sign of the Pagans*, 1959). This producer, the casting seems to be telling us, is both a gangster and a barbarian, a suggestion confirmed by the brutish behavior of the character. The director can also have the performer play against the intertext, thus exploiting a realm of tension not available to the novel. To appreciate the force of this difference, we need only contemplate the consequences of other casting choices. What would have happened if Fritz Lang had played the Prokosch role in *Contempt* or if Marlon Brando—or Pee Wee Herman—had played Humbert Humbert in *Lolita?*

Along with character and performer, the cinema offers still another entity denied the novel: the dubber (postsynchroniser), allowing for further permutations of character and voice. In India playback singers, who dub the moving lips of the stars on the image track, become famous in their own right. This third instance enables filmmakers to make thematic points about characters. Thus Glauber Rocha, in his *Deus e Diabo na Terra do Sol (Black God, White Devil,* 1964), has actor Othos Bastos dub the voices of both the "black God" and the "white devil," thus insinuating a deeper subterranean unity linking these apparently antagonistic characters.

Both novel and film have consistently cannibalized other genres and media. The novel began by orchestrating a polyphonic diversity of materials—courtly fictions, travel literature, allegory, and jestbooks—into a new narrative form, repeatedly plundering or annexing neighboring arts, creating novel hybrids such as poetic novels, dramatic novels, cinematic novels, and journalistic novels. But the cinema carries this cannibalization to its paroxysm. As a rich, sensorially composite language characterized by what Metz calls "codic heterogeneity," the cinema becomes a receptacle open to all kinds of literary and pictorial symbolism, to all types of collective representation, to all ideologies, to all aesthetics, and to the infinite play of influences within cinema, within the other arts, and within culture generally.

The cinema is both a synesthetic and a synthetic art, synesthetic in its capacity to engage various senses (sight and hearing) and synthetic in its anthropophagic capacity to absorb and synthesize antecedent arts. A composite language by virtue of its diverse matters of expression—sequential photography, music, phonetic sound, and noise—the cinema "inherits" all the art forms associated with these matters of expression. Cinema has available to it the visuals of photography and painting, the movement of dance, the decor of architecture, and the performance of theater. Both the novel and the fiction film are summas by their very nature. Their essence is to have no essence, to be open to all cultural forms. Cinema can literally include painting, poetry, and music, or it can metaphorically evoke them by imitating their procedures; it can show a Picasso painting or emulate cubist techniques or visual dislocation, cite a Bach cantata, or create montage equivalents of fugue and counterpoint. Godard's *Passion* not only includes music (Ravel, Mozart, Ferre, Beethoven, and Fauré), but is conceived musically, and not only includes animated tableaux based on celebrating paintings (Rembrandt's *Night Watch*, Goya's *The Third of May*, and Delacroix's *Turkish Bathers*), but also expresses a painterly concern with light and color. The famous definitions of cinema in terms of other arts—"painting in motion" (Canudo), "sculpture in motion" (Vachel Lindsay), "music of light" (Abel Gance), and "architecture in movement" (Elie Fauré)—merely call attention to the synthetic multiplicity of signifiers available to the cinema.

Translations and Transformations

If "fidelity" is an inadequate trope, we must then ask, What tropes might be more appropriate? One trope, I would suggest, is "translation." The trope of adaptation as translation suggests a principled effort of inter-semiotic transposition, with the inevitable losses and gains typical of any translation.[6] The trope of translation undergirds the textual mechanisms of Godard's *Le Mepris* (*Contempt*, 1963), itself an adaptation of the Moravia novel *Il Disprezzo*, a novel whose partial subject is the issue of the adaptation of Homer's *The Odyssey* for film. The film deals with various kinds of translations, literal and figurative. The translation is literal both in its implicit reference to the translation of *The Odyssey* from classical Greek into contemporary European vernaculars and in its literal inclusion of a translator (not present in the novel)—the interpreter Francesca (Georgia Moll)—who mediates linguistically between the monolingual American producer Prokosch and his more polyglot European interlocutors. (When Italian laws concerning obligatory postsynchronization led Italian dubbers to eliminate the role of Francesca, Godard disassociated himself from the Italian version of the film.) Francesca's hurried translations of Fritz Lang's poetic quotations prove that, in art as in language, "traduire, c'est trahir." Her translations invariably miss a nuance, smooth over an aggression, or exclude an ambiguity. But the film also concerns less literal translations: the generic "translation" of Homer's epic poetry into contemporary novelistic prose and the inter-semiotic "translation" of Moravia's novel into Godard's photographic images and sounds. In this sense, *Contempt* can be seen as a meditation on the richly ambiguous nature of all translation and adaptation. At the same time, the film suggests, art renews itself through creative mistranslation.

In fact, adaptation theory has available a whole constellation of tropes—translation, reading, dialogization, cannibalization, transmutation, transfiguration, and signifying—each of which sheds light on a different dimension of adaptation. For example, the trope of adaptation as a "reading" of the source novel—a reading that is inevitably partial, personal, and conjectural—suggests that just as any text can generate an infinity of readings, so any novel can generate any number of adaptations. Why should we assume that one director—for example, John Huston—has said everything that needs to be said about *Moby-Dick?* (If one has nothing new to say about a novel, Orson Welles once suggested, why adapt it at all?) A single novel can thus generate any number of critical readings and creative misreadings. Indeed, many novels have been adapted repeatedly. *Madame Bovary* has been adapted at least nine times, in countries as diverse as France, Portugal, the United States, India, and Argentina. Each adaptation sheds a new cultural light on the novel; the Hindi version, entitled *Maya* (Illusion) not only envisions Bovary through the grid of Hindu philosophy ("the veil of illusion"), but also links Emma's romanticism, quite logically, to the conventions of the Bombay musical.

Godard regarded his Moravia source novel as a banal, old-fashioned, premodernist novel, which suggests that adaptations can be motivated as much by hostility as by affection. A "reading" can also be a critique. Sergio Giral's adaptation of Cuba's first antislavery novel (Anselmo Suárez y Romero's *Francisco: El Ingenio o Las Delicias del Campo* (*Francisco: The Sugar-mill or the Delights of the Canefields,* 1839), for example, was inspired by hostility to the source novel. Although the novel, often called the "Cuban *Uncle Tom's Cabin,*" sentimentalizes slavery, the film adaptation, tellingly retitled *El Otro Francisco* (*The Other Francisco*) denounces that very sentimentality. The Giral adaptation promotes interplay between diverse generic modes of presentation: a parodically melodramatic approach, sarcastically "faithful" to the sentimental spirit of the novel; a staged (anachronistically verité) documentary about the novel's production context; and a realistic reconstruction of the historical life of the enslaved. Taken together, the three modes emphasize exactly what is suppressed in the novel: the economic motives behind the abolitionist movement, the catalyzing role of black rebellion, and the artistic mediation of the story itself. In the novel, Francisco commits suicide when he learns that his true love Dorotea has surrendered to the lust of her white master, but the documentary-style segments suggest that a slave would never commit suicide over an ill-fated romance. The film's final section stages the slave uprisings missing from the novel.

The Giral film self-reflexively, almost paradigmatically, explores the notion of adaptation as demystificatory critique. To be more precise, Giral submitted the original novel to a series of activist operations: he parodied the novel—for example, in the opening precredit sequence, by exaggerating the novel's melodramatic conventions through their filmic equivalents, overwrought acting, haloed backlighting, soft-focus visuals, and lachrymose music; he contextualized the novel by revealing the social milieu or artistic habitus out of which the novel was generated— the upper-class liberal del Monte salon; he supplemented the novel by including the author Suárez y Romero himself (or an actor impersonating him) in the film, informing us that the abolitionist author had himself inherited slaves; he inserted other contemporaneous historical figures such as the British free trade agent Richard Madden, a key figure in the background of the abolitionist movement, then in Cuba investigating the slave trade; he historicized the novel by drawing on Madden's two books on Cuban slavery in order to show slavery as a modern system of production; he documented slavery in such a way as to show us everything that the novel left out (the economic subtext of slavery and the geopolitical maneuverings of the British); he supplemented the information provided by the novel through his own research into Cuban history, revealing, for example, that Cuban independence was partially delayed due to fear of the "undue" empowerment of former slaves; he staged precisely what most frightened the Cuban elite—the history of black slave rebellion in Cuba (furthermore, he revealed that the author himself was aware of the rebellions, yet chose not to include them in his book); he resequenced the novel by having the film begin where the novel ends, with Francisco's suicide; and finally, he transformed the novel's docile central character, Francisco, into a revolutionary, the "other" Francisco of the title.

Adaptation as Intertexual Dialogism

Adaptations, then, can take an activist stance toward their source novels, inserting them into a much broader intertextual dialogism. An adaptation, in this sense, is less an attempted resuscitation of an originary word than a turn in an ongoing dialogical process. The concept of intertextual dialogism suggests that every text forms an intersection of textual surfaces. All texts are tissues of anonymous formulae, variations on those formulae, conscious and unconscious quotations, and conflations and inversions of other texts. In the broadest sense, intertextual dialogism refers to the infinite and open-ended possibilities generated by all the discursive practices of a culture, the entire matrix of communicative utterances within which the artistic text is situated, which reach the text not only through recognizable influences, but also through a subtle process of dissemination.

Intertextuality, then, helps us transcend the aporias of "fidelity." But intertextuality can be conceived in a shallow or a deep manner. Bakhtin spoke of the "deep generating series" of literature—that is, the complex and multidimensional dialogism, rooted in social life and history, comprising both primary (oral) and secondary (literary) genres—which engendered literature as a cultural phenomenon. Bakhtin attacked the limitation of the literary scholar-critic's interest exclusively to the "literary series," arguing for a more diffuse dissemination of ideas as interanimating all the "series," literary and nonliterary, as they are generated by what he called the "powerful deep currents of culture." Literature, and by extension the cinema, must be understood within what Bakhtin called the "differentiated unity of the epoch's entire culture" (Bakhtin, "Response to a Question from *Novy Mir*," in *Speech Genres and Other Late Essays* [ed. Carl Emerson and Michael Holquist, Austin: University of Texas Press, 1986], p. 3).

Building on Bakhtin and Julia Kristeva, in *Palimpsestes* (1982) Gérard Genette offers other analytic concepts useful for our discussion of adaptation. Genette proposed a more inclusive term, *transtextuality*, to refer to "all that which puts one text in relation, whether manifest or secret, with other texts." Genette posited five types of transtextual relations, some of which bear relevance to adaptation. He defined the first type, "intertextuality" as the "effective co-presence of two texts" in the form of quotation, plagiarism, and allusion. Adaptation, in this sense, participates in a double intertextuality, one literary and the other cinematic.

"Paratextuality," Genette's second type of transtextuality, refers to the relation, within the totality of a literary work, between the text proper and its "paratext"—titles, prefaces, postfaces, epigraphs, dedications, illustrations, and even book jackets and signed autographs—in short, all the accessory messages and commentaries that come to surround the text and at times become virtually indistinguishable from it. In the case of film, the paratext might include widely quoted prefatory remarks by a director at a film's first screening, reported remarks by a director about a film, or widely reported information about the budget of a film.

"Metatextuality," Genette's third type of transtextuality, consists of the critical relation between one text and another, whether the commented text is explicitly cited or only silently evoked. In this sense, *The Other Francisco* can be seen as a metatextual critique of the Suárez y Romero novel. "Architextuality," Genette's fourth category, refers to the generic taxonomies suggested or refused by the titles or infratitles of a text. Architextuality has to do with an artist's willingness or reluctance to characterize a text generically in its title. Because most adaptations of novels simply carry over the title of the original, if only to take advantage of a preexisting market, this term would seem irrelevant to our discussion. Yet in some cases a changed title signals the transformations operative in the adaptation. Giral's title *The Other Francisco* alerts us to Giral's radical transfiguration of the politics and aesthetics of the source novel. The title *Clueless* disguises the Jane Austen source (*Emma*) while signaling the film's milieu: rich, upper-middle-class adolescents. As we shall see, the title of *Man Friday*, an adaptation of *The Adventures of Robinson Crusoe*, signals a change in voice and perspective from those of the colonizer Crusoe to those of the colonized Friday, now no longer the "boy" of colonialist discourse, but a "man."

"Hypertextuality," Genette's fifth type of transtextuality, is perhaps the most suggestive of Genette's categories. It refers to the relation between one text, which Genette calls "hypertext," to an anterior text, or "hypotext," which the former transforms, modifies, elaborates, or extends. In literature the hypotexts of *The Aeneid* include *The Odyssey* and *The Iliad*, whereas the hypotexts of Joyce's *Ulysses* include *The Odyssey* and *Hamlet*. Both *The Aeneid* and *Ulysses* are hypertextual elaborations of a single hypotext, *The Odyssey*. Filmic adaptations, in this sense, are hypertexts derived from preexisting hypotexts that have been transformed by operations of selection, amplification, concretization, and actualization. The diverse filmic adaptations of *Madame Bovary* (by Renoir and Minnelli) or of *La Femme et le Pantin* (by Duvivier, von Sternberg, and Buñuel) can be seen as variant hypertextual "readings" triggered by the same hypotext. Indeed, the diverse prior adaptations can form a larger, cumulative hypotext that is available to the filmmaker who comes relatively "late" in the series.

Film adaptations, then, are caught up in the ongoing whirl of intertextual reference and transformation, of texts generating other texts in an endless process of recycling, transformation, and transmutation, with no clear point of origin. Let us take as an example *The Adventures of Robinson Crusoe*, one of the seminal source novels of a specific European tradition, the realistic mimetic novel supposedly based on "real life" and written in such a way as to generate a strong impression of factual reality. Yet this "realistic" novel is itself rooted in various intertexts: the Bible, the literature of religious meditation, the journalistic texts about Crusoe's prototype, Alexander Selkirk, and sensationalist travel literature, to mention just a few. Defoe's 1719 novel, rooted in this complex and variegated intertext, also generated its own textual "afterlife" or "post-text." In France the exemplars of this post-text were called Robinsonades. Already in 1805, less than a century after the publication of the Defoe novel, a German encyclopedia (*Bibliothek der Robinsone*) offered a comprehensive guide to all the works inspired by *Robinson Crusoe*. Nor did this novelistic post-text end in the nineteenth century, as both Michel Tournier's *Vendredi, ou l'Ile de la Pacifique* and Derek Walcott's *Pantomime*, in both of which *Crusoe* is reread through an anticolonialist grid, clearly attest.

The *Crusoe* post-text also has ramifications in the world of film, where a long pageant of adaptations has rung in changes on the themes of the original. *Miss Crusoe* (1919) performs a variation in gender, which is interesting because the novel, against the grain of the "desert island" genre, scarcely mentions women at all. *Little Robinson Crusoe* (1924), carrying out the logic of *Crusoe*-as-children's-book, changes the age of the protagonist, with Jackie Coogan coming to the island on wings to be worshiped by the naive natives. *Mr. Robinson Crusoe* (1932) keeps Crusoe but supplies him with a feminine companion, perhaps inevitably called not Friday, but Saturday. *Swiss Family Robinson* (1940) permutates the number and social status of the characters, changing the solitary Crusoe to an entire family. The Laurel and Hardy film *Robinson Crusoeland* (1950) performs a shift in genre, from colonial adventure story to slapstick comedy. Similarly, *Robinson Crusoe on Mars* (1964) turns the novel into science fiction: the "pioneer" on earth becomes a pioneer in space. In *Lieutenant Robinson Crusoe* (1965) there are transformations both professional and zoological, as Defoe's protagonist becomes the sailor played by Dick van Dyke, and Crusoe's parrot is replaced by a chimpanzee.

In *Robinson Crusoe* Daniel Defoe created one of the West's archetypal colonial-adventurer heroes. Crusoe, we often forget, had become wealthy through trade in slaves and Brazilian sugar. Cast away on an island, his first thought on seeing human footprints after years of solitude is that he might "get a servant." He names "his" islander "Friday" in memory of the day he saved the native's life, as a clear reminder of the rationale for enslaving him. It should not be surprising, therefore, that latter-day adaptations submit the novel to a kind of ideological critique. Luis Buñuel's film adaptation of the novel, *Robinson Crusoe* (1952), casts satiric doubt on Crusoe's religion but leaves unquestioned certain aspects of the film's colonialist discourse. Jack Gold's *Man Friday* (1975), meanwhile, turns Defoe's puritanical fable-cum-colonial-romance into an anticolonialist allegory. The film mocks Crusoe for his ledger-book mentality, his obsession with property, his racism, his chauvinism, and his puritanical phobias (he spends years on a tropical island without removing his fur clothing). *Man Friday* also draws out the novel's homoerotic subtext. As has often been noted, Defoe's Crusoe seems less erotically energized by his wife, whom he marries and dispatches in a single sentence, than by Friday, whom he describes as "handsome" and "well-shaped." In *Man Friday* Crusoe's fears of homosexual attraction lead him to rampant paranoia and (literal) self-flagellation, to the bemusement of Friday, who, not sharing Crusoe's erotic neuroses and inhibitions, offers himself as sexual solace.

Film adaptations can be seen as a kind of multileveled negotiation of intertexts. Therefore, it is often productive to ask these questions: Precisely what generic intertexts are invoked by the source novel, and which by the filmic adaptation? Which generic signals in the novel are picked up, and which are ignored? In the case of Fielding's *Tom Jones*, we are dealing with precisely the counter-tradition to *Robinson Crusoe*, the Cervantic tradition that is explicitly rather than surreptitiously intertextual. Henry Fielding called *Tom Jones* a "comic epic poem in prose:" comic in the sense both of a happy ending in plot and of ironic distance in style, epic in the sense of the periodic grandeur and elegance of the novel's epic similes, a poem in the sense of "creative work of the imagination"—a poem this time not in stanzaic poetry, but in euphonious prose.

Interestingly, the Richardson and Osborne adaptation, often hailed as a model of sensitive adaptation, picks up some intertextual cues, but not others. It picks up some aspects of the novel's reflexivity, partially by borrowing the language of the novel both for intertitles and for voice-over narration, but it also mingles the literary cues with specifically filmic devices in such a way as to find the filmic equivalents of literary techniques. Albert Finney's complicit winks to the spectator "cinematize" Fielding's direct address to his "dear reader." Fielding's irreverent play with chapter titles ("Containing Five Pieces of Paper," "Containing the Time of a Year") becomes in the film a virtuoso display of a specifically cinematic device, the optical wipe, here rendered as spirals, bars, and scissors. Fielding's Cervantic (and Hogarthian) freezing of specific actions is rendered in the film by the literal freeze-frame: for instance, when the philosopher Square is caught in flagrante delicto in Molly's closet. Fielding's *exercises de style* (with excursuses into pastoral, meditative, philosophical, and literary styles as well as that of Homeric simile) become in the film forays into cinematic stylistics: the accelerated motion of Mack Sennett, the iris-in on the villain. The novel's parody of Samuel Richardson's sentimental fictions becomes in the film the parody of silent period melodrama, rendered by means of overheatedly moralistic intertitles, improbable plot turns, and histrionic performance. Just as Fielding makes parodic allusions to his literary forebears, so Richardson and Osborne allude to their film antecedents through the use of archaic devices: Fielding's epic similes allude to the ancient Homeric roots of the western tradition, whereas Richardson and Osborne's use of archaic devices points to the tradition of the silent cinema.

The Grammar of Transformation

To sum up what has been argued thus far, one way to look at adaptation is to see it as a matter of a source novel hypotext's being transformed by a complex series of operations: selection, amplification, concretization, actualization, critique, extrapolation, analogization, popularization, and reculturalization. The source novel, in this sense, can be seen as a situated utterance produced in one medium and in one historical context, then transformed into another equally situated utterance that is produced in a different context and in a different medium. The source text forms a dense informational network, a series of verbal cues that the adapting film text can then take up, amplify, ignore, subvert, or transform. The film adaptation of a novel performs these transformations according to the protocols of a distinct medium, absorbing and altering

the genres and intertexts available through the grids of ambient discourses and ideologies, and as mediated by a series of filters: studio style,
ideological fashion, political constraints, auteurist predilections, charismatic stars, economic advantage or disadvantage, and evolving technology. The film hypertext, in this sense, is transformational almost in the
Chomskian sense of a "generative grammar" of adaptation, with the difference that these cross-media operations are infinitely more unpredictable and multifarious than they would be were it a matter of "natural language."

Central to the transformational grammar of adaptation are permutations in locale, time, and language. The Renoir and the Chabrol
adaptations of *Madame Bovary* feature continuity between the language
and locale of the source novel and the language and locale of the film
adaptations. The Minnelli adaptation, by contrast, features discontinuity; studio lots "stand in" for France, and the actors speak English, with
occasional use of French words and intermittent use of French accents.
The filmmaker adapting a novel written in another country and in
another language is confronted with a series of options: Should the director find performers from the country in question? Should he have actors
from the "home" country speak with an accent? Or should the adapter
"Americanize" the source novel? The bored provincial protagonist of
Woody Allen's *Purple Rose of Cairo* (played by Mia Farrow), deluded by
artistic fictions, can on some levels be seen as an American Bovary. The
director must also confront questions of temporality and epoch. Is the
film adaptation a costume drama that respects the historical time frame
of the original, or does it "update" the novel? The history of the theater
features innumerable updatings of Shakespeare, for example, yet the
practice is less common in film. Of the recent spate of Jane Austen films,
only *Clueless* updated the original, but without referencing the novel
explicitly.

Although some broad genres (comedy, tragedy, and melodrama)
are shared between novel and film, other genres are specifically filmic
(e.g., the animated cartoon) because they depend on specific cinematic
features such as the moving image, film editing, and so forth. The complexity of these intertextual negotiations becomes manifest in the case
of the Spielberg adaptation of Alice Walker's *The Color Purple*. The
novel interweaves any number of intertexts, literary and extraliterary,
each with its own network of connotations and implications: the epistolary novel, implying not only a specific orchestration of voice, but also
such themes as patriarchal oppression (as in *Pamela* and *Clarissa*), the
structural principle of procrastinated rape (here not procrastinated, but
rather placed on the very first page), and class consciousness; the historical romance, implying a past setting but here domesticated and rendered quotidian; the autobiographical slave narrative, implying the per-
sonalization of social protest; the realistic novel, with its connotations

of democratization, stylistic dignity, and the respectful treatment of the everyday life of people of "lower" social strata; the bildungsroman, or novel of development, evoked by Celie's coming-of-age story; the reflexive novel, found in the direct thematization of Celie's wrestling with language and writing; the fairy tale, implied by the once-upon-a-time quality of the girl-child's fantasies; inspirational literature (religious, secular, and feminist), implied by the overall homiletic drift of the novel; and the blues, cited literally and emulated figuratively as a vernacular art. The novel also engages in what Bakhtin calls "hidden polemics," for example, by critiquing antecedent racist representations, discourses, and stereotypes about black women and about the black family. The portrait of African religion as highly mystical, for example, argues against the stereotypical view of African religions as overly physical, superstitious, and hysterical.

In his adaptation Spielberg picks up some of these cues, ignores others, and "adds" specifically filmic allusions and protocols. He pushes the source novel toward the heightened emotions and Manichean moralism of melodrama and underscores this generic option through the lush, richly symphonic music of the Quincy Jones soundtrack. Spielberg maintains the conventions of the epistolary novel but cinematizes it with recurrent shots of the mailbox and the letters themselves while imbuing the tradition with the grain of specific voices such as Whoopie Goldberg's. In terms of specifically filmic genres, we catch the stereotypical echoes of the "all-black musical" (e.g., *Hallelujah* and *Cabin in the Sky*), especially in the gospel sequences. Here we sense that the director's experience of black people, at least at that time, had largely been mediated by film, and specifically by film of a tradition that makes the black rural community the locus of spiritual and physical vibrancy. The more bluesy-jazzistic sequences recall a different tradition, one that renders blacks not as rural and primitive, but rather as urban and sophisticated and Afromodernist.[7] The film is also inflected by the specifically filmic tradition of slapstick farce and minstrelsy, as exemplified by Harpo's repeated pratfalls and by "Mister's" ponderously comic efforts to cook for Shug. At the same time, the film adds a literary supplement through literary references not made in the source novel, notably through references to Dickens' *Oliver Twist*.

The question of intertext also brings up the question of parody. Although some adaptations, such as the Richardson and Osborne *Tom Jones*, pick up on the parodic cues of their source novels, others ignore them. Both the Chabrol and the Renoir adaptations of *Madame Bovary*, for example, do surprisingly little with a recurrent feature of the source novel, its rendering of Emma's interior consciousness, in *le style indirect libre*, through parodic exaggerations of the stylistic vices of such writers as Chateaubriand and Sir Walter Scott. Minnelli emphasizes Emma's early reading of romantic novels, but has James Mason's voice-over condemn her "illusions" and "dreams" in a univocal fashion that has little to do with Gustave ("Madame-Bovary-c'est-moi") Flaubert's "complicitous critique" of his heroine. Kubrick's version of *Lolita*, similarly, does almost nothing with the densely parodic prose of the Nabokov source novel or, for that matter, with all the self-flauntingly cinematic and self-referential ideas proposed in Nabokov's screenplay, partly as a function of Kubrick's instrumental view (at the time) of prose style as what the artist uses to fascinate the beholder and thus to convey feelings and thoughts.[8]

Transmutations of Plot and Character

Much of the literature on adaptation has concentrated on specifically textual operations having to do with plot events and characters. Often we find a kind of condensation of characters. The many Okie families of *The Grapes of Wrath* are foreshortened into the Joads of the John Ford version. The bevy of female lovers of Jules and Jim in the Henri Pierre Roche novel are condensed into Catherine (Jeanne Moreau) in the Truffaut adaptation. Film adaptations have a kind of "Sophie's choice" about which characters in the novel will live or die. But although adaptations tend to sacrifice "extra" characters from novels, occasionally the opposite process takes place, as we saw in the case of *El Otro Francisco*. The Minnelli version of *Madame Bovary* adds the character of Flaubert himself, who is being tried for obscenity in the courts of France. Godard adds the character of the translator Fracesca in *Contempt*, precisely in order to highlight the polyglot ambiance of international coproductions in the 1960s, as well as to make a more metaphorical point about adaptation as a process of translation.

Characters can also be subtly changed. The white judge in Thomas Wolfe's *Bonfire of the Vanities* became the black judge played by Morgan Freeman in the Brian de Palma adaptation, presumably as a way of sidestepping and warding off the accusations of racism leveled against the novel. Film adaptations often ignore key passages in the source books. None of the *Madame Bovary* adapters, to my knowledge, chose to stage the opening passage in which a group of pupils "nous étions a l'étude, quand le Proviseur entra, suivi d'un nouveau. . . ." And most of the adaptations downplay Charles's first wife in order to concentrate on the relationship between Emma and Charles.

Film adaptations usually make temporal changes as well. Therefore, two months in the Alberto Moravia source novel become just two days in the Godard adaptation (*Contempt*), part of a Brechtian "theatricalization" of the source novel. On the other hand, events in the source novel can be amplified, as when, in the case of *Tom Jones*, a few sentences regarding Squire Western's love of hunting became in the film the pretext for a spectacular fox hunt staged in an attempt to make the film more "cinematic" but also in order to strengthen the satire of the landed gentry. Film adaptations can also add events—for example, in the form of Peter Sellers's inspired improvisations in the Kubrick *Lolita*. These additions can have any number of motivations: to take advantage of a brilliant actor, to suggest contemporary relevance, or to "correct" the novel for aesthetic reasons. In the case of Godard's *Masculine Feminine*, supposedly an adaptation of a Guy de Maupassant story, very little was retained from the source novel. Godard kept only a few of the characters' names and almost nothing else, to the point that those who sold the rights concluded that those rights had not even been used.

There is also the complex question of point of view. Does the film adaptation maintain the point of view and the focalization (Genette) of the novel? Who tells the story in the novel vis-à-vis the film? Who focalizes the story —that is, who sees within the story? Genette distinguishes between the instance that tells (the narrator), the instance that sees and experiences (the character), and the instance that knows (the filter). In Godard's *Contempt* there is a clear shift in point of view or, to change the metaphor, to a change in voice, a "transvocalization." Although the novel is narrated as a reminiscence in the first person by screenwriter Ricardo Molteni (Paul in the film), the film is neither narrated in the first person, nor is it a reminiscence, nor is it told from any particular point of view except that, perhaps, of the cinema itself. What was therapeutic first-person rumination in the novel—"I decided to write these memoirs in hopes of finding [Camille] again"—becomes a kind of no-person point of view in the film. The unreliable narrator of the novel —we slowly realize that he is highly disturbed, paranoid, almost hallucinatory—gives way to the impersonal narration of the film, all as part of a drift toward a Brechtian depersonalization and depsychologizing. The emphasis shifts from one character's mind to the relations between five characters belonging to the same film milieu.

This is not the place to attempt to perform an ambitious extrapolation of Genette's categories concerning novelistic discourse to filmic discourse. Suffice it to say that such categories as "variable focalization" and "multiple focalization" are very suggestive for film analysis. The former evokes the tag-team approach to point of view that characterizes Hitchcock's films, moving between major characters such as Mitch and Melanie in *The Birds* but also moving to minor characters such as the boy who whistles at Melanie in the opening shots, the man who observes her from the dock at Bodega Bay, or even the birds who oversee her departure in the shot/reverse shot structure of the final sequence. "Multiple focalization" evokes not only the multiple perspectives of a film such as *Rashomon* or *Citizen Kane*, but also the multiple focalizations of a dispersed narrative such as that of Altman's *Nashville*.

Film adaptations of novels often change novelistic events for (perhaps unconscious) ideological reasons. In the case of the Minnelli *Madame Bovary*, Charles Bovary is made to refuse to operate on Hippolyte (whereas in the novel he bungles the operation), presumably out of respect for Hollywood pieties concerning the pater familias figure. Film adaptations of novels thus become entangled in questions of ideology. Does the film "push" the novel to the left or the right in terms of sexual, racial, and class politics? Spielberg's *The Color Purple* plays down the lesbianism of the Alice Walker novel. And by having Shug reconcile with her censorious preacher father, the adaptation "repatriarchalizes" a feminist novel. The John Ford version of *The Grapes of Wrath* shies away from the socialist drift of the Steinbeck novel. But the drift is not always rightward. *Man Friday*, as we have seen, pushes *Robinson Crusoe* to the antiracist, anticolonialist, antireligious left. The narrative sequencing can also be rearranged, with clear ideological overtones. The circular structure of the Kubrick *Lolita* clearly draws attention away from Humbert Humbert's nympholepsy and toward the murderous rivalry between Humbert and Quilty in ways that lead one to suspect that this was a sop to the censors. In the John Ford *Grapes of Wrath*, as has often been pointed out, the sequencing of the three camps—the Hooverville, the New Deal "Wheatpatch," and the Keane Ranch—is altered so as transform what was a spiraling descent into oppression into an ascent into New Deal benevolence and good order.[9]

Just as interesting as what in the source novel is eliminated or bypassed is why certain materials are ignored. The intercalary, essayistic chapters of *The Grapes of Wrath* were largely eliminated from the John Ford adaptation, presumably because they were seen as "uncinematic" but also because those chapters happen to be the places in which John Steinbeck's (then) socialist opinions were most in evidence. The philosophical meditations that dot Melville's *Moby-Dick* were largely ignored in the John Huston adaptation, again because of their "uncinematic" nature but also perhaps because film producers assumed that the mass audience would not be "up to" such lofty and allusive materials. The adaptations of reflexive novels such as *Tom Jones* or *Lolita*, in the same vein, tend to downplay the literary-critical excursuses that mark the source novels. Although reflexive in certain respects, the Osborne and Richardson *Tom Jones* does not try to recreate the film equivalents of Fielding's essays in literary criticism—for example, by proffering film criticism—presumably because tampering too much with the filmic illusion would spoil the "sport" of the fiction.

Here we enter the fraught area of comparative stylistics. To what extent are the source novel and the film adaptation innovative in aesthetic terms, and if they are innovative, are they innovative in the same way? *Madame Bovary* was extremely innovative at its time for its decentered approach to narrative, its subversion of norms of character, its mobile approach to point of view, and its systemic frustration of the reader's expectations. To what extent do the various film versions provide an equivalent sense of such innovations? To what extent do they go beyond the novel to innovate in cinematic terms? The answers to these questions become crucial when we realize that *Madame Bovary*, although written prior to the advent of the cinema, can reasonably be called protocinematic. Eisenstein famously cited the "agricultural fair" chapter in the Flaubert novel as a brilliant precinematic example of montage. The concept of the "cinematic novel" has, admittedly, often been abused, bandied about so imprecisely as to mean anything from a book that has sharply imagined physical action to a book that uses certain techniques reminiscent of film. Despite this danger, it is nonetheless fruitful, I think, to see a novel such as *Madame Bovary* as protocinematic. Flaubert was an author at a crucial transitional moment within the history of the novel, one distinct from both the sober documentary realism of Defoe and the playful reflexivity of a Cervantes or a Fielding. I am referring to the moment when a kind of mobilized regard crystallized the altered perceptions associated with modernity—an altered gaze associated both with impressionism in painting, where the artist is attentive to what intervenes between the object and the eye, and with modernism in the novel, where point of view and filters of consciousness become paramount organizing principles—instantiating a subjectification and a relativization of the stabilities of the classical realist model.

Flaubert's *Madame Bovary* might be called both proleptically modernist and protocinematic in a number of senses: in its film script –like notation of precise gestures (see, for example, the account of Charles Bovary's first arrival at Emma's family farm); in its artful modulation, à la Hitchcock, of point of view, whereby we experience flickering moments of identification not only with major characters such as Emma and Charles, but also with minor characters and even with unnamed characters who never again appear in the text; in its precise articulation, reminiscent of camera "setups," of character vantage points within voyeuristic structures (for example, the two gossips who observe Emma from their attic post or the "curieux" of the final pages who peeks at Charles from behind a bush); in its kinetic, destabilized portraiture of characters as a kind of flowing composition in time; in its verbal recreation of the "feel" of seeing, especially encumbered seeing (Emma's squinting, her intermittent loss of focus, her attempts to discern objects in the distance); in its "impressionist" attention to the vapors and gases jostling one another in the atmosphere, as well as to the dynamic agency of light in modifying appearances, as seen in the use of such light-active words as *blanchissaient, vernissait,* and *veloutant;* in the corporeal empathy with which it identifies the reader with the very body of the heroine (for example, the account of Emma's milky orgasm with Rodolphe); in the kinesthetic quality of Flaubert's prose, its manner of mobilizing the reader's gaze (for example, the accounts of the passing world as seen from the moving *hirondelle*); and in the ironic manipulation of "focal length"—for instance, in the abrupt move from the long view of the cab containing the fornicating Leon and Emma to the close view of "the torn-up note," followed by the extremely long view that turns Emma into a generic "femme" descending from a vehicle.

Compared with the novel, the film adaptations of *Madame Bovary* are much less innovative, and much more concerned with adapting the text to a mainstream audience. In other words, the phenomenon of "mainstreaming" is not limited to ideological issues; there also exists the phenomenon of aesthetic mainstreaming. Despite its surface modernity and its technological razzle-dazzle, dominant cinema has maintained, on the whole, a premodernist aesthetic corresponding to that of the nineteenth-century mimetic novel. In its dominant mode it became a receptacle for the mimetic aspirations abandoned by the most advanced practitioners of the other the arts. Film inherited the illusionistic ideals that impressionism had relinquished in painting, that Jarry had attacked in the theater, and that Proust, Joyce, and Woolf had undermined in the novel. Aesthetic censorship, in this sense, might be in some ways more severe and deeply rooted than political self-censorship. Adaptation, in this sense, seems to encounter the most difficulty with modernist novels such as Joyce's *Ulysses*, Nabokov's *Lolita*, or Duras's *L'Amant*. When Jean-Jacques Anauld turns Marguerite Duras's modernist, feminist novel *L'Amant* into a linear, masculinist, mainstream film, we are not entirely wrong to regret that the director has misrecognized the most salient traits of Durasian *écriture*. When a modernist, discontinuous novel is made relatively continuous through the dumb inertia of convention; when a filmic adaptation is thought to need a sympathetic male protagonist in order to be palatable for a mass audience (whence Minnelli's idealized Charles Bovary); when the hero cannot die or the villain must be punished; when a digressive, disruptive style must be linearized into a classical three-act structure with exposition, conflict, and climax; when morality must be reconfigured to suit preestablished Manichean schemas; when a difficult, reflexive novel must be made transparent and redundant; when the spectator must be led by the hand—in such cases, I would suggest, we find a kind of ideologically driven failure of nerve to deal with the aesthetic implications of novelistic modernism.

By adopting the approach to adaptation I have been suggesting, we in no way abandon our rights or responsibilities to make judgments about the value of specific film adaptations. We can—and, in my view, we should—continue to function as critics; but our statements about films based on novels or other sources need to be less moralistic, less panicked, less implicated in unacknowledged hierarchies, more rooted in contextual and intertextual history. Above all, we need to be less concerned with inchoate notions of "fidelity" and to give more attention to dialogical responses—to readings, critiques, interpretations, and rewritings of prior material. If we can do all these things, we will produce a criticism that not only takes into account, but also welcomes, the differences among the media.

NOTES

1. See Christian Metz, *The Imaginary Signifier* (Bloomington: Indiana University Press, 1977), p. 12.

2. Georges Pérec, *Les Choses* (Paris: L. N. Julliard, 1965), p. 80 (translation mine).

3. One of the side effects of reading a novel after having seen its cinematic adaptation, for me at least, is that I tend to "hear" the music track as I read.

4. Julio Bressane, in his film adaptation of the Machado de Assis novel *Memorias Postumas de Bras Cubas*, professed a lack of interest in the novel's plot while rigorously attempting to find film equivalents of its devices. The literary device of the posthumous narrator, for example, is "translated" by a filmmaker's sound boom's banging up against a skeleton.

5. For a critique of medium-specificity arguments, see Noel Carroll, *Theorizing the Moving Image* (Cambridge: Cambridge University Press, 1996).

6. For a systematic, even technical, exploration of adaptation as translation, see Patrick Cattrysse, *Pour une Théorie de l'Adaptation Filmique: Le Film Noir Américain* (Paris: Peter Lang, 1995).

7. See James Naremore's chapter on *Cabin in the Sky* in his *The Films of Vincente Minnelli* (New York: Cambridge University Press, 1993), pp. 51–70.

8. One regrets that the later, more reflexive, Kubrick of *Clockwork Orange* and *Dr. Strangelove* did not return to the Nabokov text and process it through a more stylistically self-conscious grid.

9. See Warren French, *Filmguide to* The Grapes of Wrath (Bloomington: Indiana University Press, 1973).

Adaptation in Practice

Richard Maltby

"To Prevent the Prevalent Type of Book": Censorship and Adaptation in Hollywood, 1924–1934

As a literary study in stark realism and exposition of ani-
mal passions running wild, the novel has considerable
merit. . . . As a screen proposition, An American
Tragedy, with its shameless wallowings in the sex gutters,
its debauchery and insistent dwelling on the baser sides of
human nature, would seem impossible of conversion into
anything resembling wholesome or appealing entertain-
ment for the majority of picture followers.
Harrison's Reports, *April 18, 1931*

In June 1932, furious at Paramount's travesty of his most recent novel, Theodore Dreiser denounced "The Real Sins of Hollywood" to readers of Bernard Macfadden's *Liberty* magazine. Producers, he reported, were quite uninterested in transferring an author's ideas to the screen and would be much happier if they had to pay for only the title of a play such as Eugene O'Neill's *Strange Interlude.* Then they could have their writers fashion a movie script with a plot bearing only the vaguest resemblance to the original. When asked to justify this defamation, they claimed that the play itself was "far above the head" of the average moviegoer, who in any case knew no more about it than that a play of that title had been a big success in New York. Such barbaric treatment of literature, concluded Dreiser, "spells the end of art, does it not?"[1]

Dreiser's familiar scenario is one of Hollywood's most frequently told tales, a genre piece in its own right. Few Eastern writers seemed to feel that their profitable sojourn in Hollywood was complete until they had published an account of their mistreatment at the hands

From *American Quarterly*, Vol. 44, No. 4 (December 1992), pp. 544–83. © 1992 The American Studies Association. Reprinted by permission of Johns Hopkins University Press.

of studio executives or their scenario departments. In 1930 Stephen Vincent Benét rejected his agent's suggestion that he write such a piece, saying, "I'd rather be the person who went there and didn't." O'Neill, who embodied the commercial success of the creative artist on Broadway, was a recurring icon of such pieces. Robert E. Sherwood suggested in 1929 that if a studio could hire him, they would doubtless turn O'Neill loose on *Rebecca of Sunnybrook Farm*. Another staple ingredient of the genre was a denunciation of the way Hollywood adapted the author's material. Leda Bauer explained in *The American Mercury* in 1928 that the original story was completely rewritten: "When there is no longer any connection with the story on which the screen play was based, it is pronounced perfect, the title is changed to something short, spicy, and completely inapplicable, and the original story is resold to another company to go through the same process."[2]

Conventional criticism of Hollywood's practices of adaptation has also been preoccupied with assessing the adequacy of a movie to its source material. A metaphor of failed or inverted alchemy recurs in this criticism: whatever the quality of the original material, Hollywood's apprentice sorcerers are seldom credited with producing anything but "disappointing lead." This critical discourse operates at a relatively untheorized level, assuming that the literary work possesses a stable, transhistorical meaning. A movie's fidelity to its original source is conventionally measured by how well it captures the "letter and the spirit" of the text, as though adaptation was, in critic Dudley Andrew's phrase, "the rendering of an interpretation of a legal precedent."[3]

At a number of distinct discursive levels the critical examination of adaptation has privileged the authority of the precursor text, endorsing the attitudes of writers who derived their idea of the profession of authorship from the New York literary marketplace. What Barbara Herrnstein Smith has called "evaluative authority" has been conferred on their opinions of Hollywood's procedures; claiming to speak from the cultural center, they have been called upon "to devise arguments and procedures that validate the community's established tastes and preferences, thereby warding off barbarism and the constant apparition of an imminent collapse of standards." Herrnstein Smith suggests that those who possess evaluative authority represent their opinions as "a consensus based on objective value" and pathologize other positions as deficient, "suffering from crudeness of sensibility, diseases and distortions of perception, weaknesses of character, impoverishment of background-and-education, cultural or historical biases, ideological or personal prejudices, and/or underdeveloped, corrupted, or jaded tastes."[4] Eastern writers and the critics who have followed them would endorse every term of this description as an accurate representation of the experience of adaptation in Hollywood. The villains of their scenario have almost always been a combination of philistine producers and petty industry censors, the "self-regulators" of the "Hays Office," bowdlerizing art in the name of the innocence and ignorance of the great American public.[5]

On the assumption that the Hays Office's function was to prevent particular kinds of representations from reaching the screen, industry censors have been blamed almost as frequently as the producers for Hollywood's failure to transcend itself. Describing the Alfred Hitchcock-David O. Selznick adaptation of Daphne duMaurier's *Rebecca*, for example, Robin Wood declares that "we know that the change from the novel was dictated by the Motion Picture Production Code, not anyone's actual desire."[6] Wood characterizes the Production Code and its administrators as dictatorial, but neither desiring nor desirable; they are credited with no intention other than the repression of meaning. The discursive framework of censorship has been one of the mechanisms by which Hollywood has been blamed for what it was not rather than blamed, endorsed, or simply acknowledged for what it was. But those who have castigated Hollywood as imitative rather than innovative, conservative rather than progressive, repressive rather than liberating, have seldom explained how it could have occupied any location in American cultural topography other than its assigned place as the primary instrument of the mass culture against which modernist cultural leadership and innovation defined itself.

By way of contrast to these accounts, which assume that what motivated Hollywood's practice of adaptation was a form of aesthetic ineptitude, this chapter describes that practice as belonging to a conscious ideological project. Through its trade association, the Motion Picture Producers and Distributors of America, Inc. (MPPDA), the American film industry deliberately sought to "prevent the prevalent type of book and play from becoming the prevalent type of picture." This project, documented in detail in the case files of the Production Code Administration (PCA) and its precursor, the Studio Relations Committee (SRC), arose from the industry's position as a purveyor of fictions for mass consumption. In a speech the MPPDA often quoted, its president, Will Hays, argued that "when you buy a book by a certain author, you have at least a general idea of what it is about and of what sort of psychology is going to be offered to you." But although novelists and dramatists appealed to "a more or less limited group" of "sophisticates," motion pictures had "a following infinitely more numerous," made up of "the vast majority of Americans, who do not fling defiance at customs and conventions, but who cling with fine faith and devotion to the things that are wholesome and healthy and who live lives similar to those of their forefathers, who made America what it is."[7]

Hays, the Hoosier Presbyterian elder who had masterminded Warren Harding's election campaign of 1920, had an apparently inexhaustible supply of such rhetorical homilies. Underlying them, however, and disguised by their banality was a recognition that the industry's practice of adaptation formed an important part of its defensive posture toward those civic and religious groups such as the General Federation of Women's Clubs that had designated themselves as parentally in charge of the nation's culture. Although sophisticates might object to the effect of censorship "befuddling . . . what has gone not only unchallenged but approved in literature and on the stage," the industry did not recognize the cultural authority of New York's literati, nor did it adopt their evaluative criteria.[8] It merely paid them wages. The seemingly endless story conferences that Eastern authors found so objectionable in Hollywood's practices of adaptation and narrative construction were the occasions on which, as Jeffrey Sconce has put it, the economic capital of the studio was used "to convert the cultural capital of the novel back into the economic capital of a successful motion picture." The production company's interest was satisfied if the source material was adapted to the conventions of its movie genre and the expectations of the audience: "While such an adaptation might inspire a few people to return to the novel, the chief concern was that it enticed them to return to the moviehouse."[9] Beyond such commercial vulgarities, the industry was less concerned with the adaptation of a work than with its adaptation to a set of external political conditions. The regulations it devised to render objectionable books or plays unobjectionable sought both to maximize commercial advantage and to distribute an affirmative cultural vision Hays shared with the clubwomen. "The manhood and womanhood of America is sound and wholesome," Hays declared in 1925, "and it wants wholesomeness in its entertainment in accord with the wholesomeness in its life."[10]

What Hays called the "organized industry"—the major vertically integrated companies constituting the industry's oligopoly power and comprising the dominant membership of the MPPDA—maintained a consistent attitude toward the practices of adaptation and regulation throughout the 1920s and 1930s. The fundamentals of its position had been established in the previous two decades. Since Chicago's first censorship ordinance of 1907, the public debate over movie content had always been conducted around the question of whether the motion picture industry was ethically fit to control the manufacture of its own products. In a 1915 decision that determined the constitutional status of the medium for the next thirty-seven years, the Supreme Court had declared that motion pictures were "mere representations of events, of ideas and sentiments, published and known," and therefore not to be afforded the protection of the First Amendment. The Court's decision did more than establish the constitutionality of prior censorship. In declaring that the motion picture industry was "a business, pure and simple . . . not to be regarded . . . as part of the press of the country, or as organs of public opinion," the Court confirmed a widely held Progressive opinion that "pure" entertainment—amusement that was not harmful to its consumer—was a commodity comparable to the pure meat guaranteed by the Food and Drug Administration, and its manufacture and distribution were just as liable to the incursions of government regulation.[11]

Led by its exhibition sector, the industry had recognized the economic sense of maintaining its own procedures for the regulation of content since the formation of the Motion Picture Patents Company in 1908. The National Board of Censorship, financed through industry trade associations but staffed by volunteers from civic groups, had performed this regulatory function with some success until its effectiveness was severely damaged by the public controversy over *The Birth of a Nation* in 1915. Two other short-lived trade associations had subsequently sought to resist the implementation of federal and state censorship legislation by pledging themselves to voluntary codes of practice governing screen content. The MPPDA was established in 1922 to safeguard the political interests of the emerging oligopoly, and although censorship and the regulation of content were important aspects of its work, the association's central concern was with the threat of legislation or court action to impose a strict application of the antitrust laws to the industry. It pursued policies of industrial self-regulation in matters of arbitration and intraindustry relations as well as film content, and Hays firmly attached the movies to the "associative state" fostered by Herbert Hoover's Department of Commerce. In pursuit of its avowed intent "to establish and maintain the highest possible moral and artistic standards of motion picture production," the association also constructed an elaborate public relations operation by which it established contact with nationally federated fraternal, educational, and religious organizations in order to make them "a friendly rather than a hostile critic of pictures."[12]

In its scale and its apparent openness the MPPDA's public relations policy was indicative of the larger project of culturally legitimating the amusement industry it represented. This strategy presumed a degree of cultural consensus about appropriate behavior and appropriate texts, or what Hays called "fundamental agreement about what is right and what is wrong."[13] One site where such agreement did not exist, however, was on the Broadway stage of the middle and late 1920s. Another was on the fiction best-selling lists. On both, cultural conventions were being challenged with varying degrees of maturity and durability. Works such as *The Plastic Age, The Green Hat, Elmer Gantry, Bad Girl,* or *An American Tragedy* provided the industry with a considerable problem. Their financial success made them commercially desirable and culturally appropriate for adaptation, but their content made that adaptation extremely problematic.

The studios relied on what was called "pretested" material—novels, short stories, and plays—for over half of their output, particularly of prestige and big-budget productions. Adaptations from Broadway successes, best-selling novels and nonfiction, and short stories from the mass-circulation magazines offered the best guarantee of commercial success, substantially outweighing the cost of their acquisition. As well as having already achieved public recognition, the copyright status of a well-known property was relatively easy to clarify, and companies could avoid the legal hazards sometimes attendant on unsolicited original material. The studios spent considerable sums on source acquisition, and by 1925 the motion picture rights of novels were worth an average of $5,000, whereas a successful play would sell for $20,000. Prices rose in the second half of the decade: by the early 1930s Warners spent an average of $600,000 a year on purchasing source material, and in the 1933–34 production season the industry as a whole bought 200 novels and nonfiction books at a cost of $2 million. Purchasing power on this scale made the industry an important source of revenue for both writers and publishers. Income from the sale of subsidiary rights, including movie rights, was commonly much greater than income from royalties. The publicity value of a film could also add to book sales: the movie edition of *All Quiet on the Western Front* sold 200,000 copies in two months.[14]

For both material and ideological reasons, the industry's position made it difficult to reject source material that had already proven commercially successful in another medium, but a significant proportion of both the novels and plays of the 1920s contained "unsuitable" material. The industry purchased more material than it could use, regarding the excess expenditure as an inevitable waste cost in a "style industry." There might be a variety of reasons for not producing a film from a book: a decision about the script's lack of entertainment value, the absence of a suitable star, or the failure to solve a fundamental scripting problem in condensing a novel's plot, for instance. The requirements of censorship were another such reason, one that the administrators of the Production Code understood as a generic pressure, comparable to the pressure of convention in, for example, a romantic comedy. The conversion to sound presented additional problems by increasing the industry's dependence on pretested sources for dialogue, particularly in a period when the Broadway stage was itself threatened with state censorship and denounced by Cardinal Patrick Hayes, Roman Catholic Archbishop of New York, as "reeking with filth." Early in 1927 the New York police closed three plays dealing with homosexual themes. Shortly thereafter, the Wales Padlock law prohibited the representation of "sex degeneracy or sex perversion on the stage." Producer John Golden wrote in *Theatre Magazine* that Broadway was "passing through an epidemic of sex and filth . . . due this time, they tell us, to the war, to women's rights (whatever they are), to frank talk, jazz and close-proximity dancing, short skirts, open work in clothes and open work between the sexes."[15]

The MPPDA's first regulation of motion picture content was instituted in June 1924 and dealt exclusively with the problem of adaptation. The Formula, as it was known, was a formalization of existing practice by which studios were discouraged from picturizing a book or play containing "salacious or otherwise harmful" subject matter for fear that it might have "a deleterious effect on the industry in general." The procedure was instituted because of complaints from civic groups about the adaptation of a number of novels in the 1923–24 production season, among them *Flaming Youth, Three Weeks, Black Oxen,* and *West of the Water Tower.* It was a relatively crude mechanism, effectively operating as a blacklist of works not to be filmed. In 1925 Hays claimed that the Formula had kept 160 "prevalent books and plays" with rights worth $2 to $3 million from the screen.[16]

Not surprisingly, the Formula provoked the hostility of both publishers and writers. In February 1924, for instance, Ethel Smith Dorrance accused Hays of being responsible for Universal Pictures' decision not to produce an adaptation of her novel *Damned.* Although he denied that the association had made any statement against the book, Hays acknowledged that it had been discussed by the association's board of directors, who felt that "a picture following the book with the same title would merit very severe criticism." The Authors' League of America took up the case, asking that Hays "state specifically the objections" to Dorrance's scenario of her book, which had partially sanitized the plot. They suggested that Hays was being unfair in condemning the adaptation "on the basis of the advertising, title, or contents of the book." Hays persuaded them that they had no case against the association, but they pursued the issue with Universal, arguing that it was "detrimental to an author's reputation if a picture based upon the author's work is not produced," and that a company's purchase of picture rights committed them to produce it. In reply, Universal's president, Carl Laemmle, bluntly asserted his property rights: "The matter of the producing or not producing of *Damned* is one which I alone can determine and, of course, I cannot subscribe to your statement that 'production must be considered as part of the compensation to the author.'" Laemmle also warned Hays that other producers should be dissuaded from accepting any contract provision "which could be construed as any right on the part of the author to force the producer to produce any story bought." Subsequently, the league threatened the MPPDA with an antitrust suit, and negotiations between them produced a revised version of the Formula in December 1927. This now permitted the author of a rejected story to provide a new story, with a new title that "in no way suggests the old title, containing all that is suitable in the original story and omitting all that is unsuitable for the screen. If the story is accepted and produced it will be advertised as an entirely new story and will not be presented as an adaptation or revised version of the rejected story. In none of the publicity or advertising will mention of the rejected book or play be made."[17]

By 1927 the association had extended its mechanisms for the regulation of content by compiling a code to govern production, administered by its Studio Relations Committee in Hollywood. The "Don'ts and Be Carefuls," as this code was familiarly known, synthesized the restrictions and eliminations applied by state and foreign censors. Two years later Hays initiated a further elaboration of the code, which after prolonged internal discussion emerged in April 1930 as *A Code to Maintain Social and Community Values in the Production of Silent, Synchronized and Talking Motion Pictures*. The industry's internal debates over the implementation of the Production Code revealed the extent to which producers were primarily concerned with the problems of adaptation, particularly given the new possibilities offered by sound. Metro Goldwyn-Mayer's head of production, Irving Thalberg, who had chaired the committee responsible for compiling the "Don'ts" in 1927, argued that "a character may speak delicately and exactly of subjects which he could by no stretch of the imagination indicate in pantomime." Such movies could "tread on more delicate ground" and deal "with perfect propriety . . . with human elements the silent picture was forced to shun." The additional possibilities provided by spoken dialogue therefore made it legitimate "to use any book or play which has attained wide notice or attracted general interest even though the book or play borders on the censorable," provided that in preparing it for production the story was "cleaned up so as to be appropriate for exhibition." Regarded purely as a social influence, Thalberg argued, "the decent presentation of an interesting but originally questionable story theme would do much to counteract its former unfavorable influence."[18]

In its practice of adaptation the industry had to steer a narrow course between the restrictive requirements of vocal public opinion and accusations from authors and audiences that they were attempting to obtain "attendance by deception" through "misleading, salacious or dishonest advertising." The agreement with the Authors' League regarding the apparently preposterous process by which a story was rewritten, retitled, and then sold on the basis of the value of what was no longer in it was an attempted solution. On one hand it provided for a commercially equitable relationship between the culture industries of publishing and motion pictures. On the other, by concealing the fact that *A Woman of Affairs* was adapted from Michael Arlen's *The Green Hat*, or *The Story of Temple Drake* from Faulkner's *Sanctuary*, it tried to answer the complaint of civic groups that, however much the content of films based on "salacious" sources was modified, their existence would encourage readers to turn to the corrupt original to discover the real story. The project sought to maximize mutual commercial advantage at the same time that it overtly declared itself as an exercise in the ideological recuperation of unsuitable—that is, culturally unsettling—literary material. Although the producers claimed to be "fully sympathetic" toward authors' objections to "the distorting of stories" and of authorial intentions in the process of adaptation, they maintained that "this was a condition that has always existed and . . . cannot be avoided." "Radical changes" to an author's original story arose inevitably from "the exigencies of production as well as the demands of the public [and] censorship conditions." The Formula was a means of offering authors material compensation in exchange for their abandonment of any right to control the adaptation of their original material.[19]

In practice, the Formula seldom obscured the origins of adaptations, and although the MPPDA disingenuously claimed that filmmakers were taking the responsible course and protecting the innocent from corrupting or disturbing information, their critics argued that they were cynically encouraging a sophisticated mode of audience response that involved reading through the action on the screen to identify deliberately displaced meanings. In *A Woman of Affairs*, for example, the explanation for the husband's suicide on their wedding night was changed from his having syphilis to his having perpetrated a bank fraud: whether audiences, particularly those members alert to the connotations of the book, accepted this somewhat arbitrary substitution was a matter of some debate.[20] Contrary to Thalberg's expectation that sound would expand the possibilities of delicate expression, its immediate effects were to disrupt the silent cinema's mechanisms of ambiguity and visual innuendo and to render the objectionable more explicit. As the complaints of civic and religious groups grew ever more strident after 1929, however, Hays came increasingly to feel that the assimilation of contemporary literature was far more trouble than it was worth. In 1933 he told producers bluntly that

> most of the trouble in Code observation, censorship and public disapprobation of this business grows out of bad source material. Much could be prevented if we did not start out on a bad story. Very few instances have there been where the result was worth the trouble. . . . The minute you buy a story like *Sanctuary* until the time next year when it is played in the last outpost, there is trouble. There has not been a day in the last three months when this office has not had some repercussions about *Sanctuary*—not a day.[21]

After 1933 even the Nobel Prize offered no protection: Sinclair Lewis's *Ann Vickers*, widely condemned in the Catholic press, did not escape the Production Code until its characters had been ritually denounced and burdened with a conventional morality and its thematic and narrative coherence muddied to a point of internal contradiction. Three years later MGM simply abandoned an investment of $200,000 in Lewis's *It Can't Happen Here*.

By refusing to concede equity rights to authors, the Authors' League Agreement also registered the extent to which the industry regarded literature as property. The "proper property rights of authors and dramatists" were firmly distinguished from other rights they might claim, a question that was legally laid to rest over the adaptation of Dreiser's *An American Tragedy* in 1931. The novel was exactly the kind of literary object that presented the industry's adapters with its most difficult problems. Its burdensome length (Sergei Eisenstein spoke of "Dreiser's Niagara flow of words and descriptions") was a relatively minor issue. The substance of the problem was that both its detailed actions and its thematic concerns were inappropriate to an affirmative medium. But the book's notoriety (it was banned in Boston at least three times in the 1920s) made it as attractive as it was impossible.[22] Famous Players–Lasky bought the movie rights in 1926 for $90,000, but made no attempt to produce it immediately, in part because of the protests it received from Women's Clubs and Better Film organizations. The project was, however, regularly suggested to newly arrived European émigrés; in 1930 Eisenstein prepared a script only to have the studio reject it. David O. Selznick reported that reading it had made him "so depressed that I wanted to reach for the bourbon bottle. As entertainment, I don't think it has one chance in a hundred." The studio should not finance a project "that cannot possibly offer anything but a most miserable two hours to millions of happy-minded young Americans." The MPPDA, one of whose officials described the book as being as much "a symbol of everything objectionable" as the Roscoe "Fatty" Arbuckle scandal, was anxious to delay production until after the meetings of state legislatures in early 1931. However, Paramount was committed to the production, having invested a further $60,000 in the dialogue rights, and with much consultation the studio prepared a script "shifting the emphasis of the story from the seduction, attempted abortion, murder, and execution to a relationship of Clyde and his mother . . . " that was basically acceptable to the MPPDA.[23]

Not surprisingly, Dreiser objected strenuously to Paramount's attempt to turn *An American Tragedy* into what Sergei Eisenstein had described as "'just another' . . . story of 'boy meets girl,' without going into any 'side issues.'"[24] In a letter of protest to Jesse Lasky, Dreiser argued that the film could not "possibly fail to give the impression to the millions of people throughout the world who will see this picture, that the novel on which it is based is nothing short of a cheap, tawdry, tabloid confession story which entirely lacks the scope, emotion, action and psychology of the book involved. Here is an inequitable infringement of a vested property."[25] Dreiser claimed that his contract obliged Paramount to "use its best endeavors to accept such advice, suggestions and criticisms" as he made and that there was nothing in his contract that indicated that Paramount had the right to change "the structure, or what

I may better call the ideographic plan" of the book. He recruited a jury of literati to view the film in New York, and not surprisingly they concurred with his opinion that it was not "an intelligent interpretation of the logic of the book." With that support Dreiser sued to enjoin Paramount from showing it on the grounds both of the terms of his contract and of what he called "a new principle" of "author's equity."[26]

Dreiser was asking the courts to grant him (and, he later claimed, the "thousands of authors who haven't had a square deal in having their works belittled for screen exploitation") a legal right over movie adaptation comparable to the rights granted authors by law and custom on Broadway and in Manhattan's publishing houses. The New York literary marketplace of the 1920s operated under a consensual conception of the profession of authorship that recognized authors as the creators and owners of their literary property and granted them creative control of the entire production process. An element of this authorial creative control involved a publisher's affording an author some protection from the vicissitudes of the market. A publisher, insisted Scribner's editor-in-chief, Maxwell Perkins, "must not try to get the writer to fit the book to the conditions of the trade. . . . It must be the other way around."[27]

This definition of the profession of authorship had already come into conflict with the brute economics of Hollywood on several occasions in the 1920s. Attempts by Samuel Goldwyn and Adolph Zukor to lure "eminent authors" to Hollywood in the early 1920s had ended in recriminations against "the old sausage machine" and the "entrenched bureaucracy" of scenario departments. No one, Elinor Glyn discovered, "wanted our advice or assistance, nor did they intend to take it. All they required was the use of our names to act as shields against the critics." On a more material level, the Authors' League Agreement was itself in part a response to the threat posed to the writer's traditional identity by Hollywood's more mechanized and bureaucratic approach to aesthetic manufacture. A comparable agreement was reached between the Dramatists' Guild and 152 New York theatrical producers in 1927, in part provoked by the intrusion of Hollywood money into theatrical production in the mid-1920s. The Minimum Basic Agreement guaranteed royalty and rights income and gave playwrights right of approval over basic casting, direction, and set design decisions. "In short," Richard Fine suggests, "the Guild agreement granted playwrights roughly the same basic legal rights and privileges as prevailed for authors in the publishing industry."[28]

Dreiser was arguing for an extension of this relationship and its definition of the profession of authorship to the different economic conditions of Hollywood. In *Liberty* he argued that the major companies owed part of their monopoly power and profits "to the artistic development of the film." As part of this debt, they should make "a genuine effort . . . now and then to portray a masterpiece of literature . . . in some such fashion as to widen [its] appeal." The basis of his critique was that whereas previously art had always and necessarily been the province of the artist as an individual, the motion picture had turned art into "an industry, along with coal, iron and steel." For the first time "an art, so called, is discussed as representing an investment."[29] Dreiser's analysis was hardly original and not without its own contradictions, but among New York literati the claim to an author's equity right in the determination of meaning was uncontentious enough.

It did not prove to be so in court, however. In a trial marked by heated exchanges, during which Justice Graham Witschief threatened to have Dreiser removed from the court, the author lost. The judge's legal aesthetics privileged viewers over authors:

> Whether the picture substantially presents the book or not depends on one's point of view. . . . The producer must give consideration to the fact that the great majority of people composing the audience before which the picture will be presented will be more interested that justice prevail over wrongdoing than that the inevitability of Clyde's end clearly appear.[30]

Dreiser's ire was provoked by this judicial rejection of his authorial privilege; for his readers in *Liberty* he catalogued twenty movies condemned for "not truly portraying their originals" by reason of their "failure to catch the spirit of the author, his real meaning or mood!" In a reply to Dreiser, *Liberty*'s editor in chief, Fulton Oursler, quoted the judge as saying that Paramount had "submitted the opinions of an impressive list of critics, who find that the picture is a true representation of the letter and spirit of the book." Witschief's language employed the legalistic terminology of fidelity discussed by Dudley Andrew, but the legally determining issue was a matter of who had authority over the adapted text, and in that respect Dreiser had no case. Outside the court, however, in the critical consensus of where evaluative authority ought properly to lie, the studio had no defense, and no account of Hollywood as the destroyer of writers is complete without a reference to Dreiser's case as "voicing the frustration of every novelist before and since who has found the film image of his work beyond recognition."[31]

Yet Dreiser's analysis, however commonplace it was (it shares a set of untenable assumptions about Hollywood's production practice with auteur criticism, for instance), was not particularly penetrating. This may perhaps have been because he acquired his perspective on the industry through his contact with its production branch, with which he incorrectly understood his dispute to be. Dreiser directed his hostility principally at the movie's director, Josef von Sternberg, whom he held responsible for the "distorted" and "belittling interpretation of a work which is entitled, on its face, to a far more intelligent and broadening conception of the inscrutable ways of life and chance." As Lea Jacobs has observed, it is somewhat ironic that Dreiser, embroiled as he so fre-

Figure 1. Phillips Holmes as Clyde Griffiths in the Josef von Sternberg adaptation of Theodore Dreiser's An American Tragedy *(1931). Museum of Modern Art.*

quently was in battles over the censorship of his literary production, failed to recognize the involvement of the MPPDA's censors in a production that he felt "might as well have been deliberately calculated to misinterpret not only my character and powers as a novelist, but my mental and artistic approach to life itself." This in turn may have resulted from a misperception of the differences in the organization and power structures of publishing and the motion picture industry. Given Dreiser's political persuasions, a further layer of irony is added by his failure to acknowledge the operation of economic determination in the last instance. In his *Liberty* article he recognized the hegemonic role of the MPPDA in uniting the major companies in a "purely commercial and . . . business-minded . . . tyranny over a new and even beautiful art form," but he did so in only the most general terms. Not only was he, as Jacobs argues, "never able to confront the actions of industry censors directly"; he seems also to have misunderstood the relationship within Paramount between Sternberg and "those who provide directors with their authority."[32]

The case did not lead either Eastern authors or the motion picture industry to reconsider their understanding of the position of the individual creator: for Dreiser Hollywood's sin was precisely that of pursuing the industrial logic of responding to consumer demand rather than championing a heroic creative individualism.[33] In Hollywood heroic individualism existed only inside its fictions, not in its boardrooms. Writers repeatedly accused producers of timidity and conformism in their dependence on convention, but in doing so they gave little acknowledgment to the legal constraints on the industry, understanding them only as questions of taste and evaluation. It could be argued, however, that the industry's practices of adaptation conformed to the legal definition imposed by the Supreme Court in 1915. The existence of legal censorship effectively denied producers authorial control over their products as they finally appeared before the public; as proprietors of what the Court had called "a business, pure and simple," the producers were concerned to limit their legal liability for shaping public sentiments when they were at the same time denied the legal redress accorded other expressions of opinion.

The studios' heads of production developed a number of strategies by which they attempted to evade authorial responsibility for the moral standards of their output. "We do not," maintained Thalberg, "create the types of entertainment; we merely present them." In February 1930 when the studio heads discussed the adoption of the Production Code, Jesse Lasky proposed that, given the industry's dependence on source material, responsibility for the moral standards of what was depicted in motion pictures properly lay with "the hands of the men and women writing the current fiction, the literature of the day. They are our reporters and they are the ones that set the standards for the present type of entertainment."[34] Thalberg himself, arguing that the civic groups demanding reform exaggerated the effect movies had on their audiences, insisted that

> the motion picture does not present the audience with tastes and manners and views and morals; it reflects those they already have. . . . People see in it a reflection of their own average thoughts and attitudes. If the reflection is much lower or much higher than their own plane they reject it. . . . The motion picture is literally bound to the mental and moral level of its vast audience.[35]

Whatever individual studio employees might have claimed about their own motives, the distribution and exhibition executives in the industry's center in New York and the political operatives who ran the MPPDA's public relations machinery required a far more complex understanding of the relationship between movies and their multiple audiences than writers, directors, or even Hollywood producers, since an important part of their function lay in maintaining the motion picture and its industry in the ideologically neutral space of entertainment. The industry's policy makers were neither so naïve as to believe that their products merely reflected a preexistent public opinion nor, as Eisenstein clearly understood, so subversive that they sought to produce forms of expression challenging the status quo.[36] Hays and his assistants were perpetually engaged in persuading their employers that,

> whether we like it or not, we must face the fact that we are *not* in that class of industries whose only problem is with the customer. Our public problem is greater with those out of than those in the theatre. We could commit no greater folly than to ignore the classes that write, talk, and legislate, on the basis that the mass public, as reflected by the box-office, is with us in any event. Reform elements outside, not inside, the saloon, enforced prohibition upon the country.[37]

The industry's blunt commercial interest was in occupying both a mediating position between authors and audiences and a cultural median point, in being a subject of interest, but not of concern, a topic for conversation but not action. Were it to slip from that median to a point provocatively nearer the position of negation that post-Romantic cultural theory identifies as the locus of art, it would also likely move from the periphery of the political agenda toward a place closer to the center of attention.

In his analysis of Eisenstein's adaptation of *An American Tragedy*, Keith Cohen suggests that

> adaptation is a truly artistic feat only when the new version carries with it a hidden criticism of its model or at least renders implicit . . . certain key contradictions implanted or glossed over in the original. Of prime interest, therefore, in Eisenstein's scenario is not so much its imitative fidelity or even its cinematic approximation of specifically literary effects, as its pointed distortion, reorientation of Dreiser's work.[38]

Yet despite the opinions of Paramount's tame critics, precisely the same argument could be made for the adaptation directed by Sternberg. The ideological subversion of the precursor text was very differently motivated from Eisenstein's, however. In his account of the case, Harry Alan Potamkin stressed that Paramount had drawn the court's attention to Dreiser's "high regard for the Soviet Union" and Eisenstein's "Bolshevist affiliations." For Potamkin, "the question involved in the conversion of a social novel into film is one of the treatment of an experience in which 'society has an equity,'" by which he meant "our common right to any re-incorporation of what the social entity, or any living part of it, has apprehended *textually*." The fight for the integrity of this experience, he argued, was not personal to Dreiser, or primarily related to the rights of authorship. "It is a struggle against the debasing of the intellectual and social level of an experience," and in that struggle, "the New York Supreme Court has decided to the disadvantage of the socially critical idea."[39]

From its entirely different ideological perspective, the MPPDA might well have accepted Potamkin's conclusion even as it endorsed the Court's decision. The association remained quite unrepentant about its role in the project; indeed, it regarded its involvement as a success because the film occasioned no public outcry. In an article in the MPPDA magazine *The Motion Picture, An American Tragedy* was offered as proof that "because a book or play is objected to as a book or play does not mean that it will be objectionable on the screen, for one of the obligations of producers under the Production Code is to make sure that the 'objectionable' becomes unobjectionable." The article quoted letters from clubwomen who had originally protested the adaptation, one of whom felt, ambivalently, "as though I had been at the trial of a son of my best friend." Another reported that

> when I heard this picture . . . was to be made, I rather regretted it, as I felt the book was not of sufficient value to be brought before the public. The picture has made me change my mind. I so wish many parents of our youth of today could see this picture! I have been a great believer that the parents of today are more to blame for the lack of discipline and respect of our youth than the youth itself.[40]

Rendering the objectionable unobjectionable was not unique to the movies. Rather, it was a feature of the complex negotiations involved in the dissemination of a culture of consumption. The new commodities of that culture required that the bounds of public discourse be revised, but in such a way that the commodities themselves not be blamed by cultural conservatives for the consequences of those revisions. For the movies, even before the implementation of the Formula, these negotiations often involved questions of adaptation, and they were as much concerned with the likely attitudes of audiences inside and outside the movie theater as they were with content. In order for the movies to offer the maximum pleasure to the maximum number at the maximum profit, they had not only to provide a satisfactory level of entertainment for their diverse audiences, but also to offend as small a proportion of the society's cultural and legislative leadership as possible.

In January 1923 a Universal Studios publicity release signed by Carl Laemmle and sent to newspaper editors throughout the country declared that he was "going to commit a crime that will probably bring a storm of criticism and indignation down upon my head. . . . I am going to take liberties with Victor Hugo!" Hugo, continued Laemmle, had written *The Hunchback of Notre Dame* "for an age which licked up raw meat. So he packed his story full of lust and blood and thunder and gruesome, grisly, ghoulish, to say nothing of gory, stuff. . . . Today's conditions are slightly different. The public still likes dripping red meat in its literature and even on its stage, *but not on its screen.*"[41] Adapting *The Hunchback* to "today's screen taste" without losing "all the power and virility of Hugo's masterpiece" was a "delicate surgico-screeno-literary operation." Although Laemmle acknowledged that some critics might think it criminal to take liberties with Hugo, "It is better to present a classic in a palatable form than in an undigestible mass! . . . His story will still be there, but some of the drippiest morsels of his red meat will be parboiled or even discarded entirely."[42]

There was, however, an entirely different subtext to these carnivorous metaphors. Hugo's *Notre Dame de Paris* was, like *Les Mis004erables*, in the Roman Catholic Index of Prohibited Books. Laemmle's statement was designed to ensure that any discussion of the film's variations from the novel would center on the safely aestheticized subject of whether "it was better to delete offensive things from classics rather than never attempt to produce them at all" and avoid revealing the accommodations made to Catholic sensibilities in the adaptation in case anti-Catholic editors "made the wrong use" of the information.[43]

Organized Catholicism was a prominent influence on the mediation of film content from the early 1920s. The activities of the Legion of Decency in 1934 are properly understood not as a sudden outburst of indignation, but rather as the culmination of a close relationship between the Church and the MPPDA. Throughout the 1920s, the Motion Picture Bureau of the International Federation of Catholic Alumnae (IFCA) ran a reviewing service that by 1929 provided capsule moral evaluations of two hundred films a month for 42 newspapers, 113 Catholic newspapers, and 7 radio stations. Moreover, through the MPPDA it exercised a degree of direct influence on motion picture content, not limited to specifically Catholic issues. In her monthly radio broadcast in May 1929, Rita McGoldrick, secretary of the IFCA's bureau, complimented Universal on "their willingness to cooperate with the public groups toward the ideal of better pictures" in adapting *Show Boat*, "that highly elaborate, lovely story of the Mississippi." She praised Carl Laemmle for his courage in making "a sincere effort to raise the standards of screen entertainment." Realizing the difficulty that the miscegenation theme would present in the South, he *"did not hesitate* to sacrifice what would ordinarily have been splendid motion picture material, alive with suspense, dramatic emphasis and moments of emotion."[44]

The adaptation of *Show Boat* addressed a recurrent industry concern in attempting to ensure that its product was acceptable to audiences in all parts of the country and abroad. In such concerns the sensibilities of white Southerners received disproportionate attention. *The Hunchback* was a less likely instance of the industry's fundamental problem in adaptation. If part of the literary function, as understood by Dreiser or suggested by Hugo's anticlericalism, was to provide a critique of the dominant culture, part of the motion picture industry's cultural function was quite consciously "to exercise every possible care that only books or plays which are of the right type are used for screen presentation." Although it was seldom expressed explicitly, Hays conducted the "organized industry" in a broad ideological project concisely identified by Lary May as transferring "the old moral guardianship of the small city and town to the movie corporations," making films "passionate but pure" by containing the titillations they offered their audiences within morally conventional narratives.[45] Metropolitan cynics saw Hays's job as being to "consecrate" the industry's "perfect formula" of "five reels of transgression followed by one reel of retribution." Commenting on the announcement of the Production Code in 1930, an editorial in *The Nation* declared that, leaving aside any question of art, Hays's attempts to keep the movies sexually clean had in practice left them "completely drenched with sex."

> The suggestion of everything which he has attempted to suppress has diffused itself through every scene, and the mind of the audience is encouraged to play about every idea that cannot be stated. Perhaps if an occasional film "justified adultery" or admitted that otherwise respectable girls sometimes have illegitimate children it would not be necessary for every film to deal with seduction arrested at the bedside.[46]

But the movies were, in this respect, little different from the majority of American theater, castigated by Elmer Rice in 1932 for its "timid, conventional, orthodox, and banal" treatment of sexuality, for its "canonization of bodily purity and the triumph of the institution of wedlock." Three years before, Joseph Wood Krutch had argued in similar terms that the real center of American drama was located at "that spiritual crossroads where Broadway intersects with Main Street." According to Krutch, popular successes like *Night Hostess*, "half-baked rather than hard-boiled . . . just naughty enough to seem sophisticated," encapsulated the superficial naïveté of the provincial village. But these plays were neither penetrating nor sincere, and they appealed "to an audience which still hankers after the sticky delights of romantic fiction at the very moment when it is playing at wickedness."[47] Theater critic Benjamin de Casseres's review of the 1926 stage version of *An American Tragedy* coincided with Rice's general judgment on the treatment of sex in modern drama. Describing it as "the typical American crime and sex play of last season," he observed, "I wanted to cheer when Clyde Griffith went to the chair—one American sentimental sex-idiot less."[48] This was a dramaturgy of transgression rather than transcendence, but the gulf that separated Michael Arlen's *The Green Hat* from MGM's adaptation of it as *A Woman of Affairs* was far more material than the merely aesthetic considerations that distinguished it from *Strange Interlude*. In however debased or circumscribed a manner, "the prevalent book or play" occupied the cultural position of negation, which Hays described as a "revolt from Victorianism." His account of the "lost generation" of writers expressing "a distrust in everything, including themselves," was in every sense conventional, including that of its disapproval:

> There was no God. The world was rotten. A fist was shaken at every convention of society. The sole aim of life was to get as much pleasure as possible out of it. The teachings of Freud, which in their popular conception not only stressed the importance of sex in human thought but which questioned the wisdom of all sex repressions advocated by conventional society, added confusion to thinking. . . . The cat-and-dog fight over prohibition communicated itself to other laws, with the result that there was a general decline in respect for all law. Drinking became a mark of defiance, and we found that the ancient temptation to steal apples we had been forbidden was still strong in us.[49]

The affirmative role that the motion picture industry negotiated with the bourgeois institutions of cultural politics was not only different from, but also incompatible with the position of contemporary cultural critic occupied by the readership of *The American Mercury*. Part of the hegemonic role that the industry shared with the weekly mass periodical press and advertising was quite literally to contain the spread of an urban, sophisticated culture that failed to provide an affirmative cultural vision that was acceptable or at least tolerable to the dominant cultural ideology. Therefore, it had to be prevented, and adaptation was one device for its prevention. Hollywood's cultural function was in part to contain and recuperate the negation of art into the affirmation of entertainment. The industry was not defensive about this practice of cultural paternalism. Hays reminded the "thoughtful women of Philadelphia" that "this present period has witnessed a . . . defiance of the rules and conventions under which the world has operated for ages." In print and on stage there was "extremely free discussion of topics which, previous to this particular era, were discussed in whispers, if at all."[50]

The revolt from Victorianism was by no means confined to deliberate acts of provocation in books and on stage, however. Elmer Rice pointed out that in women's magazines, which were, like the movies, sites of affirmative culture, it was the advertisements that broke cultural taboos rather than the "innocuous and infantile fiction in the adjoining columns." Frequently cast in semidramatic form, they dealt with "such distasteful subjects as bodily odors, menstruation and 'female hygiene,' the mere mention of which will, no doubt, arouse in the reader a feeling of disgust." No theatrical performance had yet attempted "to repeat upon the stage the 'confidences' which are so publicly exchanged by the heroines of the advertising pages or to reproduce the window displays of any corner drugstore." Even in its semidramatic form, advertising, the most affirmative aesthetic form of a consumer culture, occupied a cultural location far removed from artistic aspirations to either autonomy or social criticism, a location in which the breaking of a taboo might lead to a liberating purchase. Rice's list of distasteful taboos indicated that the culture of consumption was identified by its promoters and critics alike as feminine: it offered "a therapeutic renovation of sensuality," "self-realization through emotional fulfillment . . . the need to construct a pleasing 'self' by purchasing consumer goods." As Jackson Lears has suggested, advertising—"ceaselessly open to aesthetic novelty"—had by the 1920s "begun to assimilate the allegedly rebellious impulses of aesthetic 'modernism'" and, in this act of appropriation, incorporated its adversarial stance in the promotion of "a leisure world of intense private experience."[51]

What advertising was doing to cubism or *Fortune* magazine to photography—putting aesthetic autonomy to work—the motion picture industry was doing to "those books and plays which boldly flaunt their wares under the sacred name of realistic literature," circumscribing their challenge to social convention by adapting them to narrative, generic, and regulatory conventions.[52] In terms of movie content, the residue of such encounters between the Production Code and the "prevalent type of book" was most frequently the sexual suggestiveness of which *The Nation* complained. Sexual explicitness was, however, not in itself the problem. As was happening in advertising, a properly commodified sexuality was in the process of satisfactorily negotiating the boundaries of its expression, as readily susceptible to adjustment to the fashions of the moment as a hemline. The issue was less one of content than of audience, less to do with authorial intent than with likely variations in reception.[53] As Lamar Trotti, then a publicist for the MPPDA, argued in 1927,

> a book that you and I, as adults, may well read and enjoy—book that has dubious situations and words, perhaps, but which will not affect us in any wrongful fashion—may be altogether wrong for someone else with a different background and a different understanding. We may view the form of a nude figure—you and I—and be uplifted by it, inspired and made better men and women, while to the man with whom we are rubbing elbows, it may convey another and altogether distorted meaning.[54]

If it was not the young or "morons" who needed the MPPDA's parental protection, it was "the folks who represent the intelligentsia in the country towns and small cities," who, according to Carl Milliken, secretary to the MPPDA and in charge of its public relations program, were "not yet prepared to view with approval a long series of scenes including closeups which show the heroine clad only in breechclout and brassiere." Advertising its appeal to an undifferentiated market, Hollywood's ideological self-positioning obliged it to address cultural common denominators in an affirmative vision of national community, inventing the consensus that it claimed to be addressing. Unlike books and music, declared the Production Code, films could not be confined to only certain classes of people. "The exhibitors' theatres are built for the masses, for the cultivated and the rude, mature and immature, self-respecting and criminal. . . . Hence the larger moral responsibilities of the motion pictures."[55]

Quite overtly at issue in the industry's internal discussions about self-regulation was a definition of entertainment as a social function and an argument about the means by which the ideological apparatus of representation would be policed. The movies themselves were textual manifestations of that debate as well as the textual evidence around which it was conducted. The content of movies inevitably became the site of dispute, but the forces impelling the debate were not generated by the ideological superstructure of movie content. In this debate the producers did not have the sole or even the dominant voice, because it was also being conducted throughout the American press, among religious, educational, and civic groups and legislatures. Since the producers consistently denied their responsibility for creating public taste in entertainment, they made themselves subservient to a hegemonic definition of what it was they should be producing. As Hays was fond of saying, the motion picture business was everybody's business. But when he said, "The fact is, motion pictures are yours rather than ours. It is for you indeed to say what they shall be like and how far forward they may go toward their limitless possibilities. We who have the physical control of them are ready to do your bidding,"[56] he was addressing not a small metropolitan elite represented by the likes of Dreiser or the Algonquin Round Table, but the organized and culturally assertive component of those whom H. L. Mencken called the "booboisie," the clubwomen and the Parent Teacher Associations. Much of the running public debate over the regulation of the industry concerned itself with how effectively Hays had made good on his promises, but the industry had very early accepted that it needed to convince these politically influential groups of its respectability. By 1930 the producers' attempts to put limits on the social responsibility of motion pictures were in retreat, in part because of the new problems created by sound and in part because their own position in the debate almost invited activists to claim the authority to offer that definition. In his draft version of the Production Code, Father Daniel Lord, the leading figure in the revival of the Catholic Sodality youth movement, insisted on the industry's responsibility for the moral correctness of the entertainment they produced:

> The moral importance of entertainment is something which has been universally recognized. It enters intimately into the lives of men and women and affects them closely; it occupies their minds and affections during leisure hours; and ultimately touches the whole of their lives. A man may be judged by his standard of entertainment as easily as by the standard of his work.[57]

This notion of "correct entertainment" as that "which tends to improve the race, or at least to re-create and rebuild human beings exhausted with the realities of life" was common to all the groups concerned with reforming the movies in the early 1930s. However reluctantly, the industry accepted its definition of "recreation" as "the period in which a man rebuilds himself after his work . . . during which he gets the chance to rebuild himself physically . . . morally, spiritually, and intellectually."[58] A concomitant of the movies' affirmative cultural function lay in their incorporation of other cultural objects, from interior decoration to literature, into that mode. In considering the draft script for *An American Tragedy*, Hays observed that "if this production is justified at all, it is as a picturization of a terrible possibility for any boy, a picturization in fact of what is one of the tragedies often actual and always potential among the youth. . . . This whole project is going to cause real criticism. Our problem is to make certain that that criticism is not justified." If the picture was to make "a real contribution" to understanding "our social problems in America," then

> the lovemaking certainly does not have to be salacious. There need be, in my opinion, only the slightest reference to the pregnancy. Every opportunity might be sought to leave the impression that the boy was fundamentally of good character save only this trouble (if this is so the Great American Tragedy is still a Greater Tragedy). There should be no reference to abortion and only the slightest reference to the idea that they "had done everything." There need be no use of the words that per se will draw fire such as "seduce." Certainly there need be no reference to a "weak clergyman." If the chaplain is shown he should be a stronger character and a credit to his profession. . . . I think we should strive to avoid every single criticism except that which comes from the treatment of the theme at all.[59]

In the movie as well as in the court, the virtues of entertainment and moral rectitude triumphed over the vices of Dreiser's determinism. If *An American Tragedy* did indeed represent "the prevalent type of book," it had been deliberately prevented from becoming the prevalent type of picture. Insofar as it represented a conscious project to contain the spread of a metropolitan, "sophisticated" culture that rejected the dominant, affirmative cultural vision, the project of adaptation was not so much one of bowdlerization as of recuperation, in the name of a hegemony that understood American tragedies in terms very different from those of Dreiser. Speaking in 1932 for an increasingly vocal Catholic cultural influence on that hegemony, Father James Gillis, editor of *Catholic World*, advised Dreiser, and, more important, his readership, to "snap out of it. . . . Look up at the sky, take a squint at the sun, go out on the hillside and inhale deeply. Get out of the gutters. Come up from those sewers. Be decent, be clean, and America will not seem so tragic."[60]

NOTES

1. Theodore Dreiser, "The Real Sins of Hollywood," *Liberty* 11 (June 1932), pp. 6–11. Audiences might also remember that *Strange Interlude* had been banned in Boston in 1929. See Morris Ernst and Alexander Lindsey, *The Censor Marches On: Recent Milestones in the Administration of the Obscenity Law in the United States* (New York, 1940), p. 69.

2. Stephen Vincent Benét to Nannine Joseph, 20 February 1930, quoted in Richard Fine, *Hollywood and the Profession of Authorship* (Ann Arbor, Mich., 1985), p. 1; Robert E. Sherwood, "Renaissance in Hollywood," *American Mercury* (April 1929), p. 434; Leda Bauer, "The Movies Tackle Literature," *American Mercury* 14 (July 1928), p. 294. Richard Fine cites a number of representative instances of the genre, including those of Mary Roberts Reinhart and Elinor Glyn. See also Ian Hamilton, *Writers in Hollywood, 1915–1951* (London, 1990).

3. George Bluestone, *Novels into Film: The Metamorphosis of Fiction into Cinema* (Baltimore, 1957), p. 219; Dudley Andrew, *Concepts in Film Theory* (New York, 1984), p. 100.

4. Barbara Herrnstein Smith, "Contingencies of Value," *Critical Inquiry* 10 (September 1983), pp. 17–18.

5. Former Postmaster General Will H. Hays was president of the film industry trade association, the Motion Picture Producers and Distributors of America, Inc. (MPPDA), commonly known as the Hays Office and also referred to in this chapter as the association. Among its responsibilities was the administration of the Production Code or "Hays Code." In his account of the workings of the code, Jack Vizzard reports the reservations of a fellow Code administrator in the 1940s: "I don't think it's so good to be called a self-regulator. It sounds like someone who plays with himself." Jack Vizzard, *See No Evil: Life Inside a Hollywood Censor* (New York, 1970), p. 56.

6. Robin Wood, *Hitchcock's Films Revisited* (New York, 1989), p. 244.

7. Will H. Hays, "Motion Pictures and the Public," an address before the Women's City Club of Philadelphia, 20 April 1925 (New York, 1925), p. 2.

8. Wilton A. Barrett, secretary of the National Board of Review of Motion Pictures, testimony before the Committee on Education, House of Representatives, 69th Congress, 1st Session, on Bills to Create a Commission to Be Known as the Federal Motion Picture Commission, and Defining Its Powers and Duties (Washington, D.C., 1926), p. 337.

9. Jeffrey Sconce, "Narrative Authority and Social Narrativity: The Cinematic Reconstitution of Brontë's *Jane Eyre*," *Wide Angle* 10 (1988), pp. 47, 61.

10. Hays, "Motion Pictures and the Public," p. 10.

11. *Mutual Film Corp. v. Ohio Industrial Commission*, 236 U.S. 230 U.S. Supreme Court, 1915, reprinted in *The Movies in Our Midst: Documents in the Cultural History of Film in America*, ed. Gerald Mast (Chicago, 1982), p. 142. See also Garth Jowett, "'A Capacity for Evil': The 1915 Supreme Court *Mutual* Decision," *Historical Journal of Film, Radio and Television* 9 (1989), pp. 59–78.

12. Ellis W. Hawley, "Herbert Hoover, the Commerce Secretariat, and the Vision of an 'Associative State,'" *Journal of American History* 66 (June 1974), pp. 116–40; "Certificate of Incorporation of Motion Picture Producers and Distributors of America, Inc.," 10 March 1922, quoted in Raymond Moley, *The Hays Office* (Indianapolis, 1945), p. 226; "The Open Door," MPPDA pamphlet, New York, 1924, 1927.

13. Hays, "Motion Pictures and the Public," p. 5.

14. Clara Beranger, "The Story," in *Introduction to the Photoplay*, ed. John Tibbetts (1927; reprint Shawnee Mission, Kans., 1977), p. 137; Richard Koszarski, *An Evening's Entertainment: The Age of the Silent Feature Picture 1915–1928* (New York, 1990), p. 108; William James Fadiman, "Books into Movies," *Publishers' Weekly* (8 September 1934), p. 753. See also Robert Gustavson, *The Buying of Ideas: Source Acquisition at Warner Bros., 1930–1949* (Ann Arbor, Mich., 1983); Fine, *Hollywood and the Profession of Authorship*, pp. 33, 68; "The Movie Book Market," *Publishers Weekly* (20 September 1930), p. 1266.

15. *Literary Digest* (25 October 1930), p. 20. John Golden, "The Decadent Stage—Clean It or Kill It!" *Theatre Magazine* (March 1927), p. 7. Mary Beth Hamilton provides an excellent account of the cultural politics of Broadway in the late 1920s in "When I'm Bad I'm Better: Mae West and American Popular Entertainment" (Ph.D. dissertation, Princeton University, 1990).

16. MPPDA memo, 20 November 1924, 1924. Meetings—Scenarios file, Motion Picture Association of America Archive, New York (hereafter MPA); Ethel Smith Dorrance to Hays, 29 February 1924, *Damned* file, MPA; Hays 1925 Public Relations Committee file, MPA.

17. Originally published in 1923, *Damned* told the story of a "girl who was so beautiful that she meant ruin for any man who beheld her—even for Satan himself." The novel described a series of affairs leading to her death. In hell, in imitation of the *One Thousand and One Nights*, she relates her adventures to Satan. See Ethel Smith Dorrance, *Damned: The Intimate Story of a Girl* (New York, 1923). See also Hays to Dorrance, 29 February 1924; Eric Schuler, secretary, Authors' League, to Hays, 25 April 1924; Schuler to Carl Laemmle, 10 June 1924; Laemmle to Schuler, Laemmle to Hays, 11 June 1924, 1924 *Damned* file, MPA; Authors' League Agreement, 1927, in Moley, *The Hays Office*, p. 239.

18. "General Principles," a reporter's transcript of a meeting held at the offices of the Association of Motion Picture Producers, Los Angeles, 10 February 1930, p. 139, Production Code file, MPA (hereafter reporter's transcript). For a full discussion of the development of the 1930 Production Code, see Richard Maltby, "The Genesis of the Production Code," in *Prima dei Codici 2: Alle Porte di Hays/Before the Codes 2: The Gateway to Hays*, ed. Giuliana Muscio (Venice, 1991), pp. 39–80.

19. Although it was accepted within the publishing industry that in theory the economic rights, including subsidiary rights, to a literary property resided with the author, it was also accepted that when a publisher contributed to the success of an author's work, the publisher was entitled to a share of the income, often on a fifty-fifty basis. Negotiations over screen rights seldom involved authors directly, being handled by agents, publishers, or theatrical producers. See MPPDA Resolution, 24 June 1924, in Moley, *The Hays Office*, p. 239; Fine, *Hollywood and the Profession of Authorship*, pp. 33, 68; "Memorandum of conference held at MGM studio Tuesday evening, 21 August 1928, between Leroy Scott, C. B. DeMille, Jesse Lasky, Irving G. Thalberg, and Edwin J. Loeb," Books and Plays file, MPA.

20. In contravention of the Formula agreement, advertisements for *A Woman of Affairs* had identified its literary source.

21. Hays, speech to studio executives, c. 20 April 1933, Production Code file, MPA.

22. Sergei Eisenstein, *Immoral Memories: An Autobiography*, trans. Herbert Marshall (London, 1985), p. 156. Mark Fenster traces a remarkably similar recent instance in his article "Containment, Excess, Ambivalence: The Adaptation of *Less than Zero*," *The Velvet Light Trap* 28 (1991), pp. 49–64.

23. *Memo from David O. Selznick*, ed. Rudy Behlmer (New York, 1973), pp. 55–56. Eisenstein's script is printed, along with an account of its production, in Ivor Montagu, *With Eisenstein in Hollywood* (New York, 1969). Other accounts of the Eisenstein project can be found in Sergei Eisenstein, *Film Form* (New York), pp. 95ff.; Jay Leyda and Zina Voynov, *Eisenstein at Work* (London, 1982), pp. 52–59. See also Joy to Maurice McKenzie, 19 September 1930; Lamar Trotti, memo, 24 February 1931, *An American Tragedy* file, Production Code Administrative archive, Margaret Herrick Library, Academy of Motion Picture Arts and Sciences, Los Angeles (hereafter PCA).

24. Eisenstein, *Immoral Memories*, p. 156. Dreiser seems subsequently to have been more permissive about adaptations of *An American Tragedy*. Ellen Morris writes, "In 1936 he reviewed four different dramatizations (one French, one German, one Russian, one American), each with a different approach to the 'moral' of his novel, and found virtues in them all, including the Russian, which emphasized the duty of labor, the rights and godlike status of the worker, etc. 'Unfortunately,' he added, 'this dramatization is not nearly as well done as one might have hoped.'" Ellen Morris, *Two Dreisers* (New York, 1969), p. 287.

25. There is an account of Dreiser's reaction to the Sternberg version in Hamilton, *Writers in Hollywood*, pp. 53–55. See *The Letters of Theodore Dreiser*, Volume 2, ed. Robert H. Elias (Philadelphia, 1959), p. 529. Dreiser chose to ignore the qualifying phrase in the contract that required Paramount to accept his suggestions only "insofar as it may, in the judgment of the purchaser, consistently do so."

26. Among the members of the jury were George Jean Nathan, Carl Van Doren, Patrick Kearney, and psychoanalyst A. A. Brill. See Elias, *The Letters of Theodore Dreiser*, p. 530; Dorothy Spensley, "Dreiser Looks for a Fight," *Motion Picture Classic* (June 1931): 36.

27. Fine, *Hollywood and the Profession of Authorship*, pp. 69, 14; Maxwell Perkins to Marjorie Kinnon Rawlings, 26 March 1936, quoted in A. Scott Berg, *Maxwell Perkins: Editor of Genius* (New York, 1978), p. 299.

28. Elmer Rice, *Minority Report: An Autobiography* (New York, 1963), p. 179; Elinor Glyn, *Romantic Adventure* (New York, 1937), p. 291; Fine, *Hollywood and the Profession of Authorship*, p. 36; Alfred L. Bernheim, *The Business of the Theatre: An Economic History of the American Theatre 1790–1932* (New York, 1932), p. 115.

29. Dreiser, "The Real Sins of Hollywood," p. 6.

30. Elias, *The Letters of Theodore Dreiser*, p. 562. After the trial Paramount added new opening and closing scenes, apparently in an attempt to appease Dreiser. There is a detailed account of textual changes proposed by both the MPPDA and Dreiser in Lea Jacobs, "*An American Tragedy*: A Comparison of Film and Literary Censorship," in Muscio, pp. 152–57.

31. Bluestone, *Novels into Film*, p. 217, n. 3.

32. Elias, *The Letters of Theodore Dreiser*, pp. 528–29; Jacobs, *The Compound Cinema*, p. 154; Dreiser, "The Real Sins of Hollywood," p. 7. In 1929 it was reported that Dreiser was contemplating writing an exposé of the motion picture industry, using a fictionalized Will Hays as its centralized character and "divulging a lot of the inside facts on the political activities of the Hays organization over the country and especially in Washington." See *Motion Picture News*, 19 October 1929.

33. According to Keith Cohen's analysis, "Dreiser insists throughout *An American Tragedy* on the individualistic values and motives that inform Clyde Griffith's character." In conversation with Eisenstein in 1927, Dreiser insisted on the importance of the drama of the individual, "since only through the individual could the mass and its dreams be sensed and interpreted." See Keith Cohen, "Eisenstein's Subversive Adaptation," in *The Classic American Novel and the Movies*, ed. Gerald Peary and Roger Shatzin (New York, 1977), p. 254.

34. Reporter's transcript, p. 96.

35. "General Principles to Govern the Preparation of a Revised Code of Ethics for Talking Pictures," reporter's transcript, pp. 138–39.

36. Ivor Montagu reports that Eisenstein understood Lasky's proposal that he adapt *An American Tragedy* as "a sentence of final doom" on his expedition to Paramount. "It would never be permitted to foreigners, some even Russians, to make *An American Tragedy* in the way we were bound to make it. . . . [It] could never be allowed by a firm with responsibilities to the social setup such as are owed by an organization of the magnitude of Paramount." See Montagu, pp. 113–14.

37. Hays, draft of 1932 Annual Report of the MPPDA, Will H. Hays Archive, Department of Special Collections, Indiana State Library, Indianapolis.

38. Cohen, "Eisenstein's Subversive Adaptation," p. 245.

39. Harry Alan Potamkin, "Novel into Film: A Case Study of Current Practice," in *The Compound Cinema: The Film Writings of Harry Alan Potamkin*, ed. Lewis Jacobs (New York, 1977), pp. 186–87.

40. "The 'Objectionable Becomes UNobjectionable [sic]," *Motion Picture Monthly* 7 (September-August 1931), pp. 3, 8. Such testimony did not prevent *Harrison's Reports* from both denouncing the film and reveling in its box office failure. "Mr. Hays may be able to convince some simple-minded women that 'An American Tragedy' is 'Unobjection-

able.' But Paramount is finding out that the great majority of the American people take a different view of it; the box office is telling the tale. . . . Picture-goers revolted at the sight of a young man cold-bloodedly planning to murder the poor girl he had seduced so as to make himself free to marry a wealthy girl. The decency hidden within even the morbidly and sexually inclined persons revolted at the very thought of being offered as entertainment a picture showing such a dastardly act." See *Harrison's Reports*, 26 September 1931, p. 156; 20 May 1933, p. 77.

41. Robert Cochrane to Will Hays, 22 January 1923, *The Will Hays Papers* (University Publications of America [microform], 1988), 1:8, frames 646–48.

42. Ibid.

43. Ibid.

44. "Endorsed Motion Pictures," broadcast by Rita McGoldrick, 9 May 1929, IFCA file, MPA. See also Francis R. Walsh, "*The Callaghans and the Murphys* (MGM, 1927): A Case Study of Irish-American and Catholic Church Censorship," *Historical Journal of Film, Radio and Television* 10 (1990), 33–45.

45. MPPDA Board of Directors Resolution, 24 June 1924, quoted in "Agreement executed between the Authors' League of America, the Dramatists' Guild of the Authors' League, the Authors' Guild of the Authors' League and the Motion Picture Producers and Distributors of America Inc., December 15, 1927," in Moley, *The Hays Office*, p. 239; Lary May, *Screening Out the Past: The Birth of Mass Culture and the Motion Picture Industry* (New York, 1980), p. 205.

46. "Virtue in Cans," *The Nation* (16 April 1930), p. 441.

47. Elmer Rice, "Sex in the Modern Theater," *Harper's* (May 1932), p. 665; Joseph Wood Krutch, "Our Hard-Boiled Plays," *Theatre Magazine*, (February 1929), p. 20.

48. Benjamin de Casseres, "The Debasement of Crime, Sex and Money in Current Drama," *Theatre Magazine* (September 1927), p. 16. A similar opinion was expressed by Emanuel Eisenberg in "From the Front Page," *Theatre Magazine* (May 1930), p. 31. Ellen Morris reaches a comparable conclusion about the novel's relation to contemporary moral standards: "Dreiser appeared in his novel to take little account of the postwar revolution in sexual mores. . . . The murder trials that caught the fancy of the newspaper public, such as the Snyder-Gray and the Hall-Mills affairs, were those that dramatized the new rather than the old sexual code. They involved crimes of adultery, in which a faithless wife or husband was murderer or victim. But Dreiser's murders were crimes of ambition, dating from a time when the bonds of sexuality were so strong that they could be broken only by violence." See Morris, p. 210.

49. Hays, Annual Report of the MPPDA, 1931, 7, Hays Papers. For instances of similar rhetoric, see *Selected Articles on Censorship of the Theater and Moving Pictures*, ed. Lamar T. Beman (New York, 1931), pp. 280–84.

50. In Lord's draft version of the Production Code, which eventually became the text of "The Reasons Supporting the Code," he suggested that one necessity for the code was that "small communities, remote from sophistication and from the hardening process which often takes place in the ethical and moral standards of larger cities, are easily and readily reached by any sort of film." See reporter's transcript, p. 120. See also Stuart Ewen, *Captains of Consciousness: Advertising and the Social Roots of the Consumer Culture* (New York, 1977), pp. 42, 54, 190; Richard Butsch, "Introduction: Leisure and Hegemony in America," in *For Fun and Profit: The Transformation of Leisure into Consumption*, ed. Richard Butsch (Philadelphia, 1990), pp. 3–27; Michael Denning, "The End of Mass Culture," in *Modernity and Mass Culture*, ed. James Naremore and Patrick Brantlinger (Bloomington, Ind., 1991), pp. 253–68; Roland Marchand, *Advertising the American Dream: Making Way for Modernity, 1920–1940* (Berkeley, Calif., 1985), p. 341; Hays, "Motion Pictures and the Public," p. 10.

51. Elmer Rice, "Sex in the Modern Theater," p. 670; Marchand, *Advertising the American Dream*, pp. 16–24, 52–61, 206–34, 344–46; T. J. Jackson Lears, "From Salvation to Self-Realization: Advertising and the Therapeutic Roots of the Consumer Culture,

1880–1930," in *The Culture of Consumption: Critical Essays in American History 1880–1980*, ed. Richard Wightman Fox and T. J. Jackson Lears (New York, 1983), pp. 22, 27–28. See also Martin Pumphrey, "The Flapper, the Housewife and the Making of Modernity," *Cultural Studies* 1 (May 1987), pp. 179–94; Andreas Huyssen, "Mass Culture as Woman: Modernism's Other," in *Studies in Entertainment: Critical Approaches to Mass Culture,* ed. Tania Modleski (Bloomington, Ind., 1986), pp. 188–206; Gaylyn Studlar, "The Perils of Pleasure?: Fan Magazine Discourse as Women's Commodified Culture in the 1920s," *Wide Angle* 13 (January 1991), pp. 6–33.

52. Lamar Trotti, "Screenwriting," draft of article, 1927 Trotti file, MPA. Marchand, *Advertising the American Dream*, p. 140; Jeffrey L. Meikle, *Twentieth Century Limited: Industrial Design in America, 1925–1939* (Philadelphia, 1979), pp. 9, 17; Daniel Bell, "Modernism Mummified," in *Modernist Culture in America*, ed. Daniel Joseph Singal (Belmont, Calif., 1991), p. 163. Lears describes the process by which art is assimilated into advertising as requiring "the ascendance of formalism and professionalism . . . the rejection of all romantic dreams of transcendence, the dismissal of any vestigial sense of higher purpose, the acceptance of art as primarily a set of formal problems to be solved." See T. J. Jackson Lears, "Uneasy Courtship: Modern Art and Modern Advertising," in Singal, *Modernist Culture in America*, p. 180.

53. The development of a commodified sexuality directed toward a female audience is discussed in Janet Staiger, *Interpreting Films: Studies in the Historical Reception of American Cinema* (Princeton, N.J., 1992), pp. 124–38, and Miriam Hansen, *Babel and Babylon: Spectatorship in American Silent Film* (Cambridge, Mass., 1991), pp. 243–94. See also Richard deCordova, *Picture Personalities: The Emergence of the Star System in America* (Urbana, Ill., 1990), pp. 117–47.

54. Lamar Trotti, "Screenwriting," draft of article, 1927 Trotti file, MPA.

55. The MPPDA, for instance, participated actively in Americanization programs run by a variety of voluntary organizations. See Milliken to Hays, 9 October 1929, PCA *Applause* file; Marchand, *Advertising the American Dream*, pp. 4–5; reporter's transcript, pp. 119, 121.

56. Hays, "Motion Pictures and the Public," p. 3.

57. Reporter's transcript, pp. 116–17.

58. Ibid., pp. 11, 116.

59. Hays to Joy, 9 February 1931, *An American Tragedy* file, PCA.

60. James Gillis, "Sursum Corda," *The Catholic News* (6 February 1932). Quoted in William M. Halsey, *The Survival of American Innocence: Catholicism in an Age of Disillusionment, 1920–1940* (Notre Dame, Ind., 1980), p. 106.

Guerric DeBona, O.S.B.

Dickens, the Depression, and MGM's *David Copperfield*

I

Like Matthew Arnold, Charles Dickens visited America twice, and no less than Arnold he shaped the nation's ideas about culture, ameliorating tensions between the barbarians, the philistines, and the populace. He was loved by the people, but he also maintained a high level of literary prestige. As the *New World* newspaper commented at the time of his first visit, he "was read with pleasure over the whole immense extent of the States, from the British dominions on the north to the glades of Florida, and from the Atlantic cities to the cantonments and barracks on the Mississippi." He was read even by "the hunter of buffalo in the wilds . . . with a degree of intimacy that only a friend inspires."[1] For his American reading tour in 1867–68, the attendance at his welcome was outdone only at his farewell, which was witnessed by an estimated 114,000 people. Almost immediately he became a nineteenth-century Anglo-American classic, virtually the equal of Shakespeare.[2]

From the beginning the American discourse about Dickens was often expressed in class or ideological terms. He was an instant celebrity in part because he was a British author who wrote about democracy and who earned a living from his talent. As *The United States Magazine and Democratic Review* put it in April 1842, he was not an "aristocrat or millionaire":

> As to his purse, he has to fill it from time to time by a draft on his wits, like the poorest scribbler of the tribe; and as to rank, we are rejoiced that there is no other nobility about him than the universal title of simple and glorious manhood. He is neither Prince nor Lord—but there is neither Prince nor Lord in Christendom to whom we should have awarded the ovation of such a reception.[3]

Dickens's common-man aura also owed something to his performance style, which was suited to a fairly wide range of audiences. Early in his second American tour, he performed readings of his novels for a mostly highbrow group of Boston literati, including the most famous actor of the day, Edwin Booth. A cartoon drawn by C. A. Barry, which appeared in *Harper's Weekly* on 7 December 1867, shows Dickens quietly poised behind a small lectern turning the pages of a book; with his right hand mildly gesturing as he reads, he appears to be giving a lecture, not a show. A report of the performance suggests that it was a vaguely aristocratic occasion: "Though pervaded by a touch of dandyism . . . [he was] dressed in a suit of faultless black."[4] But other, less aestheticized features of his style were equally agreeable to tradespeople and the managerial middle class. "Not a breakfast table, not a parlor, not an office, not a shop," wrote a *Chicago Tribune* columnist on 11 December 1867, "can be entered without finding Mr. Dickens and his entertainment the subject of conversation; and old jokes from 'Nickleby' and 'Pickwick' are chuckled over, as if they had only just been revealed to the world." Several contemporary observers commented on his mixture of highbrow and lowbrow appeal, his ability to turn even an intellectual assembly into comedic popular theater. For example, a Boston reviewer noted that the "polished ice of that proper community has seldom cracked so loudly and cheerily."[5] The New York intelligentsia, including what the *Evening Post* called "the best" of society—Lowell, Holmes, and Longfellow—was reportedly even more animated than the Boston Brahmins, despite their complaints about Dickens's "cockneyish accent."[6]

When Dickens departed America in 1868, at least one Shakespearean scholar complained that his performances were "sedulously low-brow. He yielded to temptation to get a cheap laugh by continually playing down to his readers."[7] Even so, he guaranteed the widest possible audience. Lawrence Levine has ranked him alongside Shakespeare and Milton as one of three "highbrow" authors who most appealed to the American middle class.[8] For this reason he quickly became part of the American educational system (Edna Hays's detailed study of the requirements in English for college entrance exams lists *A Tale of Two Cities* and *David Copperfield* in 1880 and 1893, respectively). At the same time he was recognized as a liberal reformer who wrote about the poor. As one contemporary remarked, his writing asserts the "idea of human equality, under the influence of the progress of which regal palaces and baronial castles of the whole world are crumbling and destined to crumble to ruin."[9] Therefore, when Dickens died in 1870, George Templeton Strong wrote in his diary that there were at least two Dickenses, because "his genius was unquestionable; his art and method were often worthy of the lowest writer of serials for Sunday papers. . . . Few men since Shakespeare have enriched the language with so many phrases that are in everyone's mouth."[10]

As Dwight MacDonald pointed out in the *Partisan Review* in 1968, Dickens has a double appeal: "Superb comedy alternates with bathetic sentimentality, great descriptive prose with the most vulgar kind of theatricality."[11] Not surprisingly, every one of Dickens's novels was dramatized, and six of his stories reached the American stage. Immediately after the publication of *David Copperfield* and *Dombey and Son*, popular songs such as "Dora and Agnes" and "Florence" were circulated to wide acclaim.[12] The phenomenon continued well into the twentieth century. In their *What about Advertising?* (New York, 1927) Kenneth M. Goode and Harford Powell said that Americans of the Jazz Age voted Dickens as one of "the ten greatest men in history" and rated *David Copperfield* as their favorite novel. By 1930 the "Dickens Fellowship" had increased dramatically in the United States, including such organizations as *The American Dickensian* in New York, *The Chigwell Chronicle* in Boston, *The Los Angeles Dickensian* in Los Angeles, and *The Blunderstone Review* in Philadelphia.

Meanwhile, the underlying form and message of Dickens's novels may have helped to shape Hollywood cinema. At least this is what Sergei Eisenstein argued when he visited the United States in the 1930s and in his famous essay "Dickens, Griffith, and the Film Today." All American cinema, he wrote, had grown logically out of D. W. Griffith— and Griffith, in turn, was a late nineteenth-century provincial who was inspired by Dickens and Victorian stage melodrama:

> In social attitudes Griffith was always a liberal, never departing far from the slightly sentimental humanism of the good old gentlemen and sweet old ladies of Victorian England, just as Dickens loved to picture them. His tender-hearted film morals go no higher than a level of Christian accusation of human injustice and nowhere in his films is there sounded a protest against social injustice.[13]

The very form of Griffith's work, with its parallel actions and its drive toward organic unity, was, Eisenstein noted, an outgrowth of the "structure of bourgeois society," which is "woven of irreconcilably alternating layers of 'white' and 'red,'" rich and poor. In Hollywood films these parallel lines of social class never clashed or exploded into conflict. Instead, as in Dickens's novels, they were brought together through sentimental, good-hearted conclusions in which virtue triumphed over vice.

In the first half of the twentieth century, Dickens had an almost folkloric appeal for Americans—but at no point was he more important to the culture as a whole than during the Great Depression, when Roosevelt's New Deal tried to stave off revolution by introducing social reform. Cultural historian Richard H. Pells has accurately described the political situation of those years:

The Roosevelt Administration had succeeded in reducing the tension and fear which plagued the country in the early years of the depression. Through an expert use of the mass media, through the reliance on a rhetoric that was very traditional even as it introduced unprecedented reforms, through the insistence on national unity and cooperation in a time of extreme emergency, through an emphasis on order and security rather than social upheaval, the New Deal gave people the sense that their problems were at last being recognized if not yet solved.[14]

The politics of the New Deal were designed to mediate between extremes, and for that reason Dickens was particularly well suited to the times. He was a traditional yet popular British intellectual who suggested Victorian stability, and he spoke to the need for reform without revolution. There can be no question of the wide dissemination of his writings during the period. Richard B. Hovey, in recalling his education in an "average American high school" during the Great Depression, writes that Dickens was required sophomore reading and that *A Tale of Two Cities* was "nicely suited for fifteen-year-olds."[15] FDR himself was known to read *A Christmas Carol* aloud on the radio every year, and according to his assistant Harry Hopkins, "the little book was one of his priceless possessions."[16]

In the 1930s the American demand for Dickens and for Dickens-like historical novels surpassed even the popular enthusiasm for the detective story, probably because Dickens's Victorian England helped readers understand the Great Depression. James D. Hart explains this phenomenon by saying that

a period of stress and turmoil, leading people to books both for escape and explanation, favored the revival of historical novels. In a time when to face the present or the future was unpleasant, looking backward was a comparative pleasure, affording surcease from contemporary problems and an understanding that people of other ages had weathered worse times.[17]

Dickens's best-known historical novel, *A Tale of Two Cities* (1859), not only became standard high-school reading for a generation during the Depression, but was also made into a half-dozen plays and, in 1935, a major Hollywood feature by MGM. The vogue of this book is easily understood if we consider how its conservative reaction to the French Revolution could be applied to the contemporary scene. It provided adventurous escape, suggested parallels with the present, and gave many Americans a sense of childhood nostalgia for the reading of "classics"—a nostalgia that, as Lawrence Levine notes, had been on the rise in the late 1920s.[18] At about the same moment, *A Christmas Carol* became what Paul Davis calls a "culture-text," and it was eventually adapted by the mass media more than any other work in the history of English literature. This story about a family in poverty, abused by a wealthy employer, must have strongly resonated with Depression audiences. Moreover, because the story promoted the sentimental values of good-heartedness and charity, it provided a means to counteract socialist ideology and preserve a utopian faith in American enterprise.[19]

From almost their beginnings, the movies found many uses for Charles Dickens, but it is important to note that not all of them were successful.[20] In 1924 a Hollywood production of *David Copperfield* apparently confused its audience, provoking one critic to recommend that "if Dickens is ever to be popular with the masses . . . the plays and films taken from his works should be made much clearer than they are."[21] A decade later, at the height of the New Deal, MGM and David O. Selznick produced an apparently quite faithful adaptation of the same novel that proved not only clear, but also enormously popular, earning almost a million dollars in profit during its initial release. The success of the Selznick film no doubt had something to do with its unusually effective qualities as an adaptation, or even as a work of art. It survives today as arguably the best of all the screen versions of Dickens, achieving what might be described as the quintessence of "Dickens-ness." But it might never have appeared at all if it had not been perfectly suited to the politics and industrial conditions of its time. At this particular historical juncture, "Dickens-ness" served as the basis for a certain kind of charitable, largely Republican ideology that worked as a salve for hard times without proposing any radical changes to the system. In other words, a film adaptation of Dickens could respect its source and still have widespread appeal, satisfying the leaders of industry, the Arnoldian intellectuals, the respectable middle class, and even the anonymous masses.

II

In addition to having social and ideological importance, the 1935 *David Copperfield* was also an exemplary source for what Hollywood once called the "prestige production"—an idea that dates from the early days of the feature film. According to Tino Balio, the term *prestige* signified not a genre, but "production values and promotion treatment. A prestige picture is typically a big-budget special based on a pre-sold property, often as not a 'classic,' tailored for top stars."[22] By the 1930s the prestige picture was firmly established in Hollywood, and its making would become the most popular production trend of the decade, with fourteen examples listed in to *Film Daily's Ten Best.* Half of the films produced between 1934 and 1939 and close to thirty of the sixty-seven pictures on *Variety's* top-grossing films lists in the 1930s were prestige pictures. Compared with the total output of the major studios, prestige pictures accounted for a small percentage, but compared with their total production budgets, they accounted for a lion's share. Moreover, prestige pictures played a crucial role in defining the public image of a company.

Such films were especially important to the career of David O. Selznick, who was able to reap financial and aesthetic dividends from overtly literary capital. But according to Selznick's biographer, David Thomson, interest in *David Copperfield* was not at all great at MGM.[23] The studio's New York office disliked "highbrow period pieces and costume dramas that were not only costly but were deemed a bit much for the average viewer."[24] Selznick later recalled that besides the obvious cost of the film, the biggest obstacle he faced from other executives was that they could not conceive of *David Copperfield* as a star vehicle. The New York office had a point. When the movie industry had hit its rock bottom in 1933, MGM was the only major studio to make money, and it did so through star power, not literary prestige.

Selznick's project nevertheless had a certain appeal. In a memo to Loew's sales and distribution offices in February 1934, Selznick argued, "There is no question in my mind that the public has finally decided to accept the classics as motion picture fare."[25] Besides giving MGM an aura of middle-class respectability, canonical authors such as Dickens and Tolstoy also enabled the studio to achieve product differentiation and to expand its distribution and exhibition. Therefore, on 17 March 1934 Selznick sent a telegram to Arthur Loew in the Metro offices in New York stating his belief that *David Copperfield* would "add hundreds of thousands of dollars to British empire gross while still giving us a picture that would be as good for this country, and at the same time do wonders for the entire standing of our British company."[26] When the picture was finally released, the critics of the day were aware of its allure to a British audience; one review noted that *Copperfield*'s "production values are evident. It is obvious that money was spent lavishly. MGM has produced prestige building entertainment—something for the British lion and Leo to exult over."[27]

This British angle had been exploited throughout the production of *David Copperfield*, which employed British actors and an extensively researched preproduction team headed by Natalie Bucknell. Before shooting or even casting began, Selznick took his crew to Britain for a month. He also hired a much-respected British novelist, Hugh Walpole, to collaborate with Howard Estabrook on the screenplay for the film (Walpole made a cameo appearance as the Vicar), and in the trailer he had Lionel Barrymore introduce Walpole as "the distinguished author of *Captain Nicholas, Vanessa* and other great successes." When the film opened in London on 28 February 1935, a "Dickensian" publicity luncheon was held at the Savoy Hotel, complete with an English "Victorian" dessert, "The Old Charles Dickens Trifle." But Selznick also recognized the nostalgic importance of *David Copperfield* for middle-class American boys who grew up in the early twentieth century. In press releases he claimed that his father had read the book aloud to him and that throughout the production he had "lugged with me everyplace the old-fashioned, red-leather copy of *David Copperfield* which my father had given me." (Joseph Mankiewicz scoffed at this idea, saying that the famous producer never read anything but a synopsis. Ben Hecht once told Selznick, "The trouble with you, David, is that you did all your reading before you were twelve.") He also made an astute assessment of both market forces and American cultural hegemony. Literary prestige was associated in some quarters with respectability and wealth, and such prestige had long been used as a way of "reforming" films seen by the masses. Therefore Frank Dyer, vice president of the Motion Picture Production Corporation, had remarked in 1910 that "when the works of Dickens and Victor Hugo, the poems of Browning, the plays of Shakespeare and stories from the Bible are used as a basis for moving pictures, no fair-minded man can deny that the art is being developed along the right lines."[28]

Certainly it was no accident that Selznick's devoted attention to authors such as Tolstoy and Dickens coincided with the most puritanical era of the Hollywood censorship code. During this period the industry was unlikely to adapt contemporary fiction. *Harrison's Reports* for 18 April 1931 said that Dreiser's *An American Tragedy* (1925), "with its shameless wallowings in the sex gutters . . . would seem impossible of conversion into anything resembling wholesome or appealing entertainment for the majority of picture followers." To adapt Dickens into a Hollywood movie in the early 1930s was to give comfort to the numerous supporters of the Legion of Decency and participants in a general film boycott, who were disturbed by contemporary depictions of sexuality and violence; it was, in fact, a way to acquire a kind of moral prestige.[29] (As William Dean Howells, himself present at one of Dickens's readings, had said after reading *David Copperfield*, the novel was a "tasteful" book, without excessive sexual references.)

The Breen Office played a large role in shaping Hollywood's choice of fiction, but Dickens was also a safe author in American schools, and the educational community itself was publishing a number of pedagogical tools for high school film appreciation that could further help to shape the audience for Selznick's film. Already by 1928, Mary Allen Abbott's *Motion Picture Preferences for Different School Grades* (Columbia University Press) had appeared. In 1933, Edgar Dale's *How to Appreciate Motion Pictures: A Manual of Motion Picture Criticism Prepared for High School Students* was published by MacMillan. *Teaching Motion Picture Appreciation*, by Elizabeth Pollard (Ohio State University Press) and *How to Judge Motion Pictures* (Scholastic Press) were brought out the following year. But perhaps the most significant secondary educational contribution to the study of film in the 1930s was Dr. William Lewin's monograph *Photoplay Appreciation in American*

High Schools (1935). Based on Lewin's institutional self-study, new classroom units of "photoplay appreciation" were being adopted. The result was the long-running series *Photoplay Studies on Moving Picture Plays*. Under the general editorship of Max J. Herzberg, each volume featured a discussion of a particular film geared for students. Some, such as Mary Allen Abbott's *David Copperfield* (1935), even featured a teacher's manual. The series was designed as an introduction to both the film and the novel or play, and each volume contained study questions. Some of the casebooks, such as the one on *A Tale of Two Cities* (December 1935), also promoted an essay contest.

By the time of the release of *David Copperfield*, there were already *Photoplay Studies* on *Treasure Island, Great Expectations*, and *The Little Minister*. The *Photoplay Studies* were clearly a promotional device backed by movie studios, but on a scholarly level they were intelligently written. They contained historical background, biographical information about authors, detailed accounts of individual productions, bibliographies, and filmographies. One of the important functions they performed was to valorize the films discussed as adaptations. Mary Allen Abbott's volume on *David Copperfield* includes a number of facts students should know about the locale, the period, the costumes, and the characters before viewing the movie. She advises them:

> If possible, before seeing the motion picture, read the book. Read as rapidly as possible. Do not read the footnotes. After seeing the film, however, you may want to use them in a more leisurely reading. As preparation for the film, read as rapidly as possible. Read for the stories, since in Dickens' novels there are always several stories, and read for what you can learn about the characters.[30]

Abbott describes Dickens's book as a "popular classic," but she seems to have used it only as a touchstone, a guide to characterization in the film. Far from "matching" the novel with the film, she tells the students that they should "be prepared to enjoy the screen play (supposing you do enjoy it) as a separate art form."[31] She even stresses that the "the producer, the director and writer of the screenplay, and Hugh Walpole," are the most significant persons for students of Dickens to remember.

Abbott's *Photoplay* study of *David Copperfield* is particularly good at describing the details of the production. The ingenious material on the screenplay and cinematography (meant for older students) discusses "screen continuity as compared to the book." Abbott tells students of the meticulous research that MGM exerted in order to replicate the historical period: they hired ten research workers in England; they sent photographers to Yarmouth, Blunderstone, Dover, Canterbury, and London; and they matched characters' costumes to the drawings of "Phiz" (Halbot K. Browne). In addition to teaching the students about the fascinating history of *David Copperfield*'s production, Abbott goes on to talk about George Cukor's style, Oliver T. Marsh's cinematography, and even the editing techniques of Robert J. Kern. She asks the students to be attentive to close-ups, which might be there "to emphasize some important object in the narrative," as in Murdstone's turning the key in the lock after he has beaten David. She says that a close-up can also be used "to connect two scene-sequences," as in the shot of David's birth and of his father's grave.[32] To high school seniors Abbott offers certain challenges, inviting them to compare the specific details of the movie with the book. She concludes that they will "learn more about the differences between novel and drama by analyzing a single scene from *David Copperfield* than by hours of studying abstract principles of dramatic construction."[33]

The *Photoplay Study Guides* were responsible for educating thousands of students not only about *David Copperfield* and other novels and plays, but also about film. The result was a kind of fusion between Hollywood and other aspects of the culture industry, and the elevation of popular art into respectability. Throughout the process Charles Dickens functioned as a mediating influence. Again and again Dickens was portrayed in Abbott's guide as an author who healed social divisions, bridged the divide between elite and popular, and promoted concern for others. When the *Teacher's Manual* (also by Abbott) was issued as a companion to the guide, it quoted Ashley Thorndike's *Literature in a Changing Age* to the effect that Dickens was "the great democrat" who wrote "not primarily for those who are acquainted with the best that has been known and said." But the manual later observed that there was a highbrow, discriminating audience for Dickens, of which students could aspire to be part. Teachers of *David Copperfield* were told that Dickens offered a meeting point for two worlds: "the connoisseur . . . and those in a school group who have never willingly read any good novels before."[34]

III

Whatever its ideological, educational, or profit motives, there can be no doubt that the Selznick film version of *David Copperfield* works splendidly as an example of the art of adaptation. In this regard, Mary Ellen Abbott's thoughtful attention to the visual details in *Copperfield* is worth special notice, confirming Sergei Eisenstein's later observation that Dickens created "extraordinary plasticity" and that the "optical quality" in his fiction provided cinema with "parents and pedigree . . . a past."[35] And yet Dickens was not the only source of the film's images. As a general rule, those writing about film adaptation tend to think of the "precursor text" in purely literary terms, not recognizing that every movie is conditioned by a large set of influences from other media. We should keep in mind that the film of *David Copperfield*, even more than most Hollywood adaptations of nineteenth-century literature, was based not simply on a written text (however "plastic" or pictorial), but also on what Carol T. Christ and John O. Jordan have recently called the "Victorian visual imagination." Dickens "painted pictures with words" with the considerable help of Phiz, and Dickensian illustration eventually became a small industry unto itself. This industry, and the whole of Victorian visual representation, was crucially important for MGM.

David Bordwell has drawn attention to the use of visual sources in film adaptation, beginning with early film uses of *tableaux vivants,* some of which were used to create the mise-en-scène of *David Copperfield.*[36] The Selznick unit also made elaborate use of every other kind of visual record of the period.[37] The Phiz illustrations, for example, were meticulously paired to the actors and were used as guides for set designers Merrill Pye and Edwin B. Willis. (Compare Phiz's illustration for the interior of the parish church in chapter 2 with the church we see in the film.) After the film debut, Margaret Lloyd perceptively wrote in the *Christian Science Monitor* (2 February 1935) that "every reader creates his own picture as he reads, and thereafter he is adverse to accepting any other. . . . Was it the preparation of 'Drawings by Phiz' that allows us to accept the immortal characters as they are now presented?"

On another level, the film undoubtedly owes much of its visual success to director George Cukor, who once remarked: "I don't believe in 'correcting' Dickens, saving him and all that. I just had to go with the vitality of the thing."[38] The vitality of which Cukor speaks is as much a matter of performance as of language, and Cukor's work is notable for the way it selectively borrows conventions from the pantomime style of acting used in nineteenth-century theater. As one small example of the technique, notice the early scene when David and Peggotty ride off in a horse-drawn carriage while Murdstone and David's mother remain behind at the roadside: the mother waves goodby and then raises her hand to her brow in a pretty gesture of Victorian sentiment, as if she were posing for a picture; meanwhile, the tall, dark Murdstone gazes down at her like a stage villain about to gain possession of a porcelain doll. All the performances of the large cast have this same lively eccentricity (abetted by the costumes of Dolly Tree), which seems "Dickensian" without ever lapsing into a feeling of parody. Surely one of the most impressive achievements of the sort is that Lennox Pawle in the role of Mr. Dick—a sublime and saintly fool, unlike anything in the history of American movies, who seems to have stepped out of a childish but surreal cartoon.

At the same time, both Cukor and the scriptwriters managed to subordinate the Dickens text to the classical Hollywood style, which by the mid-thirties had reached its most restrained paradigm. In a certain sense, MGM rewrote Dickens into another idiom, and this—Eisenstein's famous essay on Dickens and montage notwithstanding—was no easy

Figure 2. Roland Young as Uriah Heep in David Copperfield *(1935). MGM's publicity for the film placed the leading actors alongside the original "Phiz" illustrations from the novel.* Museum of Modern Art.

task.[39] As J. Hillis Miller has argued, the novel *David Copperfield* calls the "reader's attention to the distance between the present condition of the narrator and that of the past self."[40] Its subjective narrative technique (closer to that of Wordsworth than to that of Proust), together with its multiple plots and its sheer size (it resembles what Henry James famously called a "loose baggy monster"), was hardly an ideal for the modernized, sleek narratives of Hollywood of the 1930s. Much of the film's apparent faithfulness to the novel, therefore, depends on its clever use of the "author" as a purely discursive device. The *idea* of "Charles Dickens," so thoroughly assimilated into American life, enabled Selznick, Cukor, and MGM to convert *David Copperfield* into a style that is "ominiscient, highly communicative, and only moderately self-conscious."[41] Ultimately, the production relies on the idea of a storyteller named Charles Dickens who, in Foucault's language, "seems always to be present, marking off the edges of the text, revealing, or at least characterizing, its mode of being."[42]

Of all the problems raised in redeploying David Copperfield into a Hollywood movie in the 1930s, surely the narrative technique was the most formidable. Yet from the very start of the film, Hollywood was able to appropriate first-person narration in the novel and adapt it to an omniscient form. The formal appropriation begins with what Gérard Genette calls a "paratext," which "enables a text to become a book and to be offered as such to its readers and, more generally, to the public.[43] The first shot is therefore of the book itself, showing an epigraph from *David Copperfield*'s revised preface of 1869 with Dickens's signature: "Like many fond parents, I have in my heart of hearts, a favorite child, and his name is David Copperfield." Next we see a brief shot of the opening lines of the novel: "To begin my life with the beginning of my life, I recall that I was born." Then, with the opening of the film proper, we see a pastoral image of a line of trees, and Betsey Trotwood moving through an establishing shot of the Copperfield cottage at Blunderstone in Suffolk. In this sequence the words of the author meld with those of the first-person narrator, and finally with the dramatized action. The resulting effect is what Richard Maltby describes as a typical device in classic Hollywood movies: restricted, overt acts of narration at the beginning, which give way to the "screen world."[44] This particular film presents us with a "Charles Dickens" who seems to endorse the visual project with his very signature. In collapsing the private reader into a public audience, it combines the complex, semiautobiographical elements of the novel with Hollywood conventions of temporal and spacial coherence, or with what David Bordwell refers to as "the centrality of the invisible observer."[45] Equally important, by transferring the first-person narration into a highly communicative omniscient narration, it invites the audience to think of "Charles Dickens" as the ultimate creator of the cinematic space.

Remarkably, the film gives us the emotive force of a first-person account without resorting to any further voice-over narration. Even without the ever-present novelistic "I," this version of *David Copperfield* is quite lyrical, partly because of the India ink expressiveness of Oliver Marsh's black-and-white cinematography, which sets the action in a traditional Hollywood frame. As A. Lindsley Lane said in *American Cinematographer* in 1935, the camera stimulates, through its choice of subject matter and set-up, the sense of "being at the most vital part of the experience—at the most advantageous point of perception."[46] That most advantageous point in the novel is David himself, whose consciousness becomes a kind of filter for our own emotive experience and impressions. In the film Marsh and Cukor give us a highly personalized form of dramatic showing rather than telling. The opening action, for example, positions us as secret sharers of David Copperfield's private life. We follow Betsey to the window of the cottage, where she sees her nephew's wife in the living room. With her we trespass the boundaries of a gate and a window, and then we peek into a domestic space and spy on a grieving woman. Here and elsewhere, the film does not so much abandon the subjective edge of the novel as it fully dramatizes the subjective experience of the characters' actions. From the moment we lay eyes on David as a gurgling infant, the camera pays him loving attention, selecting him out of a crowded parlor. Soon afterward we begin seeing close-ups of his reactions in almost every sequence; we view his world apart from the adults (as he makes eye contact with other children, say, in a church service), and we are introduced to important characters through him (our first glimpse of Murdstone, for instance, is a point-of-view shot from David's perspective).

David Copperfield as a novel relies as much on the central character's memory as it does on his direct sense perception. Consider the beginning of chapter 2 ("I Observe"): "The first objects that assume a distinct presence before me, as I look far back, into the blank of my infancy, are my mother with her pretty hair and youthful shape, and Peggotty with no shape at all, and eyes so dark that they seemed to darken their whole neighborhood in her face." The mature narrator's intense but recollected impression of the other characters produces a slightly hallucinatory realism, and it seems to invite the Freudian interpretation that some twentieth-century critics have applied to the novel. As Walter Allen has remarked, there is "a singular purity in the [narrator's] drawing of the adult characters as they are seen through the boy's eyes. They are, in fact, a boy's characters: fabulous beings, drawn not critically but in wonder."[47] The film captures this effect largely through the performance of the actors, beginning with the high-strung, emotive Freddie Bartholomew as David. Cast by Selznick as an unknown, Bartholomew seems a hyperaware British waif, and Cukor structures the early portion of the film around his awestruck, declamatory reactions to almost everything—such as when we first meet him at his father's grave: "Poor father! How lonely and dark it must be for him at night while we're at home by the fire." Especially in the early scenes, David views the world "in wonder," innocently commenting on the mystery of death, on the cruel abuse of the Murdstones, or on the love he has for his mother; he is both a sensitive plant and a judge of what he sees, embodying something of the double vision of the novel itself.

Inevitably, the film is more tightly organized than the novel, more directly focused on the hermeneutic problem of what will ultimately happen to David. And yet it conveys some of the discursive complexity of its source, which has an ability to split the narrative viewpoint among the young David, the mature David, and the "implied author." For example, there are moments in the film when we know more than David does—as when his mother is secretly engaged to Murdstone. (The nuptial arrangement is signaled to us by Peggotty, who speaks to Mrs. Copperfield in a sotto voce, sardonic tone while David is playing a piano in the background: "Did ya have a pleasant evening, Mum? . . . The stranger makes an agreeable change.") There are also moments when the mise-en-scène and the montage serve to comment overtly and somewhat archly on the characters in a fashion similar to that of omniscient novels. Notice, for instance, David's encounter with Dora at "The Enchanted Bird" ballet. David dotes on the beautiful young woman while we occasionally see the action on stage from her point of view. When the stage "hunter" takes aim at the bird, Dora reacts with the sort of wide-eyed innocence we associate with David as a child. "Can he be so cruel as to shoot her?" she asks. David answers, "Sometimes, love is cruel." Dora calls out, "Be careful! Be careful!" At that, the bird flies away, and Dora cries, "She's escaped! She's escaped!" David responds, "Please Miss Spendlow, may I call?" A medium shot shows the two young people standing up excitedly, while the ballet continues in the background. "Perhaps," Dora says, "if my aunts permit." The repeated cutting between the stage and the box during this scene tends to confirm what Eisenstein observed about parallel montage in Dickens himself: a bourgeois courtship is resolved into an "organic" synthesis, which is framed in a single shot at the end. But throughout the exchange between Dora and David, the action on the stage also serves as a metaphor for David's cautious, stylized pursuit of a mate. Dora herself is dressed rather like a bird, complete with a large feather fan, and her nervous, flighty behavior (skillfully executed by Maureen O'Sullivan, who seems both guileless and seductive) only intensifies the comparison. All the while, the matrons at her side snuggle up near her like two nervous hens protecting their young.

The film's ability to "match" the actors with the characters in the novel is nothing less than uncanny and has often been remarked on. (Among the most brilliant performances are those of W. C. Fields as Wilkins Micawber, Edna May Oliver as Aunt Betsey, and Roland Young as Uriah Heep). But somewhat like the novel, the film also works on a more sophisticated level to establish a strong bond between the audience and a gallery of colorful figures who are seen through the eyes of both the young and the older David. Here again the film creates a kind of "double vision." People who seem to have finished their roles—Micawber, Peggotty, Aunt Betsey, Mr. Dick, and Uriah Heep—reappear during the second half, when the mature David returns to the scenes of his childhood. When we view the second portion of the film, we feel a nostalgia that has originated not directly from the literary source text, but from the earlier portions of the reinvented filmic text; hence our feeling of the "rightness" and inevitability of the characterizations is partly confirmed by our delight in seeing old faces again, watching them perform their familiar turns. This feeling of nostalgia, however, pervades the entire narrative, despite the fact that the early episodes are shadowed by trauma and loss. Herbert Stothart's sentimental musical score helps considerably, but it is significant that the music we hear during the opening credits is composed of traditional Christmas songs, such as the "The First Noel." Before it even begins, the film invites its audience to think of *A Christmas Carol*—a story which, by the 1930s, had become part of the seasonal American ritual, invoking primal images of family home-comings and acts of Christian charity. Much of the Depression audience who saw the film were probably also engaged in another kind of nostal-gic journey—a return to a generalized idea of Dickens, who had been part of their upbringing and who seemed to represent a lost world inhabited by their ancestors.

IV

I began by equating Dickens and Matthew Arnold, and I would now like to return to that equation, because an "Arnoldian" ideology informs both the liberal culture of Victorian England and the Selznick adaptation of *David Copperfield*; indeed this is one reason the film appears so profoundly true to its source. In saying this I do not mean to suggest that anyone at MGM had actually read *Culture and Anarchy* or that the studio had a conscious desire to make use of Arnold's ideas, even in a secondhand way. My point is simply that *Copperfield*, like other pictures Selznick and Cukor had made together, offered the Depression audience a narrative about how the divisions of social class can be overcome through learning and generosity of feeling.

If the American establishment was undergoing a process of self-evaluation during the 1930s—and if certain Hollywood moguls were themselves aspiring to respectability and sophistication—Selznick and Cukor helped the process along by creating an imaginary world in which lowbrow and highbrow (or outsiders and insiders) could meet and some-times even marry. Their 1933 film, *Dinner at Eight*, seats the "barbar-ians" and the "populace" at the same dinner table. (The famous closing sequence resolves potentially explosive class tensions through a comic touch: matronly Marie Dressler, playing an aristocrat, stops in her tracks and does a double take when sexy Jean Harlow, playing a golddigger, remarks that she's just been reading a book.) The Selznick-Cukor adap-tation of Louisa May Alcott's *Little Women* made at RKO in 1933 goes even further. Bryn Mawr–educated Katherine Hepburn plays Jo Marsh, a self-taught young woman from the provinces, and the seamless fit between actor and role is rather like the synthesis achieved by the plot, in which a popular writer marries a cultivated German professor. At the level of the acting the film allows a country girl to acquire a Boston-Brahmin accent, and at the level of story it shows us a hardworking, self-sacrificing heroine who finds a cultivated spouse. In Cukor's closing sequence Jo and her family are celebrating in their house in the country when the German professor appears at the door in the midst of a rainstorm. Cukor neatly poses the couple on either side of the threshold, illustrating the divide between Germanic high culture and provincial Americana. The couple's subsequent announcement of their intention to wed gives Hollywood's utopian romance, or what Stanley Cavell calls its "pursuit of happiness," a larger social implication—a sense that love and success have been achieved through the acquisition of taste.

David Copperfield strongly resembles *Little Women* in its ability to mediate potential class conflicts. David's twin goals in *David Copperfield*, not unlike Jo's in *Little Woman*, are to achieve the Arnoldian ideals of harmonious marriage and moral education. Here we should recall that Arnold tied his notion of cultural "perfection" to a process of socialization. "The individual is required," he wrote in *Culture and Anarchy*, "under pain of being stunted and enfeebled in his own development if he disobeys, to carry to others along with him in his march towards perfection, to be continually doing all he can to enlarge and increase the volume of the human stream sweeping thitherward."[48] The Hollywood film of love and marriage, and especially the typical Selznick film of this period, had a similar project in mind. Jo in *Little Women*, for example, must find a proper mate to accompany her "development." At first she seems doomed to choose between a provincial husband and spinsterhood as a writer, but eventually she finds a way to move out of her lonely (in Arnold's terms, "indifferent") self and join the larger community. In effect, her good taste enables her not only to acquire a proper lover, but also to become a socially responsible person. In similar fashion, David Copperfield eventually becomes disillusioned by Dora's superficiality and carelessness; his combined sentiment and taste—his sweetness and light—enable him to take up the more useful but equally sophisticated responsibilities of a mature union with Agnes.

David's achievement of Arnoldian perfection is made possible because he seems to embody every level of society—the neglected poor, the decent middle class, and the polished aristocracy. His childhood fall out of comfortable circumstances and his youthful practical education among the working poor shape his adult decisions, particularly his final unmasking of Heep's embezzlement; but he also has an inherent refinement that enables him to become a kind of artist. Freddie Bartholomew's ability to convey this last quality is especially important. In a brilliant discussion of Hollywood in the 1930s, Charles Eckert has written about the "specter" of impoverished childhood during the Great Depression:

> The most persistent specter that the depression offered to those who had come through the crash with some or most of their fortunes intact was . . . that of a small child dressed in welfare clothing, looking, as he was usually depicted, like a gaunt Jackie Coogan, but unsmiling, unresponsive, pausing to stare through the windows of cafeterias or grocery stores, his legs noticeably thin and his stomach slightly swollen.[49]

Significantly, L. B. Mayer had initially approved Selznick's proposal for a film of *David Copperfield* because he thought it might make a good vehicle for Jackie Cooper, the MGM equivalent to Jackie Coogan, who had scored great success as a working-class kid in *The Champ* (1931). Freddie Bartholomew was an altogether more appropriate choice, precisely because he was an upper-class type—a fragile child who spoke with exquisite English diction and who represented the fear of falling downward on the social scale. (He was once again used this way in 1937 in MGM's highly effective adaptation of Rudyard Kipling's *Captains Courageous*, in which he literally falls from a luxury liner into a fishing boat.)

No less than Shirley Temple, Dickens's nineteenth-century waifs helped Americans emerging from the Great Depression to imagine how they might be ultimately redeemed through talent, work, and charity: Oliver Twist finds his wealthy grandfather, and Tiny Tim finally gets a middle-class home and health care. More important, however, a character such as David Copperfield is able to transcend contradiction and conflict by reforming his own social class: he is born into a solid bourgeois family, he becomes an orphan, and he moves upward again toward a "classless" world informed by what Arnold calls a "general humane spirit." Early in the film Cukor positions him in a composition similar to that seen Jo's fateful doorway sequence at the end of *Little Women:* emerging from his house to greet his mother and Mr. Murdstone, he stands on the threshold, neatly posed between Murdstone and Nurse Peggotty. The two adult figures represent two aspects of Victorian capitalism—the masculine, industrialized, "public" world, managed by the businessman, and the feminine, domesticated, "private" world, guarded by the nurse. During the course of the film David negotiates and reconciles these tensions by acquiring wide experience and humane learning and by becoming a sort of aristocrat of moral discrimination.

From the beginning David has delicate manners—he is certainly one of the most polite children in cinema history—yet he is attracted to Peggotty's atavistic world of folk culture. Early on Peggotty takes him to Yarmouth, where Dan Peggotty (Lionel Barrymore) and Ham (John Buckler) continually refer to him as Master Davey. In an impressive scene he plays on the beach with Little Emily (Fay Chaldecott), and the young girl suddenly runs off, dangerously straddling the boards of the dock overlooking the wild sea. To show us the girl's exhilaration, Cukor positions the camera at an unusually high angle behind her head. She holds up her hands ecstatically while David, refusing to walk on the wharf toward her, calls to her frantically; she then skips unharmed toward David and tells him, "That's fun, dancing near the edge." The contrast between Little Emily's spontaneity and David's reserve points to a difference between the naturalized folk and the cultivated middle class. Yarmouth is an instinctive, oral culture, filled with cockney accents and the sounds of the harsh sea; David's new household is more comfortable, but too far removed from instinctive human feeling—a stiff, quiet realm governed by Murdstone, who reads to his wife and beats David when he cannot perform mathematical calculations.

When Matthew Arnold describes the antithesis of perfection, he is describing Murdstone, the abusive, tyrannical keeper of keys, whose "bondage to machinery" and lack of "*harmonious* expansion of human nature" is related to his "inaptitude for seeing more than one side of a thing" and his "intense energetic absorption in the particular pursuit" he is intent in following.[50] The folk community at Yarmouth, however, has its own flaws. Little Emily's fitful display of fancy and her later involvement with Steerforth are symptomatic of what Arnold describes as a lack of "social" conscience. The mutual hatred that Peggotty and the Murdstones have for one another is only the clearest of many examples in the film of polarized classes who are guided by what Arnold terms "class spirit."

The first step in David's true education is his forced movement away from this divided experience at Yarmouth and Blunderstone into the "general expansion" of London, where he encounters his tutor and guardian, Mr. Micawber. In many respects Micawber represents a comic mixture of class traits: he is both gentleman and con man, both literate and impoverished, both verbal and acrobatic. After eluding his creditors on the streets of London, he does a tricky balancing act on the rooftops overlooking Saint Paul's Cathedral, then descends through a skylight into his home with a flood of elaborate language, announcing, "In short, I have arrived." As the star who incarnated Micawber, W. C. Fields achieved a similar kind of reconciliation of opposites. He had been a brilliant vaudeville juggler and one of the best of the silent comedians, but he became known in the sound era for his sardonic verbal wit. He often played a trickster who could move between classes. As a dandified, bogus professor or an articulate drunk, he could negotiate between slapstick and epigram. In the role of the verbose, acrobatic Micawber, he drew on the whole range of his abilities, meanwhile slightly anticipating what James Agee called the "fiendishly funny and incisive white-collar comedies" of his later career.[51] He therefore took on a certain resemblance to Dickens himself, who could please and reconcile diverse audiences with his performances.

But Micawber is in one sense a social failure, and his relationship with David is short-lived. David's most important guide is his Aunt Betsey Trotwood, and it seems fitting that he arrives at her doorstep in Dover after having lost all of his money and most of his clothes. With the assistance of the blissfully cuckoo Mr. Dick, Betsey takes the boy in, gives him a dose of homemade medicine, and puts him to bed, where he prays not only for himself, but for all homeless boys. Like a newborn child, he is given a bath, fed by hand, and wrapped in blankets. Mr. Dick tells him grotesque stories about the beheading of Charles I, but then casts the deciding vote in favor of his proper upbringing by saying, "Have him measured for a suit of clothes directly."

After a superbly articulate and melodramatic showdown with the Murdstones, Aunt Betsey takes charge of her nephew's life, and in this role she is vividly contrasted with the dour, heavy-eyebrowed Jane Murdstone. Both are eccentric spinsters who dislike boys, but Betsey quickly becomes lovable (in one moving sequence, she rigidly holds back her affection for the helpless David, then embraces him warmly). Jane undergoes no such metamorphosis. "Of all the boys in the world, I believe this one is the worst," she says of David, and she clings tenaciously to her imagined class superiority. She sarcastically thanks Betsey for her "very grrrrreat politeness," although she regards her as being "either intoxicated or mad." By contrast, Aunt Betsey shows compassion for outsiders such as Mr. Dick and David, and she undergoes growth and development from a strict spinster into a loving parent figure. In Arnoldian terms, she manifests "an inward spiritual activity, having for its characters increased sweetness, increased light, increased life, increased sympathy."[52]

David, who, as he says, has been "slighted and taught nothing," is now ready for the process of rebuilding and instruction. At Dover he shows the first signs of social responsibility and universal charity by praying for other homeless children. Aunt Betsey tells him that he must go to school at Canterbury because of his duty to others: "You have to be educated, Davey, and take your place in the world." In her final words to the boy, she insists that he cultivate a humane spirit to accompany his gentlemanly learning: "You must make us proud, Davey. Never be mean in anything. Never be false. Never be cruel. Avoid these three vices and I can always be hopeful of you." Eventually, as he moves toward the larger and more prosperous community (a community to which he seems always to have rightly belonged), David is given the opportunity to show his moral responsibility. In the Wickfield household his foil is not a Victorian captain of industry or a provincial capitalist such as Murdstone, but a character from the petty bourgeoisie—the accountant Uriah Heep, who has none of David's polish, and who is literally twisted with class resentment. As they discuss who will take over Mr. Wickfield's business, Heep says: "I am a very 'umble person, I'm well aware. My mother's 'umble. We live in a 'umble abode. . . . My father's former calling was 'umble."

David's frank and apparently unworldly innocence is contrasted with Heep's hypocrisy and villainy. Oliver Marsh emphasizes the melodramatic conflict by lighting Heep's eyes in horror movie style, and at one point, when Heep leaves David, the young man wipes his hand in disgust, as if he fears contamination. That gesture is a sign of David's newly acquired social and moral superiority. Heep tells us, "I have no wish to rise above my place," and from the point of view of the film's ideological project, he must stay where he is, representing a kind of rough beast. He functions as a scapegoat for all the deeper social evils David has encountered—a man who has attempted to rise above his status without possessing an aestheticized sensitivity and a humane education.

The villainous Heep was well suited to MGM's conservative ethos; for in the last analysis, the superbly crafted film version of *David Copperfield* is less about the fantasy of moving upward into the prosperous middle class than about the desire to make the economy's ruling elite behave in a humane fashion. Its hero is a man of high taste and simple virtue who falls undeservedly into the world of the poor and returns from that world to expose a vulgar financial manipulator. Such a hero was especially useful in the 1930s, when the gulf between the classes was quite visible, when the more prosperous sectors of the economy needed to develop a sort of noblesse oblige, and when, as we have seen, one of England's greatest and most popular novelists became one Hollywood's most employable talents.

NOTES

1. *New World* 8 (6 January 1844), p. 5.
2. See Lawrence W. Levine, *Highbrow/Lowbrow: The Emergence of Cultural Hierarchy in America* (Cambridge: Harvard University Press, 1988), pp. 249 ff.
3. Quoted in Michael Slater, *Dickens: On America and the Americans* (Austin: University of Texas Press, 1978), p. 8.
4. Quoted in Sidney P. Moss, *Charles Dickens' Quarrel with America* (Troy, N.Y.: Whitston, 1984), pp. 271–72.
5. Quoted in Moss, p. 272.
6. Quoted in Moss, p. 237.
7. Laurence Houseman was speaking in Sheffield on Saint George's Day at a Shakespeare Festival and is quoted in "Dickens the Low-Brow," *The Dickensian* 27:217 (Winter 1930–31), p. 167.
8. Levine, *Highbrow*, p. 233.
9. Quoted in Slater, *Dickens*, pp. 8–9.
10. Quoted in Levine, *Highbrow*, p. 233.
11. Dwight MacDonald, *Against the American Grain* (New York: Random House, 1962), p. 7. MacDonald seems really interested in advising us against Dickensian (popular) sentimentality. He provides us with another instance of how a highbrow intellectual might access Dickens.
12. James D. Hart, *The Popular Book: A History of America's Literary Taste* (New York: Oxford, 1950), p. 103.
13. Sergei Eisenstein, "Dickens, Griffith, and the Film Today," in *Film Form*, ed. and trans. Jay Leda (New York: HB, 1949), pp. 233–34.
14. Richard H. Pells, *Radical Visions and American Dreams: Culture and Social Thought in the Depression Years.* 1973 (Middletown, Conn.: Wesleyan University Press, 1984), pp. 86, 96–150. See also Robert S. McElvaine, *The Great Depression: America, 1929–1941* (New York: Random House, 1984), pp. 170–223, and Cohen, pp. 213–89.
15. Richard B. Hovey, "All the Things You Are," *Modern Age* (Summer 1993), p. 343.
16. Quoted in Page Smith, *Redeeming the Time: A Peoples' History of the 1920's and the New Deal* (New York: Viking Penguin, 1986), p. 472.

17. Hart, *The Popular Book*, p. 261.

18. Lawrence W. Levine, "Progress and Nostalgia: The Self Image of the Nineteen Twenties," in *The Unpredictable Past* (New York: Oxford University Press, 1993), pp. 189–205. Levine qualifies his argument by saying that "Americans in the twenties, as before and since, tended to turn to the past in their ideology and rhetoric more than in their actions" (p. 205).

19. According to H. Philip Boulton's *Dickens Dramatized* (1987), from 1929 to 1941 there were not fewer than twenty adaptations of *A Christmas Carol* alone. In 1988 folklore expert and historian Anne Rowbottom found that the English regarded a Victorian Christmas as the only "authentic" Christmas.

20. See Mike Poole, "Dickens and Film: 101 Uses of a Dead Author," in *The Changing World of Charles Dickens*, ed. Robert Gidding (Totowa, N.J.: Barnes, 1993), pp. 148–62. See also A. L. Zambrano, *Dickens and Film* (New York: Gordon, 1977).

21. Mary L. Pendered, "Dickens Plays and Films," *The Dickensian* 20:1 (January 1924), p. 100.

22. Tino Balio, *Grand Design: Hollywood as a Modern Business Enterprise, 1930–1939* (New York: Scribners, 1993), p. 179.

23. David Thomson, *Showman: The Life of David O. Selznick* (New York: Knopf, 1992), p. 179.

24. Thomas Schatz, *The Genius of the System: Hollywood Filmmaking in the Studio Era* (New York: Pantheon, 1988), pp. 167–68.

25. Quoted in Ibid., p. 168.

26. David O. Selznick, *Memo from David O. Selznick*, ed. Rudy Behlmer (Hollywood: Samuel French, 1989), p. 72.

27. Victor Shapiro, "Review of *David Copperfield*," *Motion Picture Daily's Hollywood Preview* (8 January 1935).

28. Frank L. Dyer, "The Moral Development of the Silent Drama," *Edison Kinetogram* (15 April 1910), p. 11. It is worth pointing out that the first *David Copperfield*, a three-reeler produced by Thanhouser for Vitagraph, appeared only a little over a year later. Eileen Bowser thinks that the 1911 production of *David Copperfield*, together with Vitagraph's *A Tale of Two Cities* (also 1911), helped to transform cinema into a prestige product. See Bowser, pp. 200–201.

29. See Leonard J. Leff and Jerold L. Simmons, *The Dame in the Kimono* (Garden City: Doubleday, 1990), pp. 3–54. According to the studio records, the Confidential Report of the Board of Censors approved *David Copperfield* without elimination in the following territories: Massachusetts (14 January 1935), Ohio (17 January 1935), Kansas (31 January 1935), New York (31 January 1935), and Pennsylvania (16 February 1935). But the international community had reservations, and the following deletions were made: Hungary (2 August 1935)—"Murdstone beating David"; Belgium (7 October 1935)—"Truck driver's hard striking of David Copperfield's hand"; Sweden (6 February 1936)—"Murdstone beating David" and the conversation between David and Mr. Dick on "the beheading of Charles I"; and Latvia (8 April 1936)—"David being beaten." See "David Copperfield," in the *George Cukor Collection*, Margaret Heller Library, Academy of Motion Picture Arts and Sciences, Beverly Hills, Calif.

30. Mary Allen Abbott, *A Study Guide to the Critical Appreciation of the Photoplay Version of Charles Dickens' Novel* David Copperfield, ed. Max J. Herzberg (Chicago: National Council of Teachers of English, 1935), p. 4.

31. Ibid., p. 5.

32. Ibid., p. 14.

33. Ibid., p. 8.

34. Ibid., p. 4.

35. Eisenstein in *Film Form*, p. 232.

36. David Bordwell, Janet Staiger, and Kristin Thompson, *The Classical Hollywood Cinema: Film Style and Mode of Production to 1960* (New York: Columbia University Press, 1985), p. 50. In discussing the *tableaux vivant* and its relationship with film pro-

duction, Bordwell says that "post-renaissance painting provided one powerful model [for composition]. Cinematographers and directors constantly invoked famous paintings as sources. Cecil B. DeMille claimed to have borrowed from Dore, Van Dyck, Corot and one 'Rubins.'" See Terry Castle, "Phantasmagoria: Spectral Technology and the Metaphorics of Modern Reverie," *Critical Inquiry* 15:3 (1988), pp. 26–31, and also Angela Dalle Vacche, *Cinema and Painting: How Art Is Used in Film* (Austin: University of Texas Press, 1996). J. Hillis Miller makes an important connection between iconography and representation in his discussion of Dickens and Cruikshank in "The Fiction of Realism: *Sketches by Boz, Oliver Twist*, and Cruikshank's Illustrations," *Victorian Subjects* (Durham, N.C.: Duke University Press, 1991), pp. 119–77, and *Illustration* (Cambridge: Harvard University Press, 1992). For an important discussion of the role of art direction in this connection, see Charles Affron and Mirella Jona Affron, *Sets in Motion: Art Direction and Film Narrative* (New Brunswick, N.J.: Rutgers University Press, 1995).

37. MGM went to great lengths to duplicate Victorian reproductions of nineteenth-century illustrations for *David Copperfield*. The studio announced that the characters were made to look like Cruikshank, but *The Dickensian* was quick to point out that they were, in fact, based on Phiz's illustrations for *David Copperfield*. Phiz's original drawings were enlarged, and then the characters were made to pose to conform to them. In addition to the well-publicized month-long production trip that Selznick, Cukor, and others took to England in order to replicate the characters and settings in *David Copperfield*, MGM's research department even consulted "street character types" in the *Illustrated London News* for 1844, 1846, and 1858 in order to authenticate Dolly Tree's costumes and Cedric Gibbons's art direction. Finally, when Dodd and Mead published *David Copperfield* in 1935 as a tie-in with the film, the publicity stills replaced Phiz's nineteenth-century ink drawings. The Victorian art direction and costumes in the film were believed to be so authentic that Reginald B. Haselden, curator of the Huntington Library, sent a letter to Selznick saying that he was "very familiar with the Dickens period and Dickens London, and I think your most valuable achievement is the way in which you have reproduced the atmosphere of the book itself." (MGM correspondence file, Margaret Herrick Library of the Motion Picture Academy, Los Angeles.)

38. Quoted in Gavin Lambert, *On Cukor* (New York: Putnam, 1972), p. 87.

39. Eisenstein's famous essay on Dickens as a kind of urtext for montage and parallel editing is based not on *David Copperfield*'s first-person, semiautobiographical form, but on the omniscient narrator in *Oliver Twist*. Brian MacFarlane believes that the connection between Griffith and Dickens by theories of adaptation "has been overestimated and under-scrutinized." See *Novel to Film: An Introduction to the Theory of Adaptation* (New York: Oxford University Press, 1996), p. 8.

40. Miller, *Victorian Subjects*, p. 99.

41. David Bordwell, "Classical Hollywood Cinema," in *Narrative, Apparatus, Ideology: A Film Theory Reader*, ed. Philip Rosen (New York: Columbia University Press, 1986), p. 22.

42. Michael Foucault, "What Is an Author?" in *The Foucault Reader*, ed. Paul Rainbow (New York: Pantheon, 1984), p. 107.

43. Gérard Genette, *Paratexts: Thresholds of Interpretation*. trans. Jane E. Lewin (Cambridge: Cambridge University Press, 1997), p. 1.

44. Richard Maltby, *Hollywood Cinema: An Introduction* (Oxford: Blackwell, 1995), p. 327. For Maltby an illustration of the paradigm is *The Pirate* (1948), with its movement from a narrated introduction of the book (telling) to the world of the movie (showing).

45. Bordwell, "Classical Hollywood Cinema," p. 32.

46. A. Lindsley Lane, "The Camera's Omniscient Eye," *American Cinematographer* 16:3 (March 1935), p. 95. quoted in David Bordwell, *Narration and the Fiction Film* (Madison: University of Wisconsin Press, 1985), p. 161.

47. Walter Allen, *The English Novel* (New York: E. P. Dutton, 1954), p. 165.

48. Matthew Arnold, *Culture and Anarchy* (Cambridge: Cambridge University Press, 1932), p. 48.

49. Charles Eckert, "Shirley Temple and The House of Rockefeller," in *Star Texts: Image and Performance in Film and Television*, ed. Jeremy G. Butler (Detroit: Wayne State University Press, 1991), p. 187.

50. Arnold, *Culture and Anarchy*, p. 49.

51. James Agee, *Agee on Film* (Boston: Beacon, 1958), p. 18.

52. Arnold, *Culture and Anarchy*, p. 64.

Gilberto Perez

Landscape and Fiction:
A Day in the Country

If previous ages looked to Giorgione or Claude, our version of pastoral landscape was painted by the Impressionists. True, that version is over 100 years old by now, but nobody has painted a newer one to replace it in our cultural imagination, and when we look at the country through the city eyes of pastoral, which see in it an idealized sweetness and peace, it is still an Impressionist picture that we tend to see. Pastoral is always a fiction, a fantasy of the country, but the Impressionists, in keeping with their time—and ours—made it a more realistic fiction, not a mythical Arcadia, but something they constructed out of the actual passing appearances—the impressions—of the world we all know. And theirs was a more democratic fiction, something that relates to the experience of anybody who can get a glimpse of a stretch of water or a piece of greenery once in a while. Made halfway along the hundred years and more since Monet and Renoir took their paints to the Forest of Fontainebleau, *A Day in the Country* looks back to the time of the Impressionists and evokes their pastoral in all its enduring appeal; but it looks back inquiringly, not just nostalgically, leading us into reflection rather than mere surrender to that appeal.

"In landscape painting I like pictures which make me want to wander about inside them," said Auguste Renoir. R. H. Wilenski commented:

> When painting landscape he [Renoir] never took a point of focus . . . and he never used the defined foreground of the classical-picturesque tradition which closed as it were the picture at the bottom and provided a point where the spectator himself could stand. . . . The entrance to the landscape depicted in his pictures is always open at all sides; and the spectator is thus tempted to enter and "wander about inside them."[1]

In Impressionist painting generally, the picture, rather than seeming contained within the frame, enclosed by it, gives us the feeling of an open

From *The Material Ghost: Films and Their Medium*, pp. 203–32. © 1998 The Johns Hopkins University Press.

field where we can imagine wandering about, inside and outside the boundaries of our view. We get much the same feeling in a Jean Renoir film. In films the frame does not mark, as it does in painting, the boundaries of the visual field: a space off screen is always implied, an indefinitely larger field of which at the moment we are seeing only a section. But most films ask us to regard that section as all we need to see for the moment, so that the frame nonetheless conventionally functions as a boundary mark enclosing not the whole, but the part that matters. Rarely have the movies moved, the camera and its subjects wandered about, with the openness of Renoir's work of the thirties; in his different medium, he accomplished a liberation from the conventional enclosures similar to that of his father and the other Impressionists. In a Renoir film, as Bazin wrote, "the action is not bounded by the screen, but merely passes through it."[2] Jean Renoir needs no prestige by association, and he has been compared to Auguste Renoir perhaps too often, but the artistic kinship between son and father is not to be slighted. *A Day in the Country* explicitly looks back to the father's work and evidently encourages the comparison.[3]

No less than the similarities, however, this film brings out the differences between the two Renoirs. It employs the period setting not so much to recapture the Impressionists as to bracket them in their own time, to help put them at a distance from which it examines their vision in a spirit at once affectionate and critical. The Maupassant story it adapts certainly regards the Impressionist countryside in a critical spirit. "The two men were friendly enough but frankly admitted they had nothing in common," wrote Jean Renoir of his father and Maupassant. "Renoir said of the writer, 'He always looks on the dark side'—while Maupassant said of the painter, 'He always looks on the bright side.'"[4] *A Day in the Country* is usually taken to brighten the writer with the painter, to answer critical detachment with a sensuous immersion in nature, but it can as well be taken to darken the painter with the writer, to answer the Impressionist pastoral with an incisive social awareness. It generates a dialogue between the beauties of nature and the conditions of society. It is not exactly a pastoral, but a film about pastoral.

Maupassant's story begins with a Parisian family—Monsieur and Madame Dufour and their daughter, together with an old grandmother and a yellow-haired young man whose apprenticeship in the family's hardware business entails an expectation of marriage to the daughter—on their way to lunch at some country restaurant near the city in the milkman's wagon they have borrowed for the day. "Here we are in the country at last!" announces Monsieur Dufour, and as they all admire the distant landscape, Maupassant describes the industrial wasteland stretching around them with its factory chimneys and its unpleasant smell. Argenteuil, the town where Monet lived in the 1870s and where Manet and Renoir also went to paint, can be seen in the distance; but the

Dufours get barely past Bezons and its rubber factory. They cross a bridge, and on the other side of the river, where the air is purer, they find a country restaurant that suits them.

The petite bourgeoisie on an outing to what was not really the country, but more like an illusion of it: Maupassant depicts a country excursion such as had become common in the later nineteenth century, and he takes toward it a disenchanting stance such as observers at the time frequently adopted. The Impressionists were well aware of the disenchanters when they painted the enchantment. "When painters went out to the countryside round Paris in the 1870s—in search of a landscape, say, or a modern *fête champêtre*—they would have known they were choosing, or accepting, a place it was easy (almost conventional) to find a bit absurd," wrote T. J. Clark in his book on Manet and his followers.[5] The Impressionists gave us a pastoral of the country outing. They chose, they accepted, the excursionist's countryside near the city, and their way of painting highlights the transient, the fluid, the casual, the impression rather than the permanency—which suggests the visitor's way of seeing and makes felt the momentariness of the enchantment they painted. (Monet in particular liked to give his painting the look of offhandedness and labored to dissemble his labors.) The Impressionists painted leisure, not the leisure of the upper class but of the ordinary people: "a day off, a trip to the country, boats, smiling women in sunlight, flags, trees in flower—the impressionist vocabulary of images," wrote John Berger, "is that of a popular dream, the awaited, beloved, secular Sunday."[6] Why is it that left-wing art critics like Berger or Clark wish that Impressionist painting had more of the solidity of Renaissance painting? The Renaissance emphasis on the corporeal, the tactile, expressed the outlook of a rising bourgeoisie that felt it could lay its hands on the world; the Impressionist emphasis on the passing moment, the colorful delight of light, expressed the outlook of a rising petite bourgeoisie that felt much less secure in the pleasures it could lay claim to.

"It is remarkable how many pictures we have in early impressionism of informal and spontaneous sociability," wrote Meyer Schapiro in a 1937 essay,

> of breakfasts, picnics, promenades, boating trips, holidays and vacation travel. These urban idylls not only present the objective forms of bourgeois recreation in the 1860's and 1870's; they also reflect in the very choice of subjects and in the new aesthetic devices the conception of art as solely a field of individual enjoyment, without reference to ideas and motives, and they presuppose the cultivation of these pleasures as the highest field of freedom for an enlightened bourgeois detached from the official beliefs of his class. . . .

As the contexts of bourgeois sociability shifted from community, family and church to commercialized or privately improvised forms—

the streets, the cafés and resorts—the resulting consciousness of individual freedom involved more and more an estrangement from older ties; and those imaginative members of the middle class who accepted the norms of freedom, but lacked the economic means to attain them, were spiritually torn by a sense of helpless isolation in an anonymous indifferent mass. By 1880 the enjoying individual becomes rare in impressionist art; only the private spectacle of nature is left.[7]

At the beginning of his book Clark quotes this passage more fully and with great admiration. But he wonders "how informal and spontaneous is the sociability depicted already in Manet's *Déjeuner sur l'herbe,* or for that matter in Monet's."[8] For informal and spontaneous sociability he should have gone to Renoir. Sociability in Manet is always uneasy. Looking is what matters in Monet, the sheer sight of something, the view from which the viewer stands back to look. Renoir brings us in. He may be said to have socialized the space of Impressionist painting as his son socialized the space of the movies.

Yet informal and spontaneous sociability is rare in the son's work. Perhaps only in the utopian *Crime of Monsieur Lange* does it prevail. Certainly not in *A Day in the Country.* Moving the setting deeper into the country, to the banks of the Loing rather than the Seine, makes it less a site of community and more the setting for an individual's private encounter with nature. And this individual—the Dufour daughter, Henriette—is just the imaginative member of the middle class Schapiro describes, reaching for freedom but lacking the economic means to attain it.

———

A Day in the Country begins on the bridge the Dufours cross into the pleasanter stretch of countryside. There are no factory chimneys anywhere around, no signs of the city other than the Dufours themselves. (A shot of them on the road from Paris is among the rushes the Cinémathèque Française recently compiled for showing, but not in the finished film as Marguerite Houllé cut it.) If the film's countryside is "a bit absurd," it is the Dufours who bring the absurdity. On the other side of the bridge nature stands unspoiled and lovely. Most of all it is the presence of nature—and the presence of Sylvia Bataille as Henriette—that sets Renoir's film apart from Maupassant's story.

From the bridge the film cuts to a lyrical traveling shot that takes the point of view of the arriving Parisians. The ambient trees sweetly float by as the visitors, and we with them, approach a country inn they have spotted for their lunch on the grass. (Marguerite Houllé, who along with Jean Renoir plays a small part in the film, can be seen coming out the inn door and down the front steps as the camera goes past.) This first impression of the place feels indeed like an Impressionist picture, both in the mobile camera's sensuous response to appearances—which provides a sort of equivalent, in black-and-white film, to the bright Impressionist palette—and in the conveyed sense of their fluidity and impermanence. No less than his father would have on canvas, Renoir celebrates this first impression, relishes this prolonged moment when nature seems to extend us an embrace. That he attributes the view to the petit bourgeois visitors does not deny its validity, but does signal its one-sidedness.

Identification is something much talked about but insufficiently understood. As in any point-of-view shot through a character's eyes, in this traveling shot we identify ourselves with the Dufour family, whose point of view we share. But how do we identify ourselves with them? Not as individuals. We have only just met them, and they are as yet scarcely individualized. We share their point of view as a group. But even as a group they are as yet scarcely particularized. Unlike the conventional point-of-view shot—which Renoir seldom uses—this traveling shot proceeds without any inserted shots of the characters looking at the scene and reacting to it such as normally would mark the view as belonging to those characters. This view does not belong to the Dufours either as individuals or as members of a particular family. It belongs to them as members of a whole social class. And it is as members of a class, the urban middle class seeking the pleasures of a day in the country, that we identify ourselves with them. That family's perspective on the inn could have been the perspective of any Sunday excursionist, could have been ours if we had been there, arriving for a *déjeuner sûr l'herbe* at that pretty country spot. Renoir implicates himself, and implicates us, in the excursionist's point of view. But he still wants us to recognize it as a point of view, a certain way of regarding things, a slant on the sights of nature rather than a universal human response.

This is made further manifest when, without having given us a closer view of the Parisians, the film cuts inside the inn to a perspective looking out from its door—the country people's reverse angle, one might call it—a reverse angle not attributed to anyone in particular, but, like the angle it reverses, construed collectively. From a visitor's perspective the film switches to an insider's, from one side of things to quite another. Inside is of course where the country people eat, lunch on the grass being a Parisian penchant on which two local young men—two *canotiers*, boatmen such as are often depicted in Impressionist painting —comment derisively.

In Maupassant's story these bare-armed *canotiers* are indistinguishable from each other; in Renoir's film they are the first characters individually drawn, Rodolphe as the more frivolous, Henri as the more serious of the two. As the two sit at table, Rodolphe opens a window that lets in, with a sudden brightness, another lovely Impressionist picture of the outdoors. Mock the Parisian pastoral though these men may, nobody could resist, we feel, the charm of that light and air, that view pouring in through the window of the visiting mother and daughter on swings. But the two men have different reactions, Rodolphe leaning out to watch, Henri taking hardly a glance outside; and the window frame intrudes to remind us that the alluring sight within its edges is after all only a picture, literally a picture for us in the audience and for the two men only a spectacle with which they have made no real connection.

For our first close look at any of the visitors Renoir singles out the daughter, Henriette, whom we see swinging on her swing, exulting in the open air, the camera empathetically following her from a low angle that enhances the sense of her soaring. And it adds to the exhilarated feeling that the camera doesn't follow her quite steadily through the air, so that its movement seems to partake of her excitement, and does not frame her quite stably on the screen, so that her excitement seems uncontainable within the bounds of the image. Like the brush strokes in Impressionist painting, and like much else in Renoir's film technique, this unsteady following and unstable framing could be deemed awkward or coarse, an unseemly showing of the artist's hand, by received standards of polish, to which in truth this is a considered alternative, capable of nuance and elegance as well as expressive force.

Henriette on her swing puts commentators in mind of an Auguste Renoir painting, *La Balançoire* (*The Swing*, 1876), which depicts a young woman standing on a swing. But the young woman in the painting is not swinging, and right beside her, in the spotted sunlight shining through the trees, are two men and a child sociably arranged. (Another group can be discerned in the background by her face and arm.) Henriette is with her family, and when she gets on the swing she attracts onlookers—Rodolphe at the window, boys gazing over a hedge, a group of seminarians passing by—but she is essentially alone as she swings up in the air. In her openness to the outdoors, her surrender to the pastoral of the country outing, she is by herself, enjoying a private experience of immersion in nature.

The woman on a swing often appears as a subject of art in the eighteenth century, a subject represented with amatory purport.[9] Fragonard's 1767 painting *The Swing*, for example, depicts a young woman swinging before a young man lying in the bushes under her and looking straight up her skirts, a plain enough representation of her giving herself to him sexually (plain enough to us, but hidden from the older man behind her who pulls her swing). This is not Auguste Renoir's swing, which evokes middle-class contentment rather than aristocratic love play. Henriette's swinging in *A Day in the Country* has none of the salaciousness of Fragonard's swing, but it carries an unmistakable sexual energy and a feeling of delighted awakening, of liberation rather than contentment. (The lonely wife's swinging on her garden swing in Satyajit Ray's *Charulata* [1964], after her husband's attractive younger brother has come to the house, expresses a rather similar delighted awakening.)

In an article comparing *A Day in the Country* with Maupassant's story, Seymour Chatman sees a problem and ponders how the film solves it: "the problem of communicating the innocent yet seductive quality of Henriette's charms."[10] This is, one might think, a problem solved by Sylvia Bataille's performance, which splendidly renders both the character's innocence and her emergent sexuality, but Chatman sees it as a problem for the camera. Henriette on her swing figures this way in Maupassant's story:

> Mademoiselle Dufour was trying to swing herself standing up, but she could not succeed in getting a start. She was a pretty girl of about eighteen, one of those women who suddenly excite your desire when you meet them in the street and who leave you with a vague feeling of uneasiness and of excited senses. She was tall, had a small waist and large hips, with a dark skin, very large eyes and very black hair. Her dress clearly marked the outlines of her firm, full figure, which was accentuated by the motion of her hips as she tried to swing herself higher. Her arms were stretched upward to hold the rope, so that her bosom rose at every movement she made. Her hat, which a gust of wind had blown off, was hanging behind her, and as the swing gradually rose higher and higher, she showed her delicate limbs up to the knees each time, and the breeze from her flying skirts, which was more heady than the fumes of wine, blew into the faces of the two men [not the *canotiers*, who haven't entered the story yet, but the father and the yellow-haired apprentice], who were looking at her and smiling.[11]

Talk about the male gaze. This narrator eyes Henriette with lust. Innocent though she may be, in this description she is seductive. Chatman remarks on the ambiguity of her "showing" her legs up to the knees—the word leaves it undecided between her showing innocently and showing with intent, leaves it open to seductive construction—and he thinks the camera incapable of conveying that ambiguity. So, he argues, the camera must adopt the point of view of a character who eyes Henriette with lust, the point of view of Rodolphe, in order that we may see the innocent young woman as seductive.

But the fact is that for most of this sequence Renoir's camera does not adopt Rodolphe's point of view. Rodolphe opens the window and looks out, but the camera remains at some distance behind him and frames Henri as well on the other side. Then the film cuts to an angle quite detached from Rodolphe's perspective and holds a long shot of the Dufour family ordering lunch, the mother sitting on her swing, the daughter standing on hers. By the time we cut to the exhilarating close view of Henriette swinging, the onlooking Rodolphe little enters our minds. "Suddenly we are very much identified with Henriette's feelings:

Rodolphe's voyeurism is forgotten," Chatman grants. But if Rodolphe's voyeurism is forgotten, Chatman's argument is in trouble. In the close view Henriette takes over: she stands apart from the others in her ride through the air, and she alone matters—her feelings, her consciousness, not Rodolphe's or anybody else's. Chatman seems to think that her sexuality can reside only in the eye of a male beholder, but Renoir vividly presents it as her own.[12]

Twice during this sequence we return to the close view following Henriette on her swing. But no single point of view governs our perception, certainly not Rodolphe's, but not her own either. She is the center of this sequence and we feel with her, but we also stand back and observe her from various points all around. We see her from below and also from eye level and from above; from close and also in long shots taken from different sides; moving with her through the air and also standing still as she swings forward and swings back; through the eyes of the passing seminarians and also through those of her most devoted watcher, the lustful Rodolphe. After the last close view following her movement, we cut to him at the window, the window that framed her like a picture or a performer when he initially opened it, and now we see *him* framed by that window like a theatrical performer. In connection with *The River*, William Rothman noted Renoir's sense of the "theatricality of viewing."[13] Rodolphe sees Henriette as performing for his benefit on a stage he intends to join as seducer, but it is his viewing rather than her swinging that strikes us as theatrical, a conventionalized performance. A frame confines; Rodolphe is confined by a role, whereas Henriette on her swing precisely rejoices in her freedom from confinement. And yet, natural and spontaneous though she may feel, when observed from Rodolphe's point of view she can be seen as theatrical, as vulnerable to theater. How real is her freedom? we may ask ourselves. How significant is her naturalness? Rodolphe's point of view is introduced not to convey Henriette's sexuality, but to qualify it. The ambiguity of her swinging is not so much between innocence and seductiveness as between freedom and convention, naturalness and theatricality.

"Wonderful invention—swings!" says Rodolphe as we watch Henriette and her mother from his point of view. "But you can't see a thing!" comments Henri. "Because she's standing," admits Rodolphe. "If she *sat*, it would be more interesting." In a moment, she sits, and we cut to a closer shot from the ground below, looking up her skirts as she swings toward us, the young man's position in Fragonard's picture. Cut to a closer shot of Rodolphe watching from the window that frames him, leering like a stage seducer and stroking his mustache, thinking of himself as the director of this show. It is he, not she, who makes theater; and yet he makes of her a theater, theater in the eye of the beholder. Now the two men start discussing amatory matters, and Henri says he's not interested in a fling. "Suppose that little one fell in love with you?" he warns Rodolphe. "You know you'd leave her . . . ruin her life." Cut to a shot of trees in the wind, and after a moment, from above the frame, Henriette swings back into view: this is the angle looking up her skirts, but now invested with a poignant sense of her vulnerability. "Enough, Henriette, come down!" we hear her mother call. As she gets down from the swing, we cut to a shot in which the window, as it did initially, frames the two women.

(The editing of this sequence, and of this film generally, is extraordinary. Renoir was fortunate to have Marguerite Houllé as his editor; what she did in his absence with *A Day in the Country* attests to how much he owed her in his other films of the thirties. His predilection for long takes and avoidance of the conventional shot breakdown have led commentators to neglect the editing of his films. This is a mistake. His style called for a different kind of editing that required special skill. Marguerite Houllé had that skill. It is time that her talent and accomplishment be recognized.)

Henriette on her swing acts out a sense of freedom inseparable from a sense of nature. Freedom, to a way of thinking we inherit from the Romantics, arises from nature: in nature we are born free, and in nature we gain freedom from the constrictions and conventions of society. On a Sunday outing we get a taste of nature and a taste of freedom, and we go back to the city renewed: the "re-creation myth," as Clark calls it, the brief immersion in nature from which we are to emerge replenished.[14] Henriette is young and naïve, and she takes her taste of nature and her taste of freedom quite seriously, as if these would not just enable her to go back and go on with her life, but would change her life. Her sense of awakening has to do with her sexuality, but something larger is involved: to reduce her feelings to the merely sexual as Rodolphe does—and he is not a villain, but only typical of what people will do—is to threaten the larger promise, the larger impulse she embodies. Thus his theater endangers her naturalness; but his is not the only theater she has to fear.

In *The Crime of Monsieur Lange,* as Bazin observed, Jules Berry plays the slick Batala in a stylized manner purposely at odds with the other actors:[15] the theatricality of the capitalist exploiter threatens the naturalness of the workers. Eisenstein did a similar thing with his caricatured capitalists and workers out of a newsreel. Mixing styles of acting is not uncommon on stage or screen. In the Astaire and Rogers musicals, for example, Fred and Ginger are less comically stylized than the other actors, so they strike us as the only normal human beings around, and therefore as right for each other. In *Boudu Saved from Drowning* Michel Simon as the tramp Boudu gives an aggressively physical performance so

Figure 3. Sylvia Bataille as Henriette in Jean Renoir's A Day in the Country *(1936). Museum of Modern Art.*

at odds with the conventionalized gentility of the bourgeois characters as to make palpable the impossibility of the tramp's domestication into their household. Fred and Ginger belong with each other, but they comfortably inhabit the same world as the other characters. Not so Boudu: in the precincts of the bourgeoisie he is an irreconcilably foreign presence.

In *A Day in the Country*, as in *Boudu*, Renoir mixes acting styles with uncommon discordance. The father and the apprentice, the petit bourgeois patriarch and the heir apparent, are bumbling figures of farce. The apprentice is pale and thin, and the father is rotund—Laurel and Hardy in the Impressionist countryside. Henriette is the daughter of this father, the woman promised to this apprentice, but no character in comedy: she is portrayed with touching conviction in a naturalistic style that would seem to belong in a different universe from this Laurel and Hardy's. The mother is somewhere in between the father and the daughter, comically stylized but not broadly farcical like the father, affecting in a way but not a serious character like the daughter. The portrayal of Rodolphe matches the mother's portrayal: these two belong together in their playfulness and their conventionality. And, as the names indicate, the portrayal of Henri matches that of Henriette: these two belong together in their seriousness and their sentiment (some have said sentimentality).

Sitting by the window that looks out on the swinging mother and daughter, Henri thinks Rodolphe irresponsible for wanting to seduce the daughter, but he considers the mother fair game and he agrees to join his friend in a pursuit of the two city women—a pursuit in which, as things develop, the couples sort themselves out for the afternoon seduction into Rodolphe and the mother and Henri and Henriette. After the Parisians have had their *déjeuner sur l'herbe*—which the film portrays not lyrically, but farcically, an occasion for gluttony rather than sociability, the father and the apprentice drunkenly recumbent in the aftermath—Rodolphe and Henri approach the mother and daughter. The women love the idea of going boating on the river, and the *canotiers* lend fishing rods to the father and the apprentice to keep them occupied and out of the way. In a held deep-focus shot we see Henriette and the four men, the two designing boatmen both with designs on her and the two bumbling city men with their borrowed fishing gear, farce and romance jostling each other on the screen. As the city men wander off into the background, toward the river, and the boatmen and Henriette follow—each *canotier* in turn grabbing her hand—all the while in the foreground the two swings, with nobody on them now, gently sway in opposite directions, slowly coming to a halt. The swings and their swaying may be taken as a metaphor for the two suitors and their pulling the young woman in opposite directions; but the swings are also Henriette herself, a reminder of her ride through the air, and their winding down suggests the impending coming down to earth of first impressions. Just as, by a law of nature, the swings slow down, so the hopes and exhilarations of the air are inevitably to meet the ground of reality.

The arrival at the country inn is enchanting, the *déjeuner sur l'herbe* a disenchantment. Nature is lovely, the father and the apprentice more than a bit absurd. *A Day in the Country* holds to no single mood or mode of representation, no settled way of seeing the landscape and the human beings in its midst. Rodolphe and the mother in one rowboat, Henri and Henriette in another, travel along the river and get off at an island where, in very different fashions, parallel seductions ensue. Unlike the story, which stays with the daughter and lets the mother recede into the background, the film cuts back and forth between the two couples. Although Henri and Henriette are romantically in earnest, Rodolphe and the mother perform a parody of a classical pastoral seduction in the woods, Rodolphe impersonating a satyr and the mother playing along as a matronly nymph.

The two couples clash, and yet each colors our impression of the other. The daughter is earnest and the mother is playful, but is not the one's palpitant sensitivity to a nightingale's song comparable to the other's giggling delight in a nymph's role? Henri is sentimental and Rodolphe is contriving, but does not the one behave as irresponsibly with an ingenuous young woman as he thought the other would have? And is not Henri's reticence, rather than Rodolphe's forwardness, just what that ingenuous young woman would fall for? One couple acts naturally and the other acts artificially, but are not both couples guided by the fantasy rather than the reality of nature? In Renoir's parallel arrangement, the two seductions make no simple contrast, but call for an inquiring comparison.

Brecht has been much discussed in connection with films, but seldom in connection with Renoir. Yet the playwright famous for his alienation effect and the filmmaker celebrated for his humane sympathy (aside from the fact that they were friends) shared important artistic concerns. In their work they both endeavored, each in his own medium and with his own outlook, toward what Brecht called "complex seeing": not a single focus, but a multiplicity of perspectives that invites from the audience active reflection rather than mere acquiescence. Mixing modes, shifting representational gears, bringing together what is not supposed to go together, served both Brecht and Renoir as a principal means to complex seeing. Breaking the consistency of a style or a tone they might have asked us to accept, they encourage us, instead, to keep in mind different ways of doing things, of regarding things. Such a mixture is difficult to bring off; it is always easier to maintain consistency than to manage diversity. *A Day in the Country* succeeds so well, with so little apparent effort, that to inattentive watchers it has seemed a simple small picture, Renoir and his actors on a Sunday outing themselves. The film is simple only in its plot, small only in its short running time, effortless only because it has the technique to take the risks it takes. Its complexity is not in the tale, but in the telling—in the seeing.

Just as Henri feared, the susceptible Henriette falls in love with a seducer, himself as it turns out; and just as he feared, her love, even though he susceptibly reciprocates it, comes to nothing after the day in the country. She goes back to the city and marries the pale apprentice: Romeo and Juliet foiled by Laurel and Hardy. The tale may be simple, but the interpretations have been conflicting. According to Leo Braudy, Henri and Henriette are too serious: they suffer from a "sentimental view of nature" and "melancholic self-indulgence in emotion," whereas Rodolphe and the mother, with their "pagan exuberance," know how to have a good time.[16] According to Alexander Sesonske, Monsieur Dufour is to be commended as a family man, Rodolphe is an innocent like Henriette, and Henri is the villain of the piece, the cynical seducer he accused his friend of being, albeit a clumsy one who has no feeling for love play and a gloomy one who infects Henriette with his self-pity.[17] According to Tag Gallagher, Henri is the hero of the piece—the tragic hero—a morose young man awakened from despondency by a beautiful woman who brings him love one Sunday afternoon, but abandons him for someone else.[18] These are all misreadings, but all have some basis in the film—misreadings that impose a simple slant on complex seeing.

Deftly balancing naturalism and farce, parody and tragedy, the film allows us no stable response. Neither a serious drama with comic relief nor a comedy with serious touches, it asks that we entertain the serious and the comical on equal terms and generates between the two a continual give and take. Of the parallel seductions one may say, after Marx, that what occurs the first time as tragedy, in the daughter's youth, occurs the second, in the mother's middle age, as farce; and Renoir, setting the farce and the tragedy side by side, insists that we keep both in mind together. Such is the give and take he later sets up in *The Rules of the Game,* where comedy and tragedy mix in a similarly unsettling way. In *A Day in the Country* the different modes are kept more separate, however, not so much mingled as juxtaposed. Henriette and Anatole, as the apprentice is called in the film, she a wholly serious character and he a clown, make the film's most incongruous juxtaposition, whose full impact is saved for the end, when we see the two married and realize with a shock that his farce is her tragedy.

In the movies place is usually but background to the fiction staged there. Sometimes place is made prominent by being deployed theatrically, as the Odessa steps are deployed in the action Eisenstein staged there, or as city streets may be deployed for the excitement of a car chase: place as spectacle rather than background. In a Renoir film of the thirties, place is neither background nor spectacle.

Natural landscape is an agreeable movie performer. It will lend itself to the pretty pictures of a love story and to the spooky atmosphere of a gothic story, to the grand vistas of a Western and to the thrilling sights of a cliff-hanger. Yet landscape in these roles is not engaged as an actual place, a stretch of the world we inhabit. Whether relegated to a background or brought forward as a spectacle, it is made to play a part in a fiction and made subservient to that fiction. The landscape may assume prominence, but only within the fictional requirements; the love story or the cliff-hanger will set the terms of our response. *A Day in the Country* is a rare film that gives primacy to the landscape and lets it have a life of its own. It does not assign it a role and a meaning defined by the fiction. Rather it has the fiction define itself and its characters against the character of a landscape that was there first.

Normally a film will start with a story and then arrange for the setting, whether in the studio or out on location. Renoir may have started with Maupassant's story, but he went out to a location that for him was there first—a place that was part of his life, a landscape with a painterly past—and the film he brought back makes that primacy felt. Landscape is a sovereign presence in *A Day in the Country*, fiction an uncertain undertaking that takes variable forms. What sort of fiction is to be enacted here? asks the film through its mixture of modes. Are we to stage a farce with the father and the apprentice and make fun of the petit bourgeois and their country outing? Are we to have a lighthearted romp in the woods with the mother and Rodolphe? Or are we to be serious and sentimental with Henriette and Henri? No mode of fiction being dominant, the landscape takes center place; each mode of fiction seeing the landscape in a different way, the landscape gains independence from any way of seeing it. Rather than a mere background to the fiction, the landscape becomes an enduring ground on which the fiction sketches tentative figures; rather than assigning meaning to the landscape, the fiction becomes a foray in quest of meaning. Setting in most films is put to the service of fiction; landscape in *A Day in the Country* puts the fictional venture to the test. Renoir makes fiction into a trope for the human attempt to connect with nature, endow it with meaning, feel at home in it, or at least feel welcome in our outings.

A sovereign presence and yet also an absence. For in a work of fiction, a story, a painting, a film, landscape can be apprehended only through fiction, and fiction in *A Day in the Country* is seen to have no secure claim on landscape. Nature cannot appear on the screen; only its representation can be seen in necessarily reductive images, but films will usually promote the impression that the images represent nature, capture it, with perfect adequacy. *A Day in the Country* declines to give us that impression and instead makes us aware of the fiction in any view of nature, any picture of it. Nature in this film, though represented with rich vividness, is yet perceived to be always in excess of its representation. Nature is there first and yet not there.

When Rodolphe opens the window, Henriette on her swing is but a picture for him, a piece of theater; when we move with her through the air, we share her feeling of freedom and forget the theatricalizing voyeur; but at the end of her swinging, our view of her is again bordered by the window frame. This not only shows her as threatened by the seducer's picture of her; it suggests that her feeling of freedom, of communion with nature, is itself a picture, an illusion, a fiction. For the window, with the reminder that we are watching a picture that its borders provide, can now be seen to frame the entire swinging sequence from beginning to end, and all the diverse views and points of view we have been getting, with Henriette at the center, become retroactively bordered by our awareness of fiction. And Henriette is especially vulnerable because, though the way she pictures herself in nature is not her own invention but a social construction, she is all alone in that picture.

Henriette is with Henri when they go off together on their boat ride. We see them in an overhead shot of their boat gliding on the water, from which we cut, movement to movement, to a shot traveling along the river and showing the grasses and trees going by on the shore. This is not a point-of-view shot—it is neither preceded nor followed by a character looking, and the characters in any case are facing backward, toward the stern of their rowboat, while the camera moves forward—but it does give us the sense of looking at the shore through the eyes of someone riding in a boat. This sense is stronger in another, more extended traveling shot that soon follows, a shot in which we gaze at the other shore, the trees overhanging the river and their reflections on the water, from what indeed feels like the perspective of a slow-moving, gently rocking rowboat. In the story the perspective is Henriette's and the sensuality of the river and the trees is attributed to her subjectivity:

> The girl, who was sitting in the bow, gave herself up to the enjoyment of being on the water. She felt a disinclination to think, a lassitude in her limbs and a total enervation, as if she were intoxicated, and her face was flushed and her breathing quickened. The effects of the wine, which were increased by the extreme heat, made all the trees on the bank seem to bow as she passed.[19]

In the film we feel the subjectivity of an individual taking in the river scenery from a boat, but Henriette (not affected by wine that we can see) is not sitting in the bow, and though she could be turning her head toward the front, the camera moves forward along the river without any inserted shots attributing the point of view to her (or to Henri, who might be glancing at the shore, too, if he could take his eyes off her). Here as in the arrival at the country inn, Renoir's camera, while adopting the position of traveling in the same vehicle as the characters, travels without bracketing or interruption by their glances or reactions, so that the camera's point of view, although associated with theirs, is not equated with it. Inserted glances and reactions are a means, which normally would have been employed here, of assimilating the setting to the fiction, making us see it in the fiction's terms—as the characters see it, as it pertains to them and their situation and only to that—but Renoir grants the fiction no prerogative to dictate terms.

Freeing the landscape from the dominance of fiction, Renoir at the same time frees the camera from its customary role as agent of that dominance, provider of views and perspectives that center on the characters and impose the priorities of the plot. Whereas the camera in most films takes its prompting from the dramatic fiction, Renoir establishes his camera, in this film and elsewhere, as an autonomous narrative agency that conducts its own transaction with the world. The normal

point-of-view shot, which gives the camera over to a character's fictional eyes, he mostly avoids; but he often employs what may be called the
loosely attributed point of view, which proposes, instead of an equation,
varying degrees of correspondence between the camera's perspective and
a character's. Renoir deserves his reputation for sympathy; his autonomous camera—and this registers as a choice, a well-felt gesture, rather
than a dramatic necessity—remains attentive to the characters, in tune
with their perceptions and sentiments; but his is a sympathy combined
with detachment. He wants us to feel with Henriette on that boat ride—
the point of view, if not quite hers, is not quite apart from hers either—
but he also encourages us to keep our distance from her so that we may
look at things with our own eyes. Just as his camera takes a path of its
own, so we, rather than simply deriving a vicarious response from the
dramatic fiction, are to consider our own response, the ways we have of
relating to that landscape along the river and to nature more generally—
the ways in which we are and the ways in which we are not in the same
boat as the characters.

In Maupassant's story we identify with the tipsy young woman
being rowed over the water by a young man who finds her pretty. But in
this identification our own position is not at stake: these are her feelings,
and we can relate to them, but they are not our feelings. Our identification with Henriette in Renoir's film is of a different kind. The scene is
presented not from her perspective, which is not ours, but from a perspective akin to hers that, imagining ourselves in a boat on that river, we
feel could well be ours. We are in a way more detached from her than we
are in Maupassant's story and in another way more identified with her:
we are not seeing through her eyes, but, from a position we recognize as
our own, we have much the same response as she has to the beauty and
sensuality of nature in summer.

In the traveling shot toward the country inn, we identify with
the arriving Parisians not as individuals, but as members of a class. On
the river we identify with Henriette as an individual, but an individual
conditioned by her society to regard nature in a certain way, a way that,
precisely, isolates the individual from society in the experience of nature. In the traveling shots along the river we are all on our own—inserted glances and reactions would have been company—for a sustained
imbibing of nature that affects us like wine. It is enchanting, this immersion in nature, and it is isolating in its enchantment. We put ourselves
in Henriette's place, see that her place could be ours, as individuals like-
wise conditioned by our society to look to nature for this kind of private
experience. She is with Henri on the river, and he may share her experience, but the experience shared by two is scarcely less private. The experience these two share cannot endure beyond the day in the country,
because it can endure only in society. To blame Henri for seducing
Henriette, or Henriette for throwing over Henri, is misguided. Renoir

does not moralize, does not put blame on individuals—not because he loves them too much, but because he sees the social picture that blaming them would obscure, because he tells the social story that determines their stories. It was in the cards, the cards society deals, that the romance of Henriette and Henri would amount to no more than a moment.

"How beautiful! I've never seen anything so beautiful!" says Henriette when she and Henri disembark on the river island. The sweet trill of Sylvia Bataille's voice matches the sound of a nightingale they hear in the woods. The camera starts moving, as if itself responding to the nightingale's call and leading the characters into the woods rather than merely following them. "All enclosed . . . like a house," notes Henriette of the surrounding verdancy. A crooked branch, rectangularly shaped, comes into view from above and marks the spot. "I come here often," says Henri. "I call it my 'private den.'" They sit down on the grass and listen to the nightingale up in a tree; he puts his arm around her waist and she removes it. Cut to the mother and Rodolphe and their parodic romance. Cut back to Henriette and Henri: she wipes a tear from her cheek while looking up at the romantic bird perched above them. Cut to Rodolphe and the mother as satyr and nymph. Cut back to Henri pressing close to Henriette: he tries to kiss her and she resists, but in a moment she gives in to him, "tremblingly, like a captured bird," as Pauline Kael wrote.[20] Cut to a very tight close-up of Henriette that, with Henri's hand on her cheek as she lies under him on the grass, her face cropped by the top edge of the frame so that we see only one tearful eye as she turns toward us, indeed compares her to a captured bird. Not that she is being coerced into sex, as some have thought: she is captured by her own feelings as well as his advances. She cries the tears of a virgin losing her virginity, and perhaps also the tears of a woman who knows that this romance she so wants cannot last. Her looking at us, however, signifies that she feels alone in this romance and in these tears.

In the aftermath of the two seductions, right after Henriette has yielded to Henri with passion and tears, the film switches away from the characters altogether. Unpeopled nature takes over in the ensuing images, first the wind-blown plants and dark clouds of a gathering rainstorm in a series of quick static shots, then the rain falling on the river and its banks with the camera backing away. This may seem an instance of the pathetic fallacy, a projection of Henriette's feelings or even, in Sesonske's plausible interpretation, a "sexual metaphor" in which the tension before the storm and the release when rain falls stand for the emotions she experiences as she resists and then surrenders to sexual passion.[21] If we switched to nature from the tight close-up of Henriette or if we returned to her after the views of nature, this interpretation might be more convincing. But from the close-up the film dissolves to a long shot of Henri and Henriette after lovemaking, and as they look away from each other, their passion spent, the film cuts to the plants and the clouds and the rain. Nature here offers no clear correlative for Henriette's emotions, whether during, or, more likely, after her first experience of sex; and besides her, three other characters, each with emotions not to be discounted, have been sexually engaged at the same time. Landscape in this film is no serviceable vehicle for the meanings of fiction.[22] At first we expect that we will soon enough return to the characters after a digression into the landscape, but gradually it dawns on us that Henriette and Henri, the mother and Rodolphe, the father and Anatole, all are being left behind. As the rain breaks and the camera retreats down the river, this sequence continues and concludes without people: the time that passes without even a glimpse of the characters works to dispel any direct associations we may entertain between their feelings and nature. Nor is this a case of nature presented as grandly impervious to the concerns of humanity (as in, say, Werner Herzog's Amazon films); to see nature as uncaring is but another form of the pathetic fallacy, to see it as meaningless but another way of assigning it a precise meaning. Nature here becomes neither too closely associated with the characters nor too far dissociated from them and the human standpoint they represent.

But the human standpoint, as Renoir here and elsewhere reminds us, is nothing universal, nothing eternal. It varies greatly according to the individual's situation, the class outlook, the premises, the conditions, the constructions of a culture and society, the sense and circumstance of a time and place. It always differs between a spectator or reader, situated outside, and a character inside a work's proposed world. Renoir brings forward this difference dividing us from the characters— rather than inducing in us the kind of identification that would dissemble it—as well as the differences dividing the characters themselves. Despite the moment of love Henriette and Henri share, her feelings and his are not truly at one; the two part ways after their encounter, not to meet again until years have sealed their mutual isolation and her unhappy marriage to Anatole. The mother and Rodolphe may be better matched in their parallel encounter, but only because neither of the two harbors any notion of oneness. Among these four individuals who all make love on that river island that summer afternoon, feelings and attitudes are split four ways.

Without hurry, savoring the appearances of summery nature, *A Day in the Country* has moved toward that river island and the moment of communion it holds for the characters. But no sooner is that consummation reached than, briskly, at an increasing pace, in three successive shots that are the film's most assertive visual maneuver, the camera travels backward as the country outing comes to an abrupt, rainy end. A meandering, exploratory progression is suddenly broken, reversed, by this decisive traveling "over the rapidly receding face of the river," as

Sesonske writes, "pierced by the myriad needles of the rain":[23] unpeopled images reverberating with a sense of loss, separation, togetherness fleetingly reached and now swiftly, in a few moments that seem to constitute a lifetime, left behind. Not only the speed and direction, but the time scale is switched here in one bold stroke: from the scale of a day, a few hours lingered over, suspended in sensual apprehension, to a few moments whose movement evokes the rush of years ceaselessly passing.

"Swiftly the years, beyond recall. / Solemn the stillness of this spring morning." In *Seven Types of Ambiguity* William Empson discusses these two lines from a Chinese poem and their juxtaposition of two different time scales—the large scale that "takes the length of a human life as its unit" and the small scale that "takes as its unit the conscious moment":

> Both these time-scales and their contrasts are included by these two lines in a single act of apprehension, because of the words *swift* and *still*. Being contradictory as they stand, they demand to be conceived in different ways; we are enabled, therefore, to meet the open skies with an answering stability of selfknowledge; to meet the brevity of human life with an ironical sense that it is morning and springtime, that there is a whole summer before winter, a whole day before night.[24]

The Chinese poem shifts from the years to the day; *A Day in the Country* shifts from the day to the years, the moment to the lifetime. In the film as in the poem, the two time scales come together in our minds. "The *years* of a man's life seem *swift* even on the small scale," writes Empson; "the *morning* seems *still* even on the large scale."[25] Disconcertingly swift on the scale of the day, the camera's retreat down the river evokes the scale of the years and seems swift on that scale, too; and conversely, the exhilaration on the swing, the imbibing of nature on the boat ride, the tender verdant privacy on the river island, are moments that seem suspended even on the scale of the lifetime. But the film's shift from the moment to the lifetime is a shift from promise to loss, from a feeling of oneness to a sense of alienation: not the serenity the poem conveys with its juxtaposition.

Autonomous but not godlike, declining to assume a superior point of vantage, Renoir's camera meets the world from a position that is always recognizably concrete, on a human plane. If it traveled up river in a rowboat, it backs away down river—as becomes significant because we register its concrete position in both cases—with the speed of a motorboat, a vehicle in which the nineteenth-century characters could not have been traveling. Although the vehicle is not shown, the departing backward views were evidently taken from an unsteady small boat, which could be the same one that traveled up river, one in which we can imagine ourselves riding on a Sunday and hurrying back when it starts to rain, but whose propelling drive in the retreat would have been unavailable to the characters. This rapid motion, especially in comparison with the leisurely progress up river, makes us note a speed beyond mere rowing, a plane of human experience attainable only since the advent of motorboats and cameras endowed with mobility to match that of an age just being born when the Impressionists were painting. At the close of an excursion it has made its own—and ours—Renoir's camera detaches itself not only from the characters, but from the whole period of the fiction: its departing motion belongs unmistakably to our century. The sense of years passing, a long span compressed into those retreating moments, extends from the characters' lives to the lives of all of us, in all the years that have passed since that time of Impressionist picnics on the grass and virginal daughters tremulously surrendering to love by the waterside. It is as if the day in the country, having begun in the nineteenth century, were ending in the twentieth—as if that river we are leaving behind were the last version of pastoral receding from our twentieth-century motorboat. Incitingly, Renoir omits the characters from this visual cadence that, no mere ornament to the story, is the film's culminant sequence, rich in associations with them but essentially addressing us, drawing us into a reflective look at things from where we stand outside the fiction.

———

Besides picturing a dramatic fiction enacted before it, the movie camera enacts the fiction of a perceiving eye, an apprehending consciousness. The dramatic fiction imitates an action; the camera imitates a gaze, a point of view, an act of perception and of consciousness. The movies are a representation both of the world and of an apprehension of the world. But usually the camera, made subservient to the drama, does little more than unfold the plot, the characters' actions and perceptions and the pertinent attendant circumstances; caught up in the movement of plot, we scarcely register the camera's point of view, the choice to look at things in this manner and succession, as a directed act of consciousness, a movement of mind. Imagine a shot that, in conventional fashion, presents something dramatically significant from a suitable angle and distance, then imagine that shot held for a moment longer than necessary to make the dramatic point: that extra moment, such as we are normally denied, would arrest the movement of plot long enough for us to gain the sense of an apprehending mind behind the camera. Renoir often gives us such extra moments, either after or before the dramatically significant thing, to which he characteristically pays no privileged attention. His camera, with its distinctive autonomous gaze, everywhere enacts an unmistakable movement of consciousness.

Rather than determining in usual fashion the point of view and the meaning, the dramatic fiction in *A Day in the Country* proposes different ways of seeing that, along with the camera's ways, partake in a complex apprehension of a landscape that seems to extend the invitation of pastoral, but conforms to no settled way of seeing it or giving it meaning. The film's movement of consciousness begins with the arriving perspective of a generalized visitor, the petit bourgeois from the city come for a pastoral day in the country. A discrepancy in points of view then starts to be made manifest, a discrepancy not only between the visitors and the locals, but among the various individuals, their differences accentuated by the different acting styles, and, moreover, a discrepancy between the characters and the autonomous camera. In such difference lies no oneness. These discordant points of view belie the harmony with nature that pastoral promises. We are made aware of a separation between nature and the consciousness that apprehends it and attempts to invest it with meaning, between a landscape that can be regarded from many different perspectives and the different perspectives from which we may regard it. Vividly represented yet always in excess of its representation, nature in *A Day in the Country* is in excess of our consciousness, of the mind's capacity to apprehend it with any conclusive adequacy. The rainstorm strikingly frustrates pastoral expectations, not only for the day, but for the years swiftly receding, and not only for the characters, but for all of us who joined them in the sunny arrival and now look upon stormy nature from the departing perspective of a visitor no longer identifiable with them, generalized beyond their circumstances and their century. That uncannily rapid departing motion of the camera—rapid like our passage through this world where we are all mere visitors—evokes the movement of a consciousness that recognizes its own foreignness amid the trees and the river and the rain, its own apartness among the things of nature.

From an imaginary plenitude, a Lacanian might say, we retreat here to the recognition of loss—loss of what was lost already, always already lost, the trees and the river that were never there on the screen, the ever-unattainable oneness felt at the mother's breast once upon a time and sought in vain thereafter. Indeed the film here pulls us back from its fiction and throws us back on our own situation as viewers of that fiction. But the Lacanian reading assumes that there was nothing there to begin with, that there can be nothing there. Taken literally, this is merely obvious: we never thought the trees and the river were actually there on the screen. Taken in its implications, it tells us we can make no real connection with the material world around us, only an imaginary connection. Henriette (incarnated, as it happens, by a woman Lacan married) was deluded from the start: just as the nature we watch on the screen can only be an illusion, so the nature that seemed to offer her freedom and tenderness was only in her head. We are all deluded from the start if we seek freedom and tenderness in the world. Alienation in this view becomes something inalterable, all but metaphysical, not a social condition, but a given of the human condition.

Between consciousness and nature, illusion and reality, where Lacanians and other theorists posit an irrevocable breach, Renoir sees a complex interplay. The famous ending of *Grand Illusion* shows the two escaped French prisoners crossing the border into Switzerland, saved from German bullets by a border quite undiscernible in the unbroken stretch of snow ("an invention of man," says one of the characters; "nature doesn't give a damn") yet quite real nonetheless. Stanley Cavell comments on

> the two figures bobbing through a field of snow, away from us. Some-where under that one white is a mathematical line, a fiction men call a border. It is not on earth or in heaven, but whether you are known to have crossed it is a matter of life and death. The movie is about borders, about the lines of life and death between German and Frenchman, between rich and poor, between rich man and aristocrat, between offi-cer and soldier, between home and absence, between Gentile and Jew. Specifically, it is about the illusions of borders, the illusion that they are real and the grand illusion that they are not.[26]

Henriette's view of nature is as much a fiction as that border and as much a matter of life and death. Just as for the men crossing that border, freedom for her hangs on that fiction. The border is a fiction made real by nations' acting on it, and the men reach freedom because the German patrol honors that fiction and lets them go. If Henriette fails to reach freedom, it is not because she pursues a fiction, but because she acts alone on that fiction, because the society that constructed that fiction by and large does not act on it.

A hundred years before the Impressionists painted the version of pastoral that is still ours, the Romantics framed the conception of freedom that is still ours: freedom as natural, freedom as a regaining of nature. The Impressionist version of pastoral, a naturalistic rather than a conventionalized pastoral, responded to that naturalistic conception of freedom and its democratic extension to the petite bourgeoisie. If nobody has painted a newer version of pastoral to replace that of the Impressionists in our cultural imagination, surely that has to do with the fact that nobody has framed a newer conception of freedom to re-place the Romantics in our political imagination. The camera that retreats from nature in *A Day in the Country,* the consciousness that recognizes its own apartness from nature, is calling into question the pastoral the Impressionists painted and the natural freedom the Roman-tics conceived.

In *Earth* Dovzhenko combined that Romantic conception—which Marxism modified but did not discard—with a peasant sense of commu-nity in nature. Tenderness is rooted in community for the virginal girl-friend in *Earth,* whereas the virginal Henriette can achieve her moment of tenderness only away from community. The view of nature expressed in *Earth* is no less a fiction than Henriette's view, and, moreover, a fiction Soviet society flagrantly did not honor, but it is a fiction Dovzhenko saw as sanctioned by a society that would act on it. For Renoir in the days of the Popular Front the freedom we can achieve in nature is a fiction as yet never realized in action. He is not prepared to discard that conception: hence our identification with Henriette, hence the sweetness and enchantment of much of the day in the country. But he is prepared to question it: hence our detachment from Henriette, hence the retreat that pulls us up short, hence her tragedy.

Maupassant's story has a brief scene in Paris two months after the day in the country. Henri is in the city and goes into the Dufour hardware store, where he talks to the mother and learns from her that Henriette has married the apprentice. Renoir had planned to film such a scene, but never got around to it, and in its place the film makes use of a title. From the camera retreating down river in the rain we fade out to these words: "Years have passed. Henriette is married to Anatole. The Sundays are now as sad as the Mondays. And on this Sunday. . . . " On this Sunday we see Henri rowing alone to the river island and finding Henriette there, too, drawn independently by the same sentimental memories the place holds for him.

Nostalgia is an emotion allegedly soft and silly, but what else are Henri and Henriette to feel on this occasion? On this Sunday the mood is not summery, but autumnal. The camera follows Henri along the same path he and Henriette followed when the nightingale sang; he pauses at the spot marked by the crooked branch, and the camera pauses with him for a moment, then swiftly moves ahead to find Henriette where he has noticed her, sitting on the grass with Anatole napping beside her; and this long take continues uninterrupted as she in turn notices Henri, gets up and walks toward him, and the camera now moves with her back to him. But this continuous path of gaze—which may be described as a double following and finding, first from his side and then from hers—leads to no togetherness except a shared yearning for what might have been. In a gesture of sentimental sympathy, the moving camera traces the form of a coming together that only underscores the missed togetherness in the lives of these two. Those who would frown on them for being sentimental should not exempt Renoir. But who are we to frown on Henri and Henriette? Who can presume to feel superior to their longing for tenderness and freedom? Renoir does not presume.

Anatole calls out, and Henri withdraws, the camera alongside him as, from a distance, he watches Henriette leaving with her clown of a husband, who compounds his ridiculousness with a petty tyrannical manner he apparently believes is the way to treat a wife. Then Henri goes over by the river and, leaning on a tree overhanging it, wistfully smokes a cigarette. As he throws away the cigarette, the camera turns in that direction, panning leftward in a movement more or less identified with his glance, but interrupted by a striking cut—a cut breaking the conventional rules of smooth editing—to another panning movement starting again from the tree he leans on but turning rightward this time, and continuing in an unhurried look at the river and its shore. A pan is like a turning of the head, and here the camera first turns its head leftward, in sympathy with Henri, and then rightward, away from him in the direction opposite to his glance. In its rightward panning the camera observes Henriette rowing away with her husband—she doing the rowing—whereupon its gaze moves down to Henri's empty boat by the shore, and on sideways to the unruffled, rippling water. These paired panning shots conclude the film. The cut between them feels like a bouncing back, with the tree as a point of stability, from Henri's melancholy contemplation, which projects onto nature an understandable but fruitless nostalgia, to an open, lingering view of nature's unceasing countenance.

NOTES

1. Renoir's remark and Wilenski's comment are quoted in Adrian Stokes, *Monet*, in *The Critical Writings of Adrian Stokes*, ed. Lawrence Gowing, vol. 2 (New York: Thames and Hudson, 1978), p. 292.

2. André Bazin, *Jean Renoir*, ed. François Truffaut, trans. W. W. Halsey II and William H. Simon (New York: Dell, 1974), p. 111.

3. In the view of some, no great artistic prestige issues from Auguste Renoir. The most popular of the Impressionists—and they are the most popular school of painting—he is often condescended to by those who like their art less popular and regard Renoir as a prettifier, complacent and crowd-pleasing, superficial and sentimental. At his worst Renoir may deserve some such characterization, but at his best he was a great painter—perhaps the only one of the Impressionists, wrote Clement Greenberg, "who was a master painter in point of craft and in joy of artisanship." The disparagement of Renoir has surely to do with a distrust of pleasure. "What a profusion of pleasure there is [in the Renoir paintings on exhibit]," marveled Greenberg at the end of his article, "and how ungrateful it is to carp at it: a foaming, pouring, shimmering profusion like nothing else in painting; pictures that are spotted and woven with soft, porous colors, and look in themselves like bouquets of flowers . . . pictures whose space is handled like a fluid that floats all objects to the surface; pictures in which our eyes swim with the paint and dance with the brush-stroke" (Clement Greenberg, *The Collected Essays and Criticism*, ed. John O'Brian, vol. 3, *Affirmations and Refusals, 1950–1956* [Chicago: The University of Chicago Press, 1993], pp. 22–26).

4. Jean Renoir, *Renoir, My Father*, trans. Randolph Weaver and Dorothy Weaver (San Francisco: Mercury House, 1988), p. 189.

5. T. J. Clark, *The Painting of Modern Life: Paris in the Art of Manet and His Followers* (New York: Knopf, 1985), p. 148. Clark's chapter "The Environs of Paris" documents the disdain many contemporary observers felt toward excursionists in the countryside the Impressionists were painting.

6. John Berger, "The Eyes of Claude Monet," in *The Sense of Sight*, ed. Lloyd Spencer (New York: Pantheon, 1985), p. 190.

7. Meyer Schapiro, "The Nature of Abstract Art," in *Modern Art: Nineteenth and Twentieth Centuries* (New York: Braziller, 1978), pp. 192–93.

8. Clark, *The Painting of Modern Life,* p. 5.

9. See Donald Posner, "The Swinging Women of Watteau and Fragonard," *Art Bulletin* 64:1 (1982), pp. 75–88.

10. Seymour Chatman, "What Novels Can Do That Films Can't (and Vice Versa)," in *Film Theory and Criticism,* 4th ed., ed. Gerald Mast, Marshall Cohen, and Leo Braudy (New York: Oxford University Press, 1992), p. 412.

11. Guy de Maupassant, "A Country Excursion," in *Sur l'eau and Other Stories,* trans. Albert M. C. McMaster et al. (London: Standard, 1922), p. 4.

12. In a footnote to his article Chatman discusses the response it elicited when he read it at a conference. Several participants charged him with sexism in the identification he proposes with Rodolphe the voyeur. After defending himself by insisting that he does not at all approve of Rodolphe, but only identifies with him for the purposes of a fiction, Chatman notes that to one participant (Roy Schafer) the close view of Henriette swinging "conveyed . . . something of *her* sexual pleasure." "Sexual pleasure" is too strong for her incipient sexuality, though the emphasis on her pleasure is apt, and the sexual does enter into her feelings for nature. See Chatman, "What Novels Can Do That Films Can't (and Vice Versa)," pp. 418–19.

13. William Rothman, *The "I" of the Camera* (Cambridge: Cambridge University Press, 1988), p. 146.

14. Clark, *The Painting of Modern Life,* p. 199.

15. Bazin, *Jean Renoir,* p. 46.

16. Leo Braudy, *Jean Renoir: The World of His Films* (Garden City, N.Y.: Anchor, 1972), p. 35.

17. Alexander Sesonske, *Jean Renoir: The French Films, 1924–1939* (Cambridge: Harvard University Press, 1980), 241–56.

18. Tag Gallagher, talk at Sarah Lawrence College, Bronxville, N.Y., 10 April 1995; idem, "Jean Renoir: The Dancers and the Dance," *Film Comment* 32:1 (1996), pp. 64–66, 72–76.

19. Maupassant, "A Country Excursion," p. 10.

20. Pauline Kael, *Kiss Kiss Bang Bang* (Boston: Little, Brown, 1968), p. 254.

21. Sesonske, *Jean Renoir,* p. 252.

22. In a sequence from *Picnic on the Grass* (1959) Renoir uses views of unpeopled nature as a metaphor for sexual intercourse. But landscape as he treats it in that film—albeit a landscape shot on location at Les Collettes, the farm in the south of France where Auguste Renoir spent the last years of his life—is mere theatrical spectacle, not the independent presence it is in *A Day in the Country.*

23. Sesonske, *Jean Renoir,* p. 252.

24. William Empson, *Seven Types of Ambiguity* (New York: New Directions, 1966), p. 24.

25. Ibid.

26. Stanley Cavell, *The World Viewed,* enl. ed. (Cambridge: Harvard University Press, 1979), pp. 143–44.

Michael Anderegg

Welles/Shakespeare/Film:
An Overview

Commenting on the proliferation of officially sanctioned cultural festivals in postwar Europe, Theodor Adorno found that culture itself, "in an effort to preserve a feeling of contrast to contemporary streamlining, . . . is still permitted to drive about in a type of gypsy wagon; the gypsy wagons, however, roll about secretly in a monstrous hall, a fact which they do not themselves notice."[1] It could be said of Orson Welles's Shakespearean films—indeed, of most of his post–*Citizen Kane* films—that they were attempts on his part to drive his gypsy wagon outside of the great hall of the culture industry. *Macbeth* (1948), from this point of view, was the last project he worked on that still remained within the hall, however much it strained to get out of it. *Othello* (1952), *Mr. Arkadin* (aka *Confidential Report*, 1955), *The Trial* (1962), *Chimes at Midnight* (1967), and *F for Fake* (1973) were, to a greater or lesser extent, compromises, at once inside and outside the hall, though Adorno would undoubtedly claim that it was no longer possible to find the "outside." Welles had in fact planned to present *Othello* on stage at the Edinburgh Festival and to produce the film under the auspices of the American National Theatre Association (ANTA), both significant manifestations of the phenomena Adorno was describing. Though neither of these plans was carried out, they indicate how aware Welles was, in the late forties and early fifties, of the limited options for producing Shakespearean films—or, for that matter, any films—then at his disposal.

The three Shakespearean films Welles completed—*Macbeth, Othello,* and *Chimes at Midnight*—appear at first sight to be less dependent on "gimmicks," more "faithful" to the plays on which they were based, than either of Welles's famous theatrical productions of the 1930s, the "voodoo" *Macbeth* and the "fascist" *Julius Caesar.* In spite of their reputations as eccentric films, each can be described as a fairly straightforward return to traditional Shakespearean performance in terms of lan-

From *Orson Welles, Shakespeare, and Popular Culture.* Copyright © 1998 by Columbia University Press. Reprinted by permission of the publisher.

guage, period setting, and thematic emphasis. Their distinctiveness lies in a different direction from the popularizing and sensationalist impulses that lay behind Welles's stage productions. The Shakespearean films reveal an aspect of Welles in some ways diametrically opposed to his democratic, populist tendencies: they exhibit an emphasis on self-expression that results in a radicalization of style, in a singular, uncompromising personal cinematic practice. Starting with *Lady from Shanghai* (1948)—some might say with *Citizen Kane* (1941)—Welles made films that, in their violation of the basic norms of Hollywood filmmaking practice, were always dangerously on the edge of putting off audiences rather than inviting them in.

That film versions of Shakespeare's plays could draw on audiences of sufficient size to justify their production seems to have been an article of faith for filmmakers from almost the beginnings of the cinema, but it was a faith sorely and continuously tested. Paradoxically, perhaps, the most active period of film/Shakespeare collaboration was the silent era: Shakespeare without words—or, at least, without spoken words—did not seem to be a contradiction in terms. But why should the movies have been interested in Shakespeare at all? In the very earliest days of film, one might argue, following Lawrence Levine,[2] Shakespeare was still positioned at a cultural crossroads, or at least could still be claimed as disputed territory, no longer truly popular as he seems to have been in the nineteenth century, but not yet fully co-opted for highbrow culture. At the turn of the century, as Pearson and Uricchio have observed, "Shakespeare may have been far more accessible to a diverse spectrum of viewers than may be apparent from a late twentieth-century perspective."[3] Furthermore, Shakespeare's plays could be reduced, by what might be called a process of "retroadaptation," to the relatively simple tales and brief narratives from which many of them had been initially drawn: stripped of most of its language, a Shakespearean adaptation frequently reverts, intentionally or not, to an adaptation of Shakespeare's source. A one-reel (approximately twelve-minute) or two-reel version of a Shakespearean play is thus perhaps not as ludicrous as it sounds. Indeed, such a film would naturally be congruent with the "key phrase, key scene, key image approach to Shakespeare"[4] that seems to have been popular during the early part of the century.

With the advent of sound in the late 1920s, at least one more reason for Hollywood's interest in Shakespeare, one already implicit in the silent era, becomes paramount: cultural respectability for a medium under increasing attack from censors and moral arbiters of various stripes. As Graham Holderness remarks, "The repute of cinema art and of the film industry can be enhanced by their capacity to incorporate Shakespeare; the institution of Shakespeare itself benefits from that transaction by a confirmation of its persistent universality."[5] Warner Brothers' *A Midsummer Night's Dream* (1935)—the first major Shakespearean film of the sound era—can be seen, at least in part, as a response to the controversies leading to the establishment of the Production Code Administration, whose edicts were formulated in 1930 but did not become enforceable until 1934.[6] Another impulse, of course, was simply the presence of the famous German stage director Max Reinhardt in Hollywood, itself a consequence of Hitler's rise to power in Germany: Warner's film was a refurbishing of Reinhardt's frequently revived peripatetic stage production, which had most recently been mounted, with Mickey Rooney as Puck and Olivia de Havilland as Hermia, in the Hollywood Bowl, an outdoor amphitheater. The casting strategies of the film—Rooney once again as Puck and de Havilland as Hermia, James Cagney as Bottom, Joe E. Brown as Flute, and Dick Powell as Lysander—together with Mendelssohn's music and Vera Zorina's choreography, as well as the two credited directors, Reinhardt and William Dieterle, suggest that Shakespeare was still seen as somehow balanced between popularity and propriety; or perhaps the filmmakers believed they were reproducing the original conditions of the theater as a social institution in Shakespeare's time: something for the groundlings and something for the "better sort." The film was, in any case, promoted as a "class act" at the same time that Warner undoubtedly hoped for a popular success.

With MGM's *Romeo and Juliet* the following year, "class" seems to have taken over almost entirely, the casting of Andy Devine as the nurse's servant, Peter, being one of the few remnants of Warner's approach. Interestingly, it was in part the recent Broadway (and national tour) success of the Katharine Cornell *Romeo and Juliet,* in which Welles had notably participated, that had given MGM the impetus for a film version.[7] Shakespeare, after a long dry spell, was once again box office, at least in New York, as Welles's "voodoo" *Macbeth* and "fascist" *Julius Caesar* would continue to demonstrate. (Ironically, Basil Rathbone, Cornell's Romeo, appears as Tybalt in the film, the role Welles had been "demoted" to, in his case from Mercutio, when the Cornell production had opened on Broadway at the end of its national tour.) Fully conscious of the cultural significance of its production, MGM sponsored an elaborate and attractive tie-in book to accompany the film's release. In spite of the publicity—much of it free—both *A Midsummer Night's Dream* and *Romeo and Juliet* generated, however, neither film enjoyed the kind of commercial success that would encourage further experiments along the same line, and Hollywood pretty much ignored Shakespeare for the next decade or so. The Shakespearean films of Welles and Laurence Olivier would initiate another round of interest in Shakespearean adaptation, an interest that would speak to the international film culture that came to the fore in the late fifties and early sixties, with Italian, Soviet, and Japanese filmmakers bringing a new and distinctive approach to filmed Shakespeare.

In addition to these social and cultural considerations, filmmakers seem to have believed—as numerous commentators have subsequently asserted—that Shakespeare's plays are in some essential way "cinematic." Unlike the modern dramatists, so the argument goes, Shakespeare, like other Elizabethan playwrights, builds up his actions in brief scenes and organizes both time and space in an extremely fluid fashion: *Antony and Cleopatra*, for one notable instance, has over forty scenes and its action covers some ten years. Shakespeare is thus naturally suited to the cinema.[8] Actually, of course, the analogy is not really apropos, for it emphasizes what are in fact only incidental properties of both Shakespeare and the film medium. The essence of Shakespeare's dramaturgy can have only a tangential relationship to these rather obvious dramatic conventions. Besides, many of Shakespeare's plays involve very few locations and take place in a quite short period of time: *Twelfth Night*, *Othello*, and *The Tempest* quickly come to mind. More to the point, Shakespeare's plays actually unfold in no specific place at all, at least in no place that needs to be specified or particularized. *Antony and Cleopatra* can move from Egypt to Rome and back quite easily because those places are defined metaphorically rather than materially.[9] Shakespeare's plays are set, literally and figuratively, in an essentially bare, abstract performing area, far removed from the concrete, detailed "realism" the cinema very early on discovered to be one of its major resources and attractions.

The analogy between Shakespeare's plays and film also lacks conviction when considered from the film side as well. Although it is a popularly held conviction that film depends on rapid movement from place to place together with a unique ability to expand, compress, or in a variety of ways distort time, neither of these factors is necessary to film. The error comes from confusing what is possible for a given medium with what is essential to it. All that can truly be said to be essential to the cinema is its mechanism: the camera, lights, projector, celluloid, and all the other paraphernalia required to produce that which we finally see projected in front of us. The supposed affinity between Shakespeare's plays and film simply does not hold up, which may at least help us to understand why Shakespearean films have always fallen short of the theory that would make such films inevitably successful.

In one of the first important studies of Shakespeare and film, Jack Jorgens described some of the traditional ways Shakespearean adaptations have been categorized in terms of stylistic modes and approaches: the "theatrical," the "realistic," and the "filmic." The theatrical mode "uses film as a transparent medium" to "capture the essence of a theatrical performance"; the realistic mode "'takes advantage of the camera's unique ability to show us *things*—great, sweeping landscapes or the corner of a friar's cell, a teeming marketplace or the intimacy of a boudoir, all in the flash of a moment'";[10] and the filmic mode demonstrates what he calls the work of the "film poet, whose works bear the same relation to the surfaces of reality that poems do to ordinary

Figure 4. Orson Welles and cast in Macbeth *(1948).* Museum of Modern Art.

conversation."[11] Immediate objections can be raised to this scheme, of
course: no medium is transparent; realism cannot be so easily defined;
all films are, by definition, filmic. Jorgens, who presents these categories
without embracing them, is the first to admit that "good Shakespeare
films often move fluidly between modes and styles, merge several simultaneously, so that it is not possible to make simple judgments."[12] These
categories, nonetheless, can help point to distinct elements in each of
Welles's films: *Macbeth* as "theatrical," *Chimes at Midnight* as "realistic," and *Othello* as "filmic."

   These primarily formal strategies are closely related to the distinct production histories of each of Welles's Shakespeare films. With
Macbeth, the unlikely sponsor (Republic Pictures, known primarily for
its cliff-hanger serials and B westerns), the modest budget, and the brief
(three-week) production schedule, all encouraged Welles to adopt an enclosed, claustrophobic, highly set-oriented, long-take method of filming.
The look and mood of this film—the papier-mâché sets, the tackily incon-

sistent costumes, the wide-angle and deep-focus photography, the wildly variable quality of style and performance—can be seen to have had their origin in the means of production even while they serve to express Welles's vision of Shakespeare's play. In adapting *Macbeth*, Welles, in the words of Lorne Buchman, "shortened the play by two-thirds, cut entire scenes, excised characters, added others, [and] rearranged what remained of the play."[13] Welles constructed a deliberately deglamorized world for Macbeth; the whole production has a lean and hungry look. The film's style, rightly described as "expressionistic,"[14] has analogues to films like Edgar G. Ulmer's *Detour* (1945) and William Cameron Menzies' *Invaders from Mars* (1953), both of which employ expressionist techniques in part as a defense against minimal budgets. Although *Macbeth* was not, like *Detour*, a bottom-drawer production, Welles employed a B picture approach in order to keep what would have been a potentially expensive film within reasonable bounds.

The very different style evident in *Othello* in part derives from a very different production context. Rather than working within a preset, clearly defined budget and within the institutional constraints of a specific studio or production organization, Welles had at his disposal varying amounts of money over several years. Reflecting Welles's peripatetic existence as a Hollywood outsider and exile from America, *Othello* exhibits evidence of having been filmed in different locations at different times, even within a single scene. In contrast to the claustrophobic unity of *Macbeth*, *Othello* appears open and fundamentally fragmented in terms of both time and space. Welles, once again, drastically cuts and rearranges Shakespeare's text, eliminating, for example, virtually all of Iago's self-justifying soliloquies. He creates a sound design that has the effect of making what dialogue remains difficult to follow. His methods result in an "opening up" of one of Shakespeare's most tightly constructed plays. If the visual style of *Macbeth* has affinities with the Hollywood B movie, the visual style of *Othello* finds its affinities in the European art cinema tradition.

With *Chimes at Midnight* we have a production history that can be conceived of as a kind of composite of those of the other two films. As with *Macbeth*, Welles was working within a reasonably firm, limited budget and a precisely delineated, albeit more generous, time frame. The filming itself was restricted in terms of space as well: a few Spanish locations and an equally restricted number of studio sets. And, as he had with *Macbeth*, Welles had at his disposal, and drew on, a recent theatrical production of the same material. As with *Othello*, on the other hand, Welles was working outside the dominant Anglo-American traditions of Shakespearean production. The entire film was produced in Spain, and the casting included Spanish, French, and other European performers, along with established Shakespeareans such as John Gielgud (Henry IV) and Ralph Richardson (narrator). As with *Othello*, Welles therefore relied heavily on dubbing non-English-speaking actors, frequently with his own voice. Even more drastically than with *Othello*, Welles also chose to deemphasize the linguistic dimension of Shakespeare and to rely more on visual equivalents to the written text.

In both *Othello* and *Chimes at Midnight*, Welles's effectual de-stabilization of narrative form, thematic consistency, and unity of char-acter is carried out to an extent that it can resemble incoherence. On the one hand, Welles restructures Shakespeare's plays so as to present us with the ending at the beginning—particularly in *Othello*, which opens with the funerals of Othello and Desdemona, but also in the opening of *Chimes*, where we can see and hear the aged Shallow and Falstaff speak-ing lines from the fourth act of *Henry IV, Part II;* he then proceeds, on the other hand, to construct in each film a narrative that precisely fails to explain what the initial scene has shown us. The need for explication is much stronger in *Othello*, and in both films an implicit, intricate act of closure is gradually revealed by the end of the narrative not to be clo-sure at all. In these late Shakespearean films (perhaps in all his films), Welles resists the sense of inevitability, of the already done, that critics of mass culture like Adorno have sometimes identified as the essence of cinema.[15]

Another way of understanding the differences between Welles's three films would be to suggest that each reproduces in formal terms the central thematics of the Shakespearean text upon which it is founded. In *Macbeth* the mise-en-scène and photography combine to recreate the self-enclosed and self-referential world of its protagonists. *Othello*, filmed with off-kilter camera angles, discontinuous editing, elliptical sound bridges, and vertiginous compositions, plays out the growing disorienta-tion that becomes the focus of Othello's experience in Cyprus. *Chimes at Midnight* articulates the essential dynamics of the Hal-Falstaff rela-tionship through a style that emphasizes the physicality of the body and at the same time separates out distinctly opposed spaces through a mise-en-scène that contrasts the court and tavern worlds. Eschewing both the artificially "theatrical" space of *Macbeth* and the essentially naturalistic and geographically identifiable world of *Othello*, *Chimes* opts for a style less dependent either on the manipulation of obvious artifice or on the foregrounding of formal cinematic techniques than its predecessors.

As an alternative to Jorgens's primarily stylistic distinctions, Shake-spearean films in general could be categorized by pointing to the materi-al circumstances of their production. To simplify matters somewhat, we could identify two basic types: those made from the center and those made at the margins. The former merge the cultural authority of Shakespeare with institutional support, whether commercial (major stu-dio), governmental (Kosintsev's *Hamlet and King Lear*, for instance), or both (Olivier's *Henry V*). In these works the cultural authority is both assumed and reinforced: the performance of Shakespeare's text is simultaneously an affirmation of the value and status of that text. The marginal films, among which Welles's figure prominently, challenge, or at least qualify, the cultural supremacy of Shakespeare by, to one extent or another, pushing the source text toward its own margins or by revealing, through the film's low-budget strategies and absence of gloss and finish, the fragmentary and tentative authority of the original. As we have been relearning in the past few decades, Shakespeare's plays themselves, as they have come down to us, can be defined as extremely unstable texts, never entirely "finished," works in progress, playhouse documents, even sketchy blueprints for an edifice that we can never satisfactorily reconstruct. But this, needless to say, is not the image of Shakespeare as he is understood in the larger culture. When Kenneth Branagh's *Hamlet* (1996) is publicized as including the full, original text, what is ignored is that we have no way of knowing precisely what the original text is. Branagh's film, for all its virtues, presents a Shakespeare in full high-Victorian garb—a Shakespeare that Sir Henry Irving and Sir Herbert Beerbohm-Tree would have been proud to produce. Welles, on the other hand, presents a Shakespeare from hunger—what we might term, paraphrasing Jerzy Grotowski, a "poor" Shakespeare.

No film in commercial release, one must concede, could ever be as "poor" as a theater presentation can be: Welles's Shakespearean films were not precisely cheap (though they were cheaper than most): I am referring, rather, to certain stylistic considerations and production circumstances that give us a "poverty effect" (just as, in Roland Barthes's terms, specific narrative devices and techniques can give us a "reality effect").[16] Although a long take, as with the ten-minutes-plus take of the murder of Duncan in Welles's *Macbeth*, may serve a variety of useful purposes, it registers as an effect of minimal resources: Welles filmed the scene that way, some viewers will assume, in order to save money. Actually, long-take filming can be just as time-consuming, and hence expensive, as breaking the scene down into numerous setups, but the impression of cheapness and speed is what I am getting at here. The obvious absence of synchronous sound in so much of *Othello* and *Chimes at Midnight* provides the viewer with a similar projection of this "poverty effect." And Welles, as the record clearly shows, did cut corners in his Shakespearean films, employing, for example, stand-ins for reverse shots simply because he could afford to hold onto his actors only for brief periods of time. My point is simply that Welles's Shakespeare films, as marginal products, are not surrounded by the same aura of class and respectability that surrounds most Shakespearean adaptations.

Welles's Shakespearean trilogy is comparable in ambition if not in effect to the trilogies of Laurence Olivier, Franco Zeffirelli, and Kenneth Branagh. In contrast to Welles, however, Olivier and Branagh project, in different ways, issues of national purpose and national identity:

"Britishness" of one sort or another. Olivier's films—especially *Henry V* —are intimately linked to Shakespeare's unmatched place in English history and culture as well as to his high value as a cultural export. Branagh, although—as a Belfast boy—ostensibly reacting against the very English, respectful, traditional attitude Olivier supposedly brings to Shakespeare, nevertheless falls rather easily into what Harold Bloom would term the "anxiety of influence." He surrounds himself with paternal and maternal figures drawn from the great tradition of British Shakespeare—John Gielgud, Paul Scofield, Derek Jacobi, Judi Dench—while he makes a gesture toward a more international Shakespeare by casting, usually in minor roles, such Americans as Denzel Washington, Keanu Reeves (in *Much Ado About Nothing*, 1993), Jack Lemmon, Billy Crystal, and Robin Williams (in *Hamlet*). Both Olivier and Branagh provide, albeit in somewhat different ways, an official Shakespeare. As John Collick notes, "Most people have been brought up to equate Shakespeare with great British actresses and actors dressed in period costumes and speaking in mellifluous accents."[17] The films of Olivier and Branagh, though they reveal specific and distinctive cultural and formal strategies and styles of their own (Olivier draws from art-historical design in *Henry V*, Freudian theory in *Hamlet*, televisual staging in *Richard III*; Branagh associates King Henry V with Tim Burton's *Batman*), are also intimately associated with the establishment British Shakespeare of the Old Vic (Olivier) and the Royal Shakespeare Company (Branagh) insofar as the genesis of their films comes from previous stage productions and from the iconography of the classical British acting fraternity.

Zeffirelli's Shakespearean films would seem to offer a specifically European approach in that the Italian director inherits his style simultaneously from a neorealist film aesthetic and from opera, so that, especially in *Taming of the Shrew* (1966) and *Romeo and Juliet* (1968), we are presented with a carefully observed, highly detailed material world in conjunction with a sweeping romantic tone underlined by a strong emphasis on music and spectacle. Zeffirelli, however, exhibits almost as much of the traditions of British Shakespeare as he does a more specifically Italian one; he has, after all, spent a good part of his working life in England, directing Shakespeare and opera on the London stage, and he has expressed his admiration for Olivier's Shakespearean films.[18] As a result, Zeffirelli's Shakespearean productions have something of the air of "Euro-pudding" about them: the variety of influences and the emphasis on spectacle do not add up to anything like a stylistic unity. By the time of *Hamlet* (1990), most traces of neorealism and opera have disappeared, and in spite of his location filming, he produces a Shakespearean film that has more in common (in its mise-en-scène, at least, especially costumes and setting) with Victorian and Edwardian stage productions than with his two earlier films, at the same time that the casting of Mel Gibson and Glenn Close, together with an orthodox group of British

Shakespeareans, has obvious appeal for a primarily Anglo-American market.

To place Welles's Shakespearean films in their specific cinema-historical contexts, we can compare the circumstances of their production with the nearly simultaneous Shakespearean films of Laurence Olivier, Akira Kurosawa, and Sergei Yutkevitch. Olivier's *Henry V* (1944), *Hamlet* (1948), and *Richard III* (1955) were all financed by the two major British producers J. Arthur Rank and Alexander Korda, with significant governmental encouragement and institutional support. Each film was conceived of as a prestige production expected to bring honor and, hopefully, some American dollars, to Great Britain. Each film (especially *Hamlet*) was provided by its distributor with a carefully orchestrated publicity campaign. *Hamlet* was released in the United States under the auspices of the prestigious Theatre Guild, a highly unusual step by that organization. Handsome illustrated booklets were prepared as press kits, and *Hamlet* generated not one, but two, lavishly illustrated hardcover volumes, one of which included both Shakespeare's play and Olivier's script.[19] *Richard III* had its U.S. premiere on NBC television in 1956, an event publicized as a significant cultural moment both for Shakespeare and for television, and one that returned a quick half million dollars to Olivier's backers.

Kurosawa's *Throne of Blood* (1957), an adaptation of *Macbeth*—and a film that is often pointed to as an ideal Shakespearean adaptation in spite (because?) of the fact that it does not include on its sound track a single word written by Shakespeare—was produced, distributed, and exhibited under, once again, highly favorable conditions. As an "art cinema" artifact, *Throne of Blood* received extensive cultural support; it was embraced by Shakespeareans in part because its translation to another medium was so complete that comparisons to the original could be made in general rather than specific terms. Yutkevitch's *Othello* (1955) was produced at a government-run studio and was the product of a cultural moment when the Soviets, partially freed from the shadow of Stalin, were in the process of redefining their relationship to culture in general and to the West in particular.[20] Significantly, none of these "successful" Shakespearean films reached a large enough popular audience so as to make a lot of money (an accomplishment perhaps more tricky than Bernstein [Everett Sloane], in *Citizen Kane*, quite realized). The undoubted critical success of a number of these films has served to obscure the fact that they were either barely profitable or not profitable at all, their seeming popularity artificially inflated by careful handling and publicity. Though Olivier's *Hamlet* ran in New York for over a year, it played at one theater only and hence could never generate large grosses. And even though an estimated 62.5 million people saw *Richard III* on television, Olivier's film still lost money.[21]

Welles's approach to filming Shakespeare may be more closely related to the circumstances of early modern theatrical practice than are those of the more orthodox projects of his contemporaries. In a very real sense, as a number of critics have recently emphasized, Shakespeare's plays themselves flourished first in the actual margins of Tudor and Stuart cultures, at the edges of the city of London proper. "The popular theatre in particular . . . was a threateningly liminal space, whose 'mingling of kings and clowns' . . . blurred a whole range of distinctions, evoking the specter of adulterating, crossbreeding, and hybridity."[22] Welles's Shakespearean films, regarded in this light, are part of a counter-tradition of Shakespeare, what might be thought of as "Shakespeare from the provinces," a tradition that includes amateur and school productions, abbreviated texts, "foreign" (i.e., non-Anglo-Saxon) stagings— almost any Shakespeare taking place outside the theater capitals of London (including London and Ontario) and New York. These forms of "derivative creativity," to employ Michael Bristol's term,[23] have, in fact, always been around: Shakespeare's own company engaged in provincial performance, employed severely cut texts, performed in makeshift acting spaces, and so forth.

Welles's Shakespearean films could be further marginalized as provincial in the sense that they are products of an American sensibility. Actually, there is very little that can be characterized as specifically American about Welles's approaches to Shakespeare's texts; the films combine traces of Hollywood genre elements (this is particularly true of *Macbeth*) with European art cinema practices. The marginal status of these films lies precisely in a simultaneous awareness and incorporation of the "great tradition" of British Shakespeare (Gielgud and Richardson in *Chimes*, for example) and a decisive movement away from the center. This is precisely what is meant by marginal: not outside the circle, but at the edges of it, reaching simultaneously toward the center and outside the line. Even *Othello*, which might seem most divorced from theater practice, is not innocent of theatrical traditions. Having Roderigo and Iago witness the elopement of Othello and Desdemona is an interpolation that goes back at least to Oscar Ashe's London production in 1907; Welles makes much of having based his visual design on the work of the Renaissance painter Carpaccio, but Beerbohm Tree did the same in 1912; in the nineteenth century the French actor Charles Fechter, playing in London, made use of a mirror to emphasize Othello's growing consciousness of racial difference, and a mirror figures prominently in Welles's film.[24]

Perhaps because Welles appears to have one foot in each camp, to be both at the center and at the periphery, practitioners of cultural studies and various other modes of poststructuralism have been hesitant to embrace his Shakespearean films. The discourse surrounding *Othello* is particularly telling: in at least four recent studies (by Vaughan, Donaldson, Collick, and Hodgdon), Welles's *Othello* has been taken to task for being insufficiently sensitive to issues of race and gender. I will not consider the race question here. The gender argument, it seems to me, is founded on little more than dubious assumptions concerning Welles's personal life and the difficulties surrounding the production of the film that have scant force as evidence. Vaughan, for example, writes: "Constructed by a male auteur who was known to have difficulty in his own relationships with women, Welles's *Othello* fetishes the female body and demonstrates the tyranny of the male gaze"; Collick claims that "the protracted search for an actress to play Desdemona hints at an indecisiveness on Welles's part and an inability to come to terms with the sexual implications of the Othello-Desdemona relationship in the film"; Donaldson supports a psychoanalytic point in this fashion: "The emphasis on the failure of the beloved's eyes to return an anxious gaze in a reassuring way may draw on Welles's memory of his dying mother's eyes"; and Barbara Hodgdon, apropos of *Filming Othello*, Welles's 1978 documentary, finds that "not only is [the film] organized as a series of male conversations or monologues, with Welles . . . at its center; but none of the three Desdemonas who worked on the film [i.e., *Othello*] appears to tell her story."[25] These comments perhaps reveal, as much as anything else, the limits of contextual criticism.

In spite as well as because of the marginal nature of Welles's Shakespearean films, they undeniably provide a more challenging reading of the plays and, not incidentally, a more useful pedagogic tool than, for example, the vast majority of the BBC-Time Life Shakespearean plays. Whereas the latter are far more "faithful" to the texts of Shakespeare than are any of Welles's films, with a few notable exceptions they are also, in their bland refusal to explore interpretive possibilities and to challenge theatrical (or even televisual) orthodoxies, dead on arrival. But because the BBC versions have the aura of "official" Shakespeare and because the videos have been aggressively marketed to schools and colleges worldwide, they have filled a significant pedagogic niche. If, however, the goal is to challenge viewers to think about Shakespeare rather than simply absorb the plays passively, Welles's films provide a far more useful model.[26] The gaps, omissions, and quirks of Welles's texts call for some kind of answering intelligence, a challenge to either Welles or Shakespeare. Although John Collick can claim that a film like Welles's *Othello* (or Derek Jarman's *The Tempest*, 1979) is "as institutionalized within the economy of commercial cinema as any other movie," thereby ironing out rather significant differences in production, distribution, and exhibition, he nevertheless recognizes that "it is in these fragmented and contradictory movies that the coherence and apparent consensus over what constitutes culture, Shakespeare, and film, breaks down to reveal an uncertain and grotesque vision of society and social relationships."[27] Welles's films, to put the matter somewhat differently, are unlikely to be perceived as definitive versions of the Shakespearean texts from which they derive.[28]

Welles's Shakespeare films, as we will see, have been more celebrated in Europe than in England and North America, in part because they place less emphasis on language and in part because the theatrical understanding of Shakespeare in Europe—and here I am thinking of such venues as the Deutsches Theater (Berlin), the Piccolo Teatro (Milan), and the Théâtre de Soleil (Vincennes)—is far bolder and more experimental, more playful and elastic, than the equivalent venues in Great Britain and North America. As Dennis Kennedy has observed,

> the authoritative and thorough-going rethinkings of the plays we associate with Leopold Jessner or Giorgio Strehler or Ariane Mnouchkine have not occurred to the same degree in the home countries. Even Peter Brook, reinventing the plays in English since 1945, has done his most radical work on Shakespeare in French.[29]

At the same time, of course, it needs to be acknowledged that Shakespeare has a rather different cultural status in Europe, that his plays are often presented in modern translations, and that French cinéastes, in particular, are less likely to be familiar with Shakespeare's original text than are most English-speaking reviewers and critics. No European critic, in short, is likely to be bothered by the fact that Welles, like many of the producers of Shakespeare in non-English-speaking countries, has virtually translated Shakespeare into another idiom.

Welles's Shakespearean films, in short, circulate more clearly within a range of European postwar appropriations of Shakespeare than they do within an Anglo-American tradition of Shakespearean performance. Or, perhaps more accurately, they exhibit, as do many contemporary Shakespearean productions, "a tension between a decentering aesthetic and the desire to retain the plays as touchstones of traditional Western culture."[30] Bringing the witches back at the very end of his film of *Macbeth*, which echoes the similar employment of voodoo drums in the Harlem *Macbeth* in 1936, may not have been an interpretive invention on Welles's part, but it is a strategy that has been latterly associated[31] with the theatrical influence of Samuel Beckett and the critical influence of Polish critic Jan Kott; the ending of Polish-born director Roman Polanski's 1971 film of *Macbeth*, which shows us Malcolm's younger brother, Donalbain, drawn to an encounter with the witches just as his older brother is being crowned king of Scotland, makes the point explicit, but it was already implicit in Welles's film.

European cinephiles, furthermore, who were quick to enshrine Welles in a pantheon of auteurs, easily incorporated the Shakespeare films into the Wellesian cinema, recognizing in them themes and dramatic emphases present as well in *Citizen Kane, The Magnificent Ambersons, The Stranger, Lady from Shanghai, Touch of Evil,* and *Mr. Arkadin*: the destructive consequence of power, even when employed in a just cause; the inevitability of betrayal; the loss of paradise. All of these films are, in their own way, Shakespearean texts, if in no other sense than in the way they impose a large, poetic intensity on questions of family and domesticity and thus wed the social with the personal. So Henri Lemaitre, for example, could write: "Perhaps the most Shakespearean film in the history of the cinema is not one of those drawn from his works, but rather a creation of the most Shakespearean of the masters of the camera, Orson Welles—the film, *The Lady from Shanghai*."[32] In the specific context of a discussion of *Touch of Evil*, Robin Wood has captured the general affinities between Welles and Shakespeare by pointing to "the efforts to create a visual-poetic world equivalent to the 'world' of a Shakespearean tragedy; in the constant reaching out for a tragic weight and grandeur; in the attempts to find a cinematic style that will fulfill a creative function analogous to that of Shakespeare's verse." (Wood, however, suggests that *Touch of Evil* may be closer in spirit to Shakespeare's near-contemporary John Webster, "in whose plays the Elizabethan creative energies degenerate into morbidity and decadence.")[33] What Welles's films and Shakespeare's plays perhaps share most directly, apart from their interest in power relations, is a compelling evocation of evil as something at once attractive and horrifying, both in terms of its appeal to characters within the fiction and to audiences outside of it.

Whether produced at the center or from the margins, however, one thing is certain: Shakespearean films, as Welles was no doubt aware, have seldom been big box office. Only such a presumption explains the methods he employed to produce *Macbeth* at Republic: a low budget was all that could justify making a Shakespearean film at all. That Welles returned to Shakespeare twice again, and planned other projects along the way, shows a tenacity quite divorced from sound business acumen. If Warner Brothers and MGM were not able to succeed with Shakespeare, who could? Certainly the conjunction of Shakespeare and Welles's modernist, avant-garde, and even postmodern cinematic practice was almost guaranteed to produce films of narrow commercial appeal. Welles made few concessions, in these films, to the requirements of popularity. After *Macbeth* he was working completely outside mainstream Hollywood and had gone over, willingly or not, into the European personal cinema, a cinema that was poised to make an extraordinary cultural, though never truly popular, international impact. This picture is complicated, however, by Welles's having positioned himself, or been positioned, as an international maverick during much of the period in question. His limited access to more or less standard modes of production, distribution, and exhibition severely compromised his European films, which were often financed by dubious speculators, processed in not always reliable labs, and released in piecemeal fashion by organizations and people ill suited to the task.

Welles's Shakespearean films, in other words, were not rationalized productions, even when compared not to Hollywood, but, more appropriately, to the international art cinema of the 1950s. It is worth noting, in this context, that the important European and international auteurs who came to prominence in the 1950s—Ingmar Bergman, Federico Fellini, and Akira Kurosawa, notably—made films that were produced, distributed, and exhibited under comparatively ideal conditions, either because of government subsidy (Bergman), major studio backing (Kurosawa), or, with Fellini, a film industry enjoying, by the end of the 1950s, a renaissance both in terms of prestige and commercial popularity that allowed it to support offbeat projects. These highly individualistic filmmakers did not, for the most part, have to struggle to find minimum financing, essential facilities, or sympathetic distributors. Welles, on the other hand, in each of the three instances in which he adapted Shakespeare to film, did so within formal constraints that virtually demanded as well as allowed an expressionist, highly fragmented solution to the questions posed by the Shakespearean text.

Hollywood's earlier experiences with Shakespeare, in other words, would have suggested both to Welles and to Republic Studios that, given the size of the potential market for Shakespeare on film, containing costs was the crucial issue. Welles knew that filming Shakespeare successfully in Hollywood would involve creative production techniques. The desire to see Welles's *Macbeth* as originating from a conflict between the commercial imperatives of Hollywood, on the one hand, and the aesthetic aspirations of the artist-genius, on the other, thus needs to be resisted. Welles was just as sensitive as studio head Herbert J. Yates and producer Charles K. Feldman to commercial values, even if he was often unable or unwilling to turn that knowledge into practice. Welles's purpose in filming *Macbeth* at a studio known primarily for its low-budget movies was precisely to demonstrate that a financially successful adaptation of Shakespeare could be made in Hollywood. The conflict, in other words, was not over whether Shakespeare could be transformed into popular art, but over how best to accomplish that goal. Welles and Republic were both, in their own ways, attempting to reach a large, popular audience for Shakespearean films.

By the time of *Othello* and *Chimes at Midnight*, the project I ascribed to Welles at the outset of this study—reconciling Shakespeare (high culture) with popular culture—was no longer viable. Neither film is "accessible" in the way the earlier *Macbeth*—at some point in time—was meant to be. Indeed, the motives behind the 1992 "restoration" of *Othello* (and the plans to "restore" *Chimes at Midnight*), I argue, testify to the irreconcilable differences between these Shakespearean films and the popular audience one might hope to discover for them. An ironic reversal takes place here. Shakespeare, essentially a popular artist, is rescued by Welles from the late nineteenth-century high classicism that had threatened to imprison and limit him, had threatened to turn him, in Gary Taylor's words, into "the badge of cultural elitism and the instrument of pedagogical oppression,"[34] but in the process the sixteenth-century playwright now becomes a distinctly modernist figure. The deconstruction Welles performs on Shakespeare's *Othello* and "Henriad" plays (and, to a lesser extent, on *Macbeth*) produces a series of irresolutions and complexities that elucidate and sharpen the tensions already present in Shakespeare while at the same time undermining the narrative and structural foundations of Shakespeare's dramaturgy.

Macbeth, Othello, and *Chimes at Midnight* have been well served by much recent attention paid both to Welles and to the filming of Shakespeare. Among a number of outstanding discussions, I would select those by James Naremore and Anthony Davies on *Macbeth,* Jack Jorgens, Peter Donaldson, and Lorne Buchman on *Othello,* and Joseph McBride and Samuel Crowl on *Chimes at Midnight.*[35] Bernice Kliman and Barbara Hodgdon, in their volumes in the Shakespeare in Performance series, have provided extremely useful estimates of, respectively, *Macbeth* and *Chimes at Midnight* within the context of performance histories.[36] Welles's Shakespearean films are very much part of the recent cultural debates on Shakespeare's "transcendent" value versus his role in maintaining and justifying what Terence Hawkes has usefully termed "Bardbiz,"[37] a debate that posits Shakespeare either as "an alternative to the culture industry" or as "simply one of its more successful products,"[38] a paradoxical space that Welles himself, partly because of his Shakespearean films, continues to occupy.

NOTES

1. Theodor W. Adorno, "Culture and Administration," in *The Culture Industry,* ed. Bernstein, (London: Routledge, 1991), p. 102.

2. Lawrence W. Levine, *Highbrow/Lowbrow: The Emergence of Cultural Hierarchy in America* (Cambridge: Harvard University Press, 1988).

3. Roberta E. Pearson and William Uricchio, "How Many Times Shall Caesar Bleed in Sport," *Screen* 31:3 (Autumn 1990), p. 248.

4. Ibid., p. 258.

5. Graham Holderness, "Radical Potentiality and Institutional Closure: Shakespeare in Film and Television," in *Political Shakespeare: New Essays in Cultural Materialism,* ed. Jonathan Dollimore and Alan Sinfield (Ithaca: Cornell University Press, 1985), p. 182.

6. "The movie was produced as a conscious exercise in prestige building, not necessarily with any cynical motive but rather as an attempt to consolidate Warner's reputation as a socially responsible company with both the public and the Hays Office." See John Collick, *Shakespeare, Cinema, and Society* (Manchester, UK: Manchester University Press, 1989), p. 83.

7. Tad Mosel with Gertrude Macy, *Leading Lady: The World and Theatre of Katharine Cornell* (Boston: Little, Brown, 1978), pp. 387–88.

8. So, for example, Roger Manvell writes that Shakespeare constructed "his plays in a manner which closely resembles the structure of a screenplay." Manvell, *Shakespeare and the Film* (New York: Praeger, 1971), p. 9.

9. In the Arden edition of *Antony and Cleopatra,* editor M. R. Ridley writes of the necessity of "becoming accustomed, in Shakespeare and other Elizabethan drama, to 'non-

localised' scenes—some characters meet 'somewhere' to transact some necessary business of the play, and where the 'somewhere' is may often be of small importance" (Cambridge: Harvard University Press, 1954), p. xix.

10. Jorgens is here quoting from Arthur Knight, "Three Problems in Film Adaptation," *Saturday Review* (18 December 1954), p. 26.

11. Jack J. Jorgens, *Shakespeare on Film* (Bloomington: Indiana University Press, 1977), pp. 7–10.

12. Ibid., p. 15.

13. Lorne M. Buchman, *Still in Movement: Shakespeare on Screen* (New York: Oxford University Press, 1991), p. 6.

14. See James Naremore, "The Walking Shadow: Welles's Expressionist *Macbeth*," *Literature/Film Quarterly* 1:4 (Fall 1973), pp. 360–66.

15. "Certainly every finished work of art is already predetermined in some way but art strives to overcome its own oppressive weight as an artefact through the force of its very construction. Mass culture on the other hand simply identifies with the curse of predetermination and joyfully fulfils it." Theodor W. Adorno, "The Schema of Mass Culture," in Bernstein, *The Culture Industry*, pp. 53–84 (quotation on p. 62). Welles's entire career could be read as a refusal to accept that predetermination.

16. See Roland Barthes, "The Reality Effect," in *The Rustle of Language*, trans. Richard Howard (New York: Hill & Wang, 1986), pp. 141–48.

17. Collick, *Shakespeare, Cinema, and Society*, p. 60.

18. See Ace G. Pilkington, "Zeffirelli's Shakespeare," in *Shakespeare and the Moving Image*, ed. Anthony Davies and Stanley Wells (Cambridge: Cambridge University Press, 1994), pp. 165–66.

19. This tendency has been carried on by Kenneth Branagh, especially in the lavishly illustrated screenplay book *Hamlet by William Shakespeare* (New York: Norton, 1996).

20. See Laurie E. Osborne, "Filming Shakespeare in a Cultural Thaw: Soviet Appropriations of Shakespearean Treacheries in 1955–6," *Textual Practice* 9:2 (1995): 325–47.

21. Bruce Eder, liner notes, *Richard III*, dir. Laurence Olivier, 1955 (videodisk, Voyager, 1994). Kenneth Branagh's *Henry V* and *Much Ado About Nothing*, in part because of preselling to secondary markets like cable television and video, are exceptions to the rule that Shakespearean films cannot make money; Branagh's *Hamlet*, on the other hand, cost $24 million and only grossed $11.3.

22. Patricia Parker, *Shakespeare from the Margins: Language, Culture, Context*, p. 15.

23. Michael Bristol, *Big-Time Shakespeare*, (London: Routledge, 1996), p. 61.

24. These examples are drawn from Julie Hankey, ed., *Othello: Plays in Performance* (Bristol, UK: Bristol Classics Press, 1987), pp. 138, 91, and 237.

25. Virginia Mason Vaughan, *Othello: A Contextual History*, p. 200; Collick, *Shakespeare, Cinema, and Society* (Cambridge: Cambridge University Press, 1994), p. 96; Peter S. Donaldson, *Shakespearean Films/Shakespearean Directors* (Boston: Unwin Hyman, 1990), p. 124, note 18; Barbara Hodgdon, "Kiss Me Deadly; or, The Des/Demonized Spectacle," in *Othello: New Perspectives*, ed. Virginia Mason Vaughan and Kent Cartwright (Rutherford, N.J.: Fairleigh Dickinson University Press, 1991), p. 222.

26. Like the far more obviously "experimental" and "underground" Shakespeare films discussed by Graham Holderness ("Shakespeare Rewound," *Shakespeare Survey* 45 [1993], pp. 63–74), Welles's Shakespeare films, too, "can be used to challenge traditional notions and to provoke debate about some central issues of both text and performance" (p. 70).

27. Collick, *Shakespeare, Cinema, and Society*, pp. 63, 73.

28. And thus they are relatively safe from the danger articulated by James C. Bulman: "Because film and video allow us repeated viewings of a single performance, they encourage us to assimilate that performance to the condition of a literary text—a stable artifact rather than a contingent, ephemeral experience." See Bulman, "Introduction: Shakespeare and Performance Theory," in *Shakespeare, Theory, and Performance*, ed. Bulman (London: Routledge, 1996), p. 2.

29. Dennis Kennedy, ed., *Foreign Shakespeare: Contemporary Performance* (Cambridge: Cambridge University Press, 1993), p. 6.

30. Dennis Kennedy, *Looking at Shakespeare: A Visual History of Twentieth-Century Performances* (Cambridge: Cambridge University Press, 1993), p. 302.

31. Kennedy, ed., *Foreign Shakespeare*, p. 10.

32. Henri Lemaitre, "Shakespeare, the Imaginary Cinema and the Pre-cinema," in *Focus on Shakespearean Films*, ed. Charles W. Eckert (Englewood Cliffs, N.J.: Prentice-Hall, 1972), p. 36.

33. Robin Wood, "Welles, Shakespeare, and Webster," *Personal Views* (London: Gordon Fraser, 1976), pp. 136–52 (quotations from pp. 136–37, 152).

34. Gary Taylor, *Reinventing Shakespeare* (New York: Weidenfield & Nicholson, 1989), p. 384.

35. James Naremore, "The Walking Shadow" and *The Magic World of Orson Welles* (New York: Oxford University Press, 1978), chap. 5; Anthony Davies, *Filming Shakespeare's Plays* (Cambridge: Cambridge University Press, 1988), chap. 5; Jorgens, *Shakespeare on Film*, chap. 12; Donaldson, *Shakespearean Films/Shakespearean Directors*, chap. 4; Lorne Buchman, *Still in Movement* (New York: Oxford University Press, 1991), chap. 7; Joseph McBride, *Orson Welles* (New York: Viking, 1972), chap. 12; Samuel Crowl, "The Long Goodbye: Welles and Falstaff," *Shakespeare Quarterly* 31 (Autumn 1980), pp. 369–80, reprinted in *Shakespeare Observed: Studies in Performance on Stage and Screen* (Athens: Ohio University Press, 1992), chap. 3.

36. Bernice W. Kliman, *Shakespeare in Performance: Macbeth* (Manchester: Manchester University Press, 1992); Barbara Hodgdon, *Shakespeare in Performance: Henry IV, Part II* (Manchester: Manchester University Press, 1993).

37. Terence Hawkes, "Bardbiz," *London Review of Books* (22 February 1990), pp. 11–13.

38. Bristol, *Big-Time Shakespeare*, p. 109.

Matthew Bernstein

High and Low: Art Cinema and Pulp Fiction in Yokohama

The first American critics who reviewed Akira Kurosawa's *High and Low* (1963) expressed surprise that it was taken from Ed McBain's (Evan Hunter's) *King's Ransom,* a 1959 entry in the 87th Precinct series of police procedurals. McBain's novel was written and situated in a strictly American milieu, and as far as the critical establishment was concerned, it was little more than a potboiler, leading to a quite different sort of film from Kurosawa's 1957 adaptations of high art classics by Gorky (*The Lower Depths*) and Shakespeare (*Throne of Blood*). Kurosawa's distinctive style was the focus of their discussion, which reflected *High and Low*'s appearance at the height of the auteurist or international art cinema in late 1963. Although most critics appreciated the film as, in Howard Thompson's words, "a model of its genre," they chiefly admired what Thompson called Kurosawa's "chessboard groupings" of figures and his "masterful use of pure movie technique." *Time*'s critic commented that "the screen is alive with motion, choreographically precise and caught by his artist's eye in scene after scene of stunning composition." For Stanley Kauffmann of *The New Republic*, "Every camera angle, every composition, every cut, every performance, is—as far as I can see—brilliantly right. . . . The very motion of this motion picture is gratifying."[1]

To most reviewers, the McBain connection was incidental to the film's aesthetic success, and worth mentioning only in passing. Even Judith Crist, who alone seemed to have read the novel, praised *High and Low* as a movie that gives us more than the usual thriller: "two hours and twenty-three minutes of character and suspense drama, with no detail of frustration or personal sorrow or social morality omitted. We go beyond good guys and bad guys to consider the motives of both—in detail." For her, Kurosawa's "painstaking" treatment of the investigation created an unprecedented realism ("detection without glamour, suspense created by reality, a slow pacing") that was supposedly characteristic of Japanese cinema and culture.[2]

The critical reception of *High and Low* thus alternated between the two poles of interpretation that David Bordwell has described as typical of art cinema discourse: the picture was praised for its realism (as by Crist) or for its manifestations of the director's style and authorial commentary (as by everyone else).[3] The fact that it was also a brilliant genre film based on a popular novel was of little concern. Kauffmann expressed complete bewilderment as to why Kurosawa selected the McBain piece in the first place, and he compared Kurosawa's use of source material to François Truffaut's recent "semi-satiric, semi-reverential" *Shoot the Piano Player* (1962), based on *Down There* by American David Goodis. *Newsweek*'s critic dwelt at length on the irony of cinema artists' working with pulp fiction, speculating that other "modish" international directors would follow suit and make "crime pictures":

> Resnais presumably will make a film about a man who thinks he may have committed a crime; Fellini, a man planning to commit a crime; Antonioni, the crook who has lost his gun and wanders around looking for it; Bergman, the gangster who has a religious vision; Satyajit Ray will show the flowers blooming behind the hide-out.[4]

Most of Kurosawa's academic critics have responded in similar fashion, ignoring *King's Ransom* and avoiding serious discussion of *High and Low* as an adaptation. James Goodwin's admirable *Kurosawa's Intertextual Cinema* has little to say about *High and Low* at all. Donald Richie's chapter on the film in his pioneering *The Films of Akira Kurosawa* refers only briefly to the McBain novel, as does Stephen Prince's brilliant *The Warrior's Camera*. David Desser alone has explored the connection, sketching a comparison of novel and film in the concluding chapter of his seminal *The Samurai Films of Akira Kurosawa*; he also notes, in a discussion of Kurosawa's work in popular genres, that "cultural elitism" has meant that "a disproportionate amount of critical attention has been paid to films like *Rashomon* and *Throne of Blood* at the expense of films like *Sanjuro* and *High and Low*."[5]

We know that great films have come from pulp fiction: Orson Welles's *Touch of Evil* (1958), derived from Robert Wade and William Miller's *Badge of Evil*, comes most immediately to mind. Yet the discussion of such films is always conducted on auteurist grounds, as a way of showing how talented directors transcend their source material. In fact, one could argue that the French New Wave practice of recasting pop fiction into an art cinema mode was precisely designed to give the director priority over the writer. Kurosawa's decision to use an American thriller as the basis of his film is therefore, as the *Newsweek* reviewer noted, perfectly in line with the strategies of the international art cinema of his day. I would argue, however, that Kurosawa took the McBain novel just as seriously as he took Shakespeare or Gorky. In what follows, I want to support my argument by giving somewhat more attention than critics have usually done to the relationship between the novel and the film. My point is not to devalue Kurosawa, but to give McBain his due, showing how the film respects its source and at the same time adapts it to a different cultural context.

Although most of Kurosawa's academic critics reflect carefully on the director's complex combination of Japanese and Western narrative and visual traditions, discussions of *High and Low* have not considered how these same traditions might affect the film as an adaptation. Even if such matters were not relevant, any study of a story's variations—say, from novel to script draft, from draft to revision, and from revisions to finished film—provides fresh insight into the filmmaking process and the creation of meaning. In this case, although the story of *King's Ransom* takes up only the first seventy minutes of Kurosawa's film, McBain's novel offered many themes and narrational techniques that appealed to the filmmaker and his coscenarists (Ryuzo Kikushima and Hideo Oguni).[6] Their particular use of the novel also seems to reveal a process of cross-cultural adaptation whereby certain features of the source are retained while others are discarded according to a principle of cultural plausibility or resonance: in *High and Low*, for example, brash characters from the novel become taciturn in Kurosawa's hands, and the issue of individuality and the group is handled quite differently.[7] By examining the film and the novel in light of such issues, we can enrich our understanding of both texts.

It should be noted first of all that *King's Ransom* is already a highly "cinematic" piece of fiction, composed in a fast-paced, hard-boiled style, and consisting of a great deal of movielike dialogue. In its early chapters it creates dramatic situations that clearly form the basis for Kurosawa's mise-en-scène. Evan Hunter, who wrote the novel, was well known as the author of a book that had become a famous movie—*The Blackboard Jungle* (1955)—and was himself an important screenwriter who subsequently worked with Hitchcock on *The Birds* (1963). Everything he authored under the name of Ed McBain belongs to a fictional genre that is virtually inseparable from movies. The general atmosphere and narrative form of the 87th Precinct series grows out of a long tradition of post–World War II police procedurals, beginning with Jules Dassin's *Naked City* (1948) and culminating in such artful B pictures as Anthony Mann's *T-Men* (1947) and *He Walked by Night* (1948). More specifically, McBain seems to have been influenced by the conventions of naturalistic police dramas such as William Wyler's adaptation of the Sidney Kingsley play *Detective Story* (1951) and by the early episodes of the highly successful television show *Dragnet*, which give slightly more attention to the quotidian aspects of police work and provide opportunities for overt social commentary. In turn, his fiction influenced a number of later movies and television dramas. The 87th Precinct novels were eventually made into a 1972 Hollywood feature (*Fuzz*), an NBC series (*87th Precinct*), and a made-for-television movie (*Ed McBain's 87th Precinct*).

At the same time as it draws on movies, the novel exhibits considerable linguistic and literary skill, an ear for American speech, and an artistic self-conciousness about its generic sources. At one point a police detective in *King's Ransom* alludes to *Dragnet*. The wife of one of the criminals wonders, "When a gangster watches a gangster movie, does he identify with the police or with Humphrey Bogart?"[8] As she ruminates on her unfair life, the novel's omniscient narrator comments on the relation between life and film:

> What she wanted to cry now were the words that poured from the mouth of the gangster as he lay bleeding in the gutter. What she wanted to sob out was the criminal's straight-man dialogue designed as a setup for Jack Webb's devastating closing punch line. (p. 132)

The original reviewers of *King's Ransom* (all of them writing short notices for the readers of mystery novels) seemed to appreciate these qualities, and even remarked that this particular book was different from previous volumes in the series, as if it were aspiring to literature. "The tale itself forgoes McBain's customary 'procedural' mode for an inquiry into human motives," one critic commented. Pronouncing the book a "nice job," the *San Francisco Chronicle* observed that "there are more new angles to this set-up than you would think possible; mighty interesting they are, too, and more serious and plausible than some of McBain's others." The *New York Times* review agreed:

> This one's about a kidnapping, with quite a number of fresh variations on the Big Snatch theme. It's as immediate and convincing as any of the 87th Precinct tales, and a little more (in the best sense) theatrical than most. . . . One looks forward to a dramatic version that might be even more so.[9]

Whether or not the novel surpasses its genre, it makes good use of the police procedural's inherent tendency to "map" urban space and reveal social tensions beneath the crime plot. Situated in the entirely fictional city of Isola (a cross between Boston and New York, rendered with meticulous accuracy), it dramatizes the typical class differences of any American metropolis, and it places particular emphasis on racial or ethnic differences. McBain, a liberal author writing at the time of the U.S. Civil Rights movement and just before the Kennedy presidency, depicts the 87th as a kind of melting pot or cross-section of ethnic types. The police who investigate the crime consist of an Italian, a Jew, and an Irishman (later novels in the series would introduce an important black detective). The police force itself is not free of racism, but the heroic and most sympathetic characters in the 87th are liberals and honest civil servants at the fringe of the middle class who cope with personal problems even while they solve crimes.

Judging from the film Kurosawa made, this tendency of the novel toward social commentary must have interested him. But McBain had also written a book that offered many possibilities for bravura treatment in the film medium. What we have in *High and Low* is a "cinematic" novel from an American popular tradition that has been adapted into an equally "cinematic" film by an international art director. We might say that McBain's narrative has been transposed from West to East and from low to high culture. In the process, Kurosawa made a number of changes or modifications. To explain some of these changes, a brief summary of the film's plot in relation to the novel is in order.

Kurosawa kept the basic situation of McBain's novel for the first third of his film. Kingo Gondo (Toshiro Mifune), the rich, self-made, ruthless executive in charge of National Shoes, is faced with exorbitant ransom demands for the return of his chauffeur's son; and this happens at the very moment when he is poised to take over the corporation through a high-stakes purchase of house-mortgaging stock. (The kidnappers have taken the chauffeur's son by mistake; they intended to take Gondo's.) Gondo agonizes over whether to pay the ransom, and his struggle takes place in front of his wife, Reiko (Kyoko Kagawa), his chauffeur, Aoki (Yutaka Sada), his assistant, Kawanishi (Tatsuya Mihashi), and a group of police detectives led by Tokuro (Tatsuya Nakadai) and "Bosun" (Kenjiro Ishiyama). Initially determined not to pay, Gondo ultimately yields to the kidnapper's demands.

The early scenes of the film are confined entirely to Gondo's house, located high on a hill overlooking Yokohama and the harbor. We know only as much as Gondo's family and the police, and this highly restricted range of knowledge allows everyone to consider the ethical and practical aspects of Gondo's dilemma. He subsequently boards the "Echo Limited" bullet train, where the kidnapper gives instructions by telephone to drop briefcases of cash out the bathroom window. All the while, the police look on helplessly. Aoki's son Shinichi is subsequently recovered, and the final portion of *High and Low*, over an hour in length, concerns the tracking and capture of the kidnapper, Takeuchi (Tsutomu Yamazaki). Here the film departs considerably from the novel, although its range of narration broadens considerably, in the fashion of the typical police procedural. We cross-cut between the detectives, the kidnapper, and Gondo. As the police eventually discover, Takeuchi is a poor medical intern who has killed off his heroin-addict accomplices with pure drugs. In the film's climactic sequence, Tokura, Bosun, and their men follow Takeuchi as he scores heroin in a teeming, noisy harbor bar and scouts out a strung-out female junkie in the harrowing "Dope Alley." Takeuchi gives the woman a fatal sample and returns to

Figure 5. Advertisement for the Japanese release of Akira Kurosawa's High and Low *(1963).* Matthew Bernstein collection.

his hideout, a villa within sight of Mount Fuji, where he believes his accomplices are still alive; and there the police capture him.

In the film's final scene, which occurs some time afterward, Gondo visits Takeuchi in prison. Only hours before his execution, the kidnapper expresses outrage at Gondo's ostentatious wealth. "It is interesting," he boasts, "to make a fortunate man unfortunate." His crime, he says, was motivated by his anger at Gondo's success, happiness, and ignorance of the misery surrounding him in the lower city. Meanwhile, Gondo, who has lost his fortune because of the kidnapping, has started over at a small shoe company. The film concludes starkly, with a dark interview screen descending in front of Gondo as the raging Takeuchi is taken away to his death.

In the intensity of its dramatic situations and the scope and misery of Yokohama uncovered in the investigative sequences, *High and Low* is both an absorbing chase film and a critique of profound social inequalities in contemporary Japan. This indictment is pronounced verbally, if only in personal terms, in the eloquent rage and desperate actions of Takeuchi, the intelligent but poor intern who seeks to defy social law and custom, much like Dostoyevsky's Raskolnikov. As Joan Mellen has noted:

> In Japan, where, as [sociologist] Chie Nakane reminds us, a vertical hierarchy governing all relationships persists and one is always first subject to a predetermined status within a collective; to demand a style of life different from that afforded by one's allotted place in the system [as Takeuchi does] constitutes extreme rebellion. In a social order which functions only so long as everyone accepts his place, to challenge one's position amounts to a revolt against the organization of the entire society.[10]

Kurosawa's critique of Japan is further dramatized in the film's plot structure, whereby Gondo's dilemma over whether to pay the ransom is displaced by the multifaceted police investigation, and Gondo's home is subsumed into the larger "stage" of Yokohama itself. David Desser has compared this shift in narrative focus with that in Alfred Hitchcock's *Psycho* (1960) for its abruptness and its upsetting of conventional expectations. It is also comparable with *Ikiru* (1952), in which one narrative line abruptly ends after Watanabe has decided to build a playground over a sewer. The narrator informs us of Watanabe's death a few months later, and the remainder of the film focuses on Watanabe's family and coworkers—that is, broader Japanese society attempting to make sense of Watanabe's behavior.[11] Watanabe's growth as a person, like Gondo's decision to pay the ransom, would make an interesting film in itself; but Kurosawa broadens the canvas in both films to show us the repercussions of the individual's action for the larger society.

High and Low's dissection of social inequality in Japan is also apparent in its visual style. The most striking instance is Kurosawa's low-key rendering of Dope Alley, where sidelit human "zombies" shuffle in groups in hopes of scoring more heroin. Throughout these sequences we hear eerie, minimalist, almost atonal music—the same theme we heard during the opening credit sequence, which consists of various shots of Yokohama from a high vantage point (the view, we realize when the credits end, from Gondo's living room window). Gondo's air-conditioned mansion (the "heaven" of the literal Japanese title, "Heaven and Hell") contrasts vividly with the lower city's sweltering heat, decay, and poverty. The expanse of the Gondo living room is opposed to the stifling "closet" apartment of Takeuchi, and the TohoScope aspect ratio of the film enables Kurosawa to emphasize luxurious space between the wealthy characters, contrasting their world with the teeming humanity that chokes the bar where Takeuchi buys the heroin to rock 'n' roll music.

McBain's novel is quite different in many respects. *King's Ransom* concludes with the recovery of the child and the immediate capture of one of the kidnappers. No ransom payment is ever made, and the story takes up three days, as opposed to Kurosawa's vague number of weeks or months. The stark conclusion of the film, in which Takeuchi refuses to respond in kind to Gondo's "Why must we hate each other?" and an interview screen descends in front of Gondo with the force of a hammer, has no counterpart in the novel. Modern, recovering Japan, the film suggests, has not completely escaped its feudal heritage; the divisions of caste between samurai, craftsman, and farmer has been replaced with that of the wealthy, the middle-class, and the absolute dregs of humanity. Not even kindness and sympathy across the classes can remedy this problem.

Considered from this standpoint, McBain's *King's Ransom* seems comparatively lacking in social critique (or perhaps less obvious about it). One of the poor kidnappers in the novel thinks that life has been unfair; the American detectives suffer in the November cold, much as Kurosawa's police sweat through the hellish summer in the lower city; and one of the detectives expresses a strong distaste for cases involving the wealthy. Still, the symbolic "heaven and hell" contrast is somewhat muted. In McBain's book Douglas King (the Gondo character) refuses to pay for the return of the chauffeur's son, even after his wife leaves him in disgust and takes their own son with her. The kidnappers are a threesome consisting of the sociopathic Sy Barrett and a younger, relatively sympathetic couple, Kathy and Eddie Folsom, who seek not so much to make King poor, but to make "the final score" that will take them to Mexico and (they tell themselves) end their life of crime. No drugs or addicts are involved, and Kathy and Eddie bear no resemblance to the rebellious outsider Takeuchi—a social rebel who feels deprived, sees the misery surrounding him, and determines to bring Gondo low.

The novel's kidnappers have great confidence in their scheme because of "the monster," a radio Eddie has assembled from parts stolen over the preceding months. When King gets in his Cadillac with a detective lying on the floor of the back seat and an empty cardboard box that is supposed to be the payment, he gets instructions from Eddie on where to make the "drop" via the monster, which transmits his voice to King's car phone. This use of a radio may well have been one source of the film's manifold examples of technologies of surveillance (the telephones at Gondo's and on the bullet train, the police radios, the bugged phones, the movie and still cameras, etc.).[12] The police of the 87th are helpless in the face of this technology until Kathy, kind to the kidnapped child, appalled at the kidnapping itself, and harassed by the lecherous Sy, shouts the waiting Sy's whereabouts into the radio microphone. She and Eddie leave the child and slip away free, while the police track down Sy, whom King chases, fights, and beats unconscious.

The novel's concluding chapter brings us back to the precinct office and the two leading 87th Precinct detectives: the bald, Jewish Meyer Meyer (who had pronounced the kidnapper "meshugah" [Yiddish for crazy] for insisting King pay anyway for the safe return of Reynolds's son), and the Italian Steve Carella. They review the case and indirectly inform us that Kathy and Eddie (whose identities remain unknown to them) have gotten away, that King's stock maneuver has gone through, and that his wife has returned to him. McBain's concluding sentence is "Outside the squadron room, the city crouched" (p. 171); crimes will go on being committed, but their social origins are not this book's explicit concern.

Besides being less symbolic and less like a social protest than Kurosawa's film, *King's Ransom* is more true to the conventions of American popular fiction by being individualistic in its approach. The uncompromising, self-made capitalist, King (about whom McBain seems distinctly ambivalent), physically chases down the head criminal and beats him unconscious. The ideology of individualism is perhaps also inscribed in the narrative structure of the novel, which employs a form of parallel action at least as old as a D. W. Griffith melodrama. As David Desser describes it, McBain's cross-cutting among King's home, the 87th Precinct office, and the kidnappers either waiting in the bushes or back at the farm they are housesitting has a "'meanwhile back at the ranch' temporal structure,"[13] in contrast to the less predictable and more dynamic structure of the film. (After the first hour of the film, we never know where the plot will take us next—a fish market, a hilly retreat near Mount Fuji, a city incinerator, or somewhere else.[14])

But these differences do not obscure some overwhelming similarities between the two texts. McBain's first chapter is virtually a shooting script for the film's opening. It takes place entirely in King's home, where we see the dispute between King and the mercenary shoe company executives who want to make cheap shoes and take over the corporation. Everything we find in Kurosawa's first scene is here—the capitalist's assistant fixing drinks for the bigwigs, the capitalist's speech about how making shoes is his entire life, the entry of the capitalist's wife as the disgruntled men leave, and the tempting of the assistant to betray his boss. Chapter 1 even begins with a lengthy description of the view of the river and the city from King's window, a prototype for *High and Low*'s opening credit sequence. This sense of place is as integral to McBain's story as it is to Kurosawa's, and it carries with it many of the same social implications.

The next chapter of *King's Ransom* takes us to the 87th Precinct office, where Detective Meyer fills out a report on stolen radio equipment. Chapter 3 brings us back to King's house, taking up where we left off, gradually revealing King's secret stock deal and developing several characters: King's wife, Diane; her best friend, Liz (who is having an affair with the assistant, Cameron); and the chauffeur, Reynolds. Like the film, this chapter shows King's son and Reynolds's playing sheriff and "Indian." King tells his son to "make his own rules," and he draws an explicit analogy between the game of cowboys and Indians and his own ruthless approach to business (pp. 33–34).[15] The chapter ends with a kidnapper (Eddie) waiting outside in the bushes. Thereafter, *King's Ransom* shifts its coordinates among the criminals, the police, and the King home. The cross-cutting climaxes with King's drive to drop off the cardboard box, and we quickly shift from Kathy and Eddie hiding in a shack with the boy to King and Detective Carella driving in the car, then to Sy waiting at the drop-off point.

Kurosawa's approach to narration is different from McBain's. Restricting the first part of his film to Gondo's home reflects, as Stephen Prince has noted, Gondo's "own class blindness, perched on his hill and confined to his wealthy home, oblivious to the city below."[16] It is only after the payment is made in the film that Kurosawa adopts the more conventional approach to investigative fiction, revealing the kidnapper to us wordlessly and very briefly, and then following in meticulous detail the various leads, successful and unsuccessful, of the police investigation. (Until the final forty minutes, we know only what the kidnapper looks like—we do not learn who he is, where he works, and so on, until the police do; in McBain's novel, on the other hand, we meet the kidnappers and learn their history quite early). The film also takes a slightly different attitude toward the technical expertise of the police. In the novel, even before King leaves to make the payment drop, we find detectives collecting paint scrapings and tire marks to identify the stolen car used by the criminals, meanwhile explaining the elaborate processes by which such deductions and lab work are done (chapters 6 and 9). By contrast, Kurosawa creates a broader sense of many types of expertise, not all of them technical, that contribute to solving the case—from that of the fisherman who knows the different fish markets the kidnapper's car drove through to that of the trolley conductor who can recognize (and even impersonate) the sound of a specific trolley car in the background of a tape of Takeuchi's telephone call.

Kurosawa treats the narration of *High and Low* in ways that are typical of his own films, which frequently alternate between showing and telling. There is probably no other major director who so constantly makes his characters tell each other stories. From the various witnesses to the outrage in *Rashomon* (1951) to the grandmother describing the bombing of Nagasaki to her grandchildren in *Rhapsody in August* (1991), Kurosawa's films are full of internal narrators or storytellers. David Desser has observed this quality in *High and Low*, and he connects it with traditional Japanese narrative and visual arts: for example, when the detectives narrate for Gondo the 16-millimeter footage of the kidnappers taken from the train, they act like a katsuben, the narrator/lecturer who accompanied silent films; and young Shinichi's crude drawing of Mount Fuji recalls kamishibai, painted pictures accompanied by narration.[17] Desser argues that the film thus invokes traditional Japanese representational practices, such as bunraku, kabuki, and noh theater, all of which relate stories in part through a narrator sitting on the side of the stage. Elsewhere in the film, Kurosawa also splits image from sound; for example, he shows us the group at Gondo's listening to a recording of the kidnapper's second phone call but does not allow us to hear the call itself. In similar fashion, he keeps us outside the phone booth on the bullet train when Gondo gets instructions (a move worthy of the manipulative Hitchcock).

As a corollary to having characters tell stories, Kurosawa often has his characters observe and comment on each other, usually in the form of groups of people who represent an outmoded conventionality and who are shocked by individual initiative. Think of the amazed villagers who watch Kambei cut his topknot in *Seven Samurai* (1954) or the useless bureaucrats who observe Watanabe negotiate the various agencies to get the playground built in *Ikiru*.[18] In *High and Low* the social situation is more complex, perhaps because of the very nature of McBain's police procedural, which is deeply expressive of modern society. As Stephen Prince has pointed out, the film's camera work "captures social process itself, defining Gondo's reduced range of options as a function of the social construction of his position within the narrative and its visual construction within the frame. The individual is clearly shown to be embedded within a network of institutional roles and expectations."[19] The Yokohama detectives also contribute to what Prince has called "complex seeing," a Bakhtinian polyphony in Kurosawa films in which events are viewed from various perspectives. These perspectives are sometimes visualized by cuts and camera movements that violate the 30 degree rule, giving the viewer a sort of cubist representation of the spatial relationships among characters.[20]

The Yokohama detectives are representatives of society, but as a group they are also dogged heroes who relentlessly track Takeuchi down. In *High and Low*, unlike other Kurosawa films, the consensus of the group is not something to be repudiated by the hero; like *King's Ransom*, the film abandons the central capitalist individual for much of the narrative and in so doing indicates the limits of even the powerful, charismatic individual to control his or her own life (*this* shoe company executive, it should be emphasized, cannot personally chase down the kidnapper and beat him senseless). The police's tracking of Takeuchi as he makes his rounds on the night of his capture parallels their constant observation of Gondo at the start of the film. Their utter devotion to capturing Takeuchi is in one sense admirable—and Kurosawa signals their determination at crucial stages with a trumpet fanfare. But the detectives carry out their task to a destructive extreme when they effectively allow yet another murder to be committed, not acting to prevent it, just as Gondo might have done if he had not paid the ransom (a point some critics have taken to imply criticism of the detectives). More generally, the police remain blind to or unconcerned about the social inequalities that motivate the criminal they track.[21]

In specifying the multiple functions of the detectives in *High and Low*, it is helpful as well to note how differently Kurosawa characterizes them from their counterparts in *King's Ransom*. Isola detective Steve Carella does not hesitate to say what he thinks as he watches King's behavior. When the executive flatly informs the police that he will not pay the ransom, Carella erupts: "But he has to! That kid hasn't got a chance unless he—" until a Lieutenant cuts him off. King affirms, "I don't *have* to do anything" (p. 97). Later, as they drive to the drop-off point, Carella tells King he is a "big turd" for not paying the ransom (p. 138).

By contrast, the Yokohama police observe and react quietly as Gondo weighs his decision, and Gondo becomes a more sympathetic character as the movie progresses. Even at the beginning of the film, Gondo does not appear to aggravate the police, who act like true guests in his home. They look at each other in silent surprise when the assistant, Kawanishi, waves around Gondo's check for several hundred thousand yen; they look down in embarrassment as Gondo refuses Aoki's pleas to ransom Shinichi; and they tell Gondo he has a right not to pay the ransom. When Gondo helps them plant telltale chemicals in the payoff briefcases, they are moved by his sacrifice. As Gondo drops his shoemaker's tool kit noisily to the floor, everyone stops what they are doing to watch him. He comments that he is "starting all over already" (because he is here reduced to using his old tools for manual labor), and each detective slowly stands in a silent salute of respect and awe. Bosun pronounces their sentiments: "Usually I waste no love on the rich, but that Gondo is okay." Their sympathy for Gondo motivates their ruthless dragnet for the kidnapper. One of the younger detectives, later viewing Gondo's house from the lower city, agrees with the kidnapper: the white mansion, perched atop a bluff overlooking Yokohama, is arrogant and offensive. But the police ultimately side with Gondo, who, like them, comes to occupy a liminal space between high and low, heaven and hell.

Several scenes in *King's Ransom* are narrated from the detectives' point of view—a technique that functions in a way analogous to Kurosawa's staging of the Yokohama police scenes. Steve Carella in particular represents a middle-class perspective on the wealthy King, and McBain's technique undoubtedly encouraged Kurosawa to give the Yokohama detectives such prominence. For example, as Detective

Carella first arrives at King's home, we are told that cases involving children and the wealthy give him "the willies"—partly because Carella himself has recently become a father, and partly because he finds the rich intimidating. The scene in which the chauffeur, Reynolds, begs King to pay the ransom—reproduced fairly closely in the film—is told as one of Carella's memories, one of the ones he would like to forget. McBain even provides Kurosawa with stage directions: Carella recalls Reynolds and King standing on opposite sides of the room during the scene, just as Kurosawa stages it, with Reynolds falling to his knees as the detective looks on.

The chauffeur is the only major character in the novel that Kurosawa took virtually intact. "Watching him," McBain writes of Reynolds, "you felt you could reach out to touch a substance at once sticky and gelatinous" (p. 29); his hesitant, hunched shoulders provide stage directions for Aoki (Yutaka Sada). He assumes his place in a list of weak-willed characters whom Toshiro Mifune despises in other Kurosawa films: the bankrupt, wifeless gambler in *Yojimbo* (1961), the mostly spineless farmers in *Seven Samurai*, and so on. Yet even here, Kurosawa develops sides of Aoki that are unthinkable in an American character like Reynolds. The morning after the first night, Aoki rescinds his desperate plea to Gondo to ransom his son Shinichi, remembering the propriety of his place in the Gondo household and revoking his outrageous demand on his employer of the night before. And after Shinichi returns, Aoki browbeats him for information to aid the police in the investigation and takes him out for dangerous detective ventures; his overwhelming sense of guilt for Gondo's misfortune governs his behavior as the police pursue their leads.

The characterization of the capitalist's wife attests to even greater cultural differences between 1960s America and Japan. In the film, Reiko displays loyal and demure qualities. She is far more the traditional, loyal Japanese wife than Diane King could ever be: beautiful, dressed traditionally and aristocratically until Gondo has made the decision to pay, Reiko constantly and respectfully reminds her husband of his better nature. She is also isolated in a house full of men. By contrast, the "damn attractive" Diane (p. 23) is an outspoken woman who confides in her adulterous friend Liz and accuses King of ruthlessness and even murder (p. 115). Although the novel provides many suggestions that Diane finds King's power seductive—his advice to his son to "pounce" on Reynolds's son during their game of sheriff and Indian is compared not only with King's business tactics, but with a quick assignation with Diane—she defies King in ways Reiko could never imagine.

In the novel, after Diane has left King and as he drives to the drop-off point, he tells the story of their relationship. King and Diane met at a USO dance during World War II; he was dirt poor, and her wealthy father disowned her for marrying him (King regrets that his father-in-law died before he rose to his highest standing at the shoe company). All of this is elided in Kurosawa's film, perhaps for reasons of plausibility, or perhaps because Kurosawa wished to focus more exclusively on the present. We do learn indirectly that Gondo has worked his way to the top and that he has married a woman used to luxury. Their respective families are nowhere in sight, suggesting that their wealth has cut them off from traditional family living arrangements, in which paternal grandparents stay in the home.

Gondo is far more likeable than Douglas King because he is quiet and taciturn, whereas King is often arrogant and pigheaded. But King is nevertheless the model for Gondo. In the novel he is described as tall, "with the wide shoulders and narrow waist of an exhibition diver" (p. 10). He has the same distinguished, gray-haired temples as Gondo. He stands up like Gondo to make his pronouncements on the executives' takeover bid, making the same speech about his devotion to shoes and expressing the same contempt for the poorly made products his rivals want to manufacture.

From the opening scene Mifune, shot typically from low or head-on angles, has a kind of grandeur that—combined with Kurosawa's choreography, setting him against the other executives—gives him the stature and mien of a noble if hard-nosed and aggressive protagonist. Unlike Mifune's Gondo, however, McBain's Douglas King becomes more repellant when he faces the prospect of paying the ransom. As the detectives ask their initial questions of King, he rudely protests that they are irrelevant, and he insults the police's competence. He wants the FBI, not "a bunch of local Keystone cops" (p. 46), and he keeps mispronouncing Detective Steve Carella's name. Carella has to refrain from punching King in the mouth and scolds him, "I know my job and I do it well, and any questions I ask you are not asked because I'm auditioning for *Dragnet*" (p. 48).

Moreover, unlike the noble Gondo, King refuses to pay the ransom, shocking the police into silence when he announces this. "What the hell do I owe humanity?" he asks Diane during their heated debate. He is contemptuous of the kidnapper, who wants money for doing nothing, and of his chauffeur, who "never learned to swim" in the world (p. 114). King insists as he drives to drop off the payment (actually an empty cardboard box) that this is no "fairy tale" and he cannot change (p. 158). And the chief irony of *King's Ransom* is that King's decision is in some sense justified, enabling him to play a major role in the capture of Sy. When Kathy yells into the car phone and King and Carella drive off after Sy, King chases the gun-toting, knife-wielding criminal into the woods. Sy slashes his coat and his skin, while King, calling him a "lousy son of a bitch," grabs him by the throat: —

> The knife flashed erratically now, searching for flesh. King's grip on Sy's throat would not loosen. A powerful man with hands that once had

cut leather, he battered Sy's head against the tree, never relaxing his grip, silently, coldly, viciously pounding the other man until the knife dropped quietly from his lax fingers. (p. 167)

Sy provides a legitimate target for all of King's "murderous" impulses, and in the best tradition of good-guy-versus-bad-guy melodrama, the police catch up with the tough, up-from-the-proletariat capitalist before he can exact morally righteous revenge.

King is a typically American character who has something in common with the rugged individualist and whose self-interest is somehow connected to the social interest. By contrast, Gondo is a far more subdued character. Even as he refuses to pay the ransom, even as he rages at the injustice of what has befallen him, he is always respectful of the detectives and their efforts. He feels compelled to justify himself to the police, a sentiment King never entertains until after Diane leaves him. Ultimately, Gondo decides to pay because he knows the answer to King's question, "What the hell do I owe humanity?" At the end of the film he appears before Takeuchi in prison as a man without bitterness who is chastened by the experience that has cost him his money and brought him low.

Kurosawa's films prior to 1963 repeatedly focused on protagonists compelled to learn Gondo's lesson, most dramatically Watanabe, the lifeless bureaucrat of *Ikiru* (1952).[22] This theme arises from Kurosawa's appreciation for the potential of individualism in postwar Japan, but it is a Japanese variant of individualism that acknowledges how ties of obligation bind individuals to the social fabric much more tightly than in America. Even though, as a rich Yokohama industrialist, Gondo owes little to his chauffeur, his final decision to pay the ransom is preordained. As Reiko tells him, "You must pay." Gondo takes on the mantle of the updated bushido code, wherein capable, powerful, superior men must help others to make society better.[23]

The price of Gondo's sacrifice is enormous not only in social terms, but also in terms of the film's specific narrative. Where King remains an active character who is crucial to the capture of Sy, Gondo becomes almost irrelevant to the chase sequences of *High and Low*.[24] We see him getting progress reports, mowing his lawn, and accidentally bumping into Takeuchi, the kidnapper, in the lower city on the night of his capture. That Kurosawa so dramatically altered the character may testify to the obligations on and limited effectiveness of the individual in postwar Japanese culture. In a similar fashion, Takeuchi, the film's kidnapper, is quite different from the apolitical trio of villains in McBain's novel; his criminality is an active, willful choice based on a perverse social outrage.

Takeuchi is most forcefully compared with Gondo himself at the end of the film, as we see each man's reflection in the prison glass window separating them: they are two sides of contemporary Japan, individuals from social classes that define themselves in opposition to each other. Yet this comparison has been suggested throughout the film. Gondo's mansion is lordly, overlooking the industrialized lower city; but the villa Takeuchi is housesitting is similarly isolated atop a hill within plain view of Mount Fuji, the national symbol of Japan. Just as we sit and wait with Reiko and Kawanishi for the call from Osaka on Gondo's stock deal to come through, we similarly spend several minutes on the dance floor waiting for Takeuchi to swap cash and drugs with his heroin dealer.

The relationship between the two characters is ultimately expressed in terms of space. The contrast between Gondo's expansive house and Takeuchi's "three-tatami-mat" apartment is at first jarring; but after Gondo has thrown the money-filled briefcases out the bullet train's bathroom window, he is shown in a medium close-up with a telephoto lens in a similarly cramped space. Even in the earlier scenes Gondo's house seems a symbol of both strength and vulnerability, both isolation and exposure to the city. At every point where Gondo announces a decision—whether to throw in with the shoe company executives, whether or not to pay the ransom—he walks to the sliding glass door, opens it, and takes in the sights and sounds of Yokohama. The comfort of this setting becomes ironic when Gondo realizes how visually exposed he is; although he is no voyeur, his sudden discovery that he can be observed by the kidnapper is comparable with Jeffries' discovery in Hitchcock's *Rear Window* (1954) when Thorwald looks his way. The irony is compounded as Gondo agonizes over the decision of whether to pay the ransom as his wife and the detectives look on; at times he paces up and down along the curtains of the window like a caged tiger amidst the stolid, impassive forms of the detectives watching him.

This informing sense of place and its impact on characters' lives extends to the very setting of Yokohama itself. As Japan's major trade port as well as the site of an American naval base, Yokohama is the gateway to the West. *High and Low* shows us a city infiltrated by Western culture. If two boys in McBain's Isola play sheriff and Indian, this fact is unremarkable; but the game takes on a slightly different meaning in Yokohama. When Gondo tells his son to play the game aggressively, the film connects predatory capitalism to the West. The alleyways Takeuchi walks through on his way home are cluttered with discarded electronics and the residue of modernity—television sets in particular. The overwhelming number of American sailors in the bar where Takeuchi scores his heroin also contributes to the film's suggestion that Japan's relationship with the West, and America in particular, has made it what it is. Hence the very choice of the McBain novel as a source seems deeply related to the film's meaning.

At one point in *High and Low*, Schubert's "Trout" symphony plays over a shot of the kidnapper Takeuchi (the trout is reputed in some Japanese circles to be a difficult fish to catch). Kurosawa's representation of Western culture here, as in his other films, encompasses both high and low realms, both old and new forms. For Kurosawa, David Desser has written, "the narrative modes characteristic of traditional Japanese storytelling practices intersect with a modern, international film culture."[25] As I hope this chapter essay has shown, however, Ed McBain's popular crime novel provided especially useful material for Kurosawa. And this process of international adaptation may well continue: even as I write, Martin Scorsese has announced his intention to direct a remake of *High and Low* from a script by David Mamet.[26] By the time the story makes another trans-Pacific crossing, who knows what interesting changes might result?

NOTES

1. Howard Thompson, "'High and Low,' a Movie of Suspense, Arrives from Japan," *The New York Times* (27 November 1963), p. 30; Brendan Gill, *The New Yorker* (14 December 1963), pp. 197–98; Stanley Kauffmann, "Japanese Drama, Domestic Japery," *The New Republic* (23 November 1963), pp. 26–29; "A Yen for Yen," *Time* (29 November 1963), p. 103; "Mysterious East," *Newsweek* (25 November 1963), pp. 104–105. It was Thompson who characterized the McBain source as "of all things."

Variety's critic, speculating that Kurosawa had added the "social angle" to McBain's plot, remarked that a "tighter film, concentrating and balancing police activity and human conflicts [i.e., not abandoning Gondo so completely in the film's second half] would have given this added distinction in arty circles," but pronounced it "a finely tooled item, made by a master craftsman," and heralded it as being in "the Alfred Hitchcock tradition" "for crime pic aficionados." See "Hawk.," *Variety* (11 September 1963).

2. Judith Crist, "87th Precinct—Japanese Style," in *The New York Herald Tribune* (8 December 1963), p. 37.

3. David Bordwell, "The Art Cinema as Mode of Film Practice," in *Film Theory and Criticism*, 5th ed., ed. Leo Braudy and Marshall Cohen (New York: Oxford University Press, 1999), pp. 716–24.

4. "Mysterious East," *Newsweek* (25 November 1963), p. 105.

5. James Goodwin, *Akira Kurosawa and Intertextual Cinema* (Baltimore: Johns Hopkins University Press, 1994); Donald Richie, *The Films of Akira Kurosawa* (Berkeley: University of California Press, 1999); David Desser, *The Samurai Films of Akira Kurosawa* (Ann Arbor: University of Michigan Research Press, 1983), pp. 6–7; see also pp. 137–39.

Stephen Prince notes the film's source in a footnote in *The Warrior's Camera: The Cinema of Akira Kurosawa* (Princeton, N.J.: Princeton University Press, 1991), p. 318, n. 44. Significantly, Prince discusses *High and Low* in a chapter on the complex forms of Kurosawa's modern films rather than in the "Experiments and Adaptations" section. Desser has elaborated on his analysis of the film with a new essay, "Narrating the Human Condition: *High and Low* and Story-Telling in Kurosawa's Cinema," in *Perspectives on Akira Kurosawa*, ed. James Goodwin (New York: G. K. Hall, 1994), pp. 157–71. Desser's essay and Prince's discussion are the most enlightening analyses of the film yet published. No English-language critic has explained how Kurosawa came across McBain's novel in the first place.

6. For brevity's sake, I discuss the adaptation choices as Kurosawa's, having here acknowledged his collaborators on the script.

7. For another analysis of cross-cultural adaptation, see Phebe Shih Chao, "Reading *The Letter* in a Post-Colonial World," in *Visions of the East: Orientalism in Film*, Matthew Bernstein and Gaylyn Studlar (New Brunswick, N.J.: Rutgers University Press, 1997), pp. 292–313. For an exemplary statement on expanding the texts analyzed to varying script drafts and finished films, see Lea Jacobs, *The Wages of Sin: Censorship and the Fallen Woman Film, 1928–1942* (Berkeley: University of California Press, 1995).

8. I quote from the 1959 paperback edition published in New York by Signet, p. 131; all subsequent quotes are referenced in the text.

9. James Sandoe, "Mystery and Suspense," *New York Herald Tribune Book Review* (22 November 1959), p. 18; Lenore Glen Offord, "The Gory Road," *San Francisco Sunday Chronicle* (20 December 1959), p. 30; Anthony Boucher, "A Report on Criminals at Large," *New York Times Book Review*, (6 December 1959), p. 42.

10. Joan Mellen, *The Waves at Genji's Door: Japan Through its Cinema* (New York: Pantheon, 1976), p. 409.

11. Desser, "Narrating," p. 162; Desser discusses *Ikiru* in terms of narration in his "*Ikiru*: Narration as a Moral Act," in *Reframing Japanese Cinema: Authorship, Genre, History*, ed. Arthur Nolletti Jr. and Desser (Bloomington: Indiana University Press, 1992), pp. 56–68.

12. Richie, *Films of Akira Kurosawa*, p. 167; Prince, *The Warrior's Camera*, p. 188.

13. Desser, *The Samurai Films*, p. 138.

14. Kurosawa is fond of such narrative structure and the idea of chance's befalling his characters; think of the way the General (Mifune) blunders into the opposing general's camp in *The Hidden Fortress* (1958), or even how the characters never can be sure what awaits them beyond the borders of the frame or even a few feet into the fog.

15. In *High and Low* a visit to the shop floor of National Shoes tells us and the detectives that Gondo is a tough but widely respected taskmaster.

16. Prince, *The Warrior's Camera*, p. 195.

17. Desser, "Narrating," pp. 157–58, 163.

18. Among Western films, John Madden's *Mrs. Brown* (1997) comes to mind as a recent example of this staging principle at work, as members of Queen Victoria's court are stunned at her groom's informalities given the rigid code of conduct in the presence of members of the royal family.

19. Prince, *The Warrior's Camera*, pp. 190–93. The quote is from p. 193.

20. Noel Burch, *Theory of Film Practice* (Princeton, N.J.: Princeton University Press, 1973); Prince, *The Warrior's Camera*, pp. 190–93.

21. Prince, *The Warrior's Camera*, p. 188.

22. To this example we might add the heroine of *No Regrets*, the seven samurai in the film of that title, the young policeman in *Stray Dog* (who feels his responsibility perhaps too much), the hero of *The Bad Sleep Well*, and even Sanjuro in *Yojimbo*, when he frees the wife of the bankrupt gambler and reunites their family.

23. Stephen Prince persuasively argues that this ethos informs all of Kurosawa's films through *Red Beard* (1965). See chap. 3, "Willpower Can Cure All Ailments," in his *The Warrior's Camera*.

24. Prince, *The Warrior's Camera*, p 190.

25. Desser, "Narrating," p. 165.

26. "Kurosawa Film May Be Reworked," *Atlanta Constitution* (14 May 1999), p. 15.

Darlene J. Sadlier

The Politics of Adaptation:
How Tasty Was My Little Frenchman

At this point, history took such a strange turn that I am
surprised that no novelist or scenario-writer has yet
made use of it. What a marvelous film it would make!
Claude Levi-Strauss, Tristes Tropiques *(1955)*

Most commentaries on literary adaptation in film are formalistic, pre-occupied with issues of textual fidelity or with attempts to explain the differences between media. From my own point of view, the study of adaptation becomes more interesting when it takes into account histor-ical, cultural, or political concerns. As one example of the kinds of films that are illuminated by such an approach, consider the career of Nelson Pereira dos Santos, one of Brazil's most admired directors, who has fre-quently been an adapter of respected literary works. Pereira dos Santos's best pictures sometimes offer brilliant translations of literature into another medium, but he is neither an illustrator of classics nor a propo-nent of what Truffaut once derided as a "tradition of quality." He is a committed director, and all of his films have liberal or left-wing sources and are largely proletarian in theme. Many of his adaptations can be seen as responses to the turbulent decades when Brazil moved from an un-stable leftist labor government to a right-wing military rule, and finally to a nascent redemocratization. Throughout the 1960s and early 70s, - Pereira dos Santos used canonical literature as an indirect way of speak-ing about contemporary social problems. He chose safely historical texts, but the texts contained themes that spoke directly to his audiences.

An obvious case in point is *Vidas Secas* (*Barren Lives*, 1963), a sort of Brazilian version of *The Grapes of Wrath* (albeit a much more raw and less sentimental narrative than we find in either John Steinbeck or John Ford). The corrupt landowning system and the brutally impover-ished peasantry described in the 1939 novel by Graciliano Ramos were still in place when the film was released; indeed the labor government headed by João Goulart proposed a partial agrarian reform system that very year, and a middle-class revolt against reforms of this nature, which included the nationalization of privately owned petroleum refineries, led to a new conservative regime in 1964.[1] Although Pereira dos Santos placed a title at the beginning of *Vidas Secas* to inform viewers that the action took place in the 1940s, most Brazilians and virtually any traveler to the country's northeastern provinces would have seen that the film was a kind of docudrama about present-day conditions and represented a direct intervention in the political debates of the day.

Following the ultraconservative crackdown in 1968, the political implications of Pereira dos Santos's adaptations became more oblique, almost allegorical. There was a certain tension or ambiguity in his choice of projects: the Brazilian government was less likely to censor his adaptations of classics (particularly when they were aimed at an intellectual or art movie audience), and it was even able to acquire a liberal aura or a degree of cultural capital not only by allowing them to be produced, but also by providing (in some cases) financial backing. At the same time, Pereira dos Santos was able to use respected literature to comment on government policies. Nowhere was his strategy more evident than in his adaptation of Machado de Assis's nineteenth-century novella, *O Alienista* (The Psychiatrist)—a satire about a foolish analyst who institutionalizes an entire population. The film was released in 1970 at a moment when the military was sending hundreds of citizens to prison for "subversive" activities. Pereira dos Santos grounded the allegory of the film and made its essential point clear through its very title: *Azyllo Muito Louco* (A Very Crazy Asylum).

Shortly after *Azyllo*, Pereira dos Santos directed his most interesting film of the period, *Como Era Gostoso O Meu Francês* (*How Tasty Was My Little Frenchman*, 1971), which is based not on a novel, but on the German explorer Hans Staden's celebrated sixteenth-century chronicle *Brasilien: die wahrhaftige Histoire der wilden, nacken, grimmigen Menschenfresser-Leute* (*Brazil: The True History of the Wild, Naked, Fierce, Man-Eating People*, 1557), describing his capture by the Tupinambá when he was living among the Portuguese in the area now known as Rio de Janeiro. According to film critic and historian Helena Salem, Pereira dos Santos had long been contemplating a film project about the Staden adventure and about the roughly contemporary formation of a Huguenot community on an island in Guanabara Bay that the director passed every day on his regular commute from Niteroi to Rio.[2] But Pereira dos Santos's imagination was also fired by newspaper accounts of the plight of an indigenous community in the northeast with which he had had contact when making *Vidas Secas*.[3] As a result of the country's attempt to bring "civilization" to the interior, an entire culture was on the verge of extinction. The situation at that time harked back to the very origins of the encounter between European modernity and the native populations of the New World; in particular, Pereira dos Santos was reminded of one of the earliest colonial records, describing the decimation by Portuguese troops of a tribe known as the Caetés, who had killed and devoured a shipwrecked Portuguese bishop. His film would therefore use the Staden text for its basic plot but would also treat a whole tradition of colonial discourse and ethnographic representation as if it were present-day news. In the process, the film would become less a "translated" adaptation of Staden than a subversive retelling of his story; it would treat the native populations of the sixteenth century in realist fashion, but it would ultimately be an experiment in pastiche and intertextuality, offering a political satire about global capitalism and the Brazilian economic "miracle" of the 1960s and 1970s.

In one sense, every film adaptation can be understood as a type of intertextuality or pastiche, if only because the very process of adaptation involves the deliberate imitation of a prior work. But *How Tasty Was My Little Frenchman* has a more complicated relation to its sources than the usual movie based on a book. It draws on a wide range of other historical narratives besides Staden, and at various junctures it becomes a stylistic hodgepodge: realistic images of Tupinambá life photographed in documentary fashion on vibrant color stock are mixed with elements of obvious burlesque, and dramatic reenactments are interspersed with title cards quoting directly from sixteenth-century sources. The film's use of colonial history is particularly dense and layered, revealing contradictions in the sources themselves. Throughout it suggests that the historical archive is as riven by conflict as contemporary politics, and it makes clear that the country's past and present-day realities are not distinct. Although the major historical trauma it exposes is a familiar one of European domination and genocide, it suggests that this irreducible violence keeps returning and repeating itself in the here and now; meanwhile, it converts the traumatic event described by the Staden text—the cannibalist act—into a provocative metaphor for resistance to a modern society of global capital and foreign consumption.

We can appreciate the complexity of Pereira dos Santos's treatment of historical narrative if we examine the brief precredit sequences of the film, which are based on the same events that Claude Levi-Strauss, whom I quote in my epigraph, thought would make a "marvelous film." On the soundtrack we hear a narrator's voice reading from a sixteenth-century text—not by Staden, but by the French Admiral Nicolau Durand de Villegaignon, in a famous letter addressed to Protestant leader John Calvin, about the religious community Villegaignon had established in 1555 off the coast of Rio. A recent convert, Villegaignon had written to Calvin in 1557 asking him to send missionaries to the island, which was to become a religious haven for Catholics and Protestants alike. But just as the island experiment got underway, fierce theological debates broke out between the two groups. The arguments were exacerbated by Villegaignon's tyrannical leadership—not to mention the daily hardships caused by unfamiliar surroundings, food shortages, disease, and the constant threat of attack by the Portuguese. Villegaignon finally drove out the Protestant missionaries. Lacking material support from the indigenous Brazilian population, whom he considered "beasts with human faces," and with the Portuguese pressing for control, Villegaignon ultimately abandoned Fort Coligny, which came under Portuguese rule in 1560.

Pereira dos Santos's use of the Villegaignon document is blatantly ironic. The original text, written in the formal style of a sixteenth-century epistle, is read by an off-screen announcer delivering the "Latest News from Terra Firme." The text vilifies the local inhabitants, but on the screen we see richly colored images of the Indians behaving hospitably to the Europeans. The text also expresses a good deal of concern about tribal "sin" and "carnal lust," while we clearly see that European explorers are trying to obtain sexual gratification from the naked Tupinambá women. (The Europeans cover up the women's nakedness with oversized, frilly shirts, and then the women run along the crest of a hill, brandishing the shirts over their heads or tossing them away.) At one point the announcer reads Villegaignon's account of a conspirator who, freed of his chains and allowed to plead his case, escaped and drowned in the sea; on the screen, the conspirator is bound with a ball and chain, read over by a priest, and summarily pushed off a hillside into the ocean. As the "broadcast" continues, scenes of exploitation and murder are accompanied by a Mozart French-horn concerto that was the popular soundtrack for the short newsreel, "Atualidades Francesas" (French Current Events), shown in Brazilian movie theaters in the 1960s.[4]

In separate studies of the film, critics Richard Peña and Randal Johnson have observed that this opening prepares us for a film that consistently challenges official history. In Peña's words, the quotations from Villegaignon are "ironic, 'historical' counterparts to the events depicted."[5] Johnson agrees, arguing that the film places "quotations of historical documents" in "ironic if not contradictory" relation to the truth.[6] In fact, however, the film's technique is more complicated, involving something other than an opposition between lying "history" and transparent "reality." Despite their sly humor and evident irony, the images we see on the screen are no less "historical" than the off-screen voice on the soundtrack; in fact, they derive from a series of well-known texts that are roughly contemporary with Villegaignon, describing what historian Philip P. Boucher refers to as "Villegaignon's much publicized Brazilian fiasco"[7]—a fiasco that has long been part of the official record in Brazil as well as in France. By juxtaposing Villegaignon's letter with a visible enactment of his tyranny, the film might be said to "adapt" a celebrated eyewitness account by the French Huguenot Jean de Léry, whose *Histoire dun Voyage Fait en la Terre du Bresil Autrement Dite Amerique* (1578) (History of a Voyage to the Land of Brazil, Otherwise

Called America) includes a transcription of Villegaignon's letter, followed by a denunciation of Villegaignon and a description of his cruel treachery. (In his book Léry also criticizes the Franciscan André Thevet, whose *Comographie Universelle* [1575], based on his brief stay in the community, sides with Villegaignon in the island religious wars and accuses the Calvinists of intrigue.) Indeed the scene showing the Indian women swinging the frilly European shirts over their heads comes directly from Léry's account.

Perhaps the best way of explaining the opening of the film would be to say that it is made up of two or more historical documents in ironic juxtaposition (framed by a burlesque newsreel) and that it favors one document over the others by granting it the status of photographic "truth." At any rate, it would be a mistake to view *How Tasty Was My Little Frenchman* as a straightforward attempt to mock the archival record. Certainly it mocks historical personages (all of them European), but on one level it is a fairly respectful attempt to adapt or interpret historical narratives. In the last analysis, it is formed by a subtle and dense interweaving of materials toward which Pereira dos Santos had a mixed attitude—and no wonder, because these materials are contradictory not only of one another, but also within themselves.

In interviews Pereira dos Santos spoke repeatedly of his use of historical sources to provide as accurate an account as possible of the period.[8] (In addition to Staden, who provides the *donne* for the plot, the film quotes and explicitly identifies various writers in the intertitles—among them the Huguenot Léry, the Franciscan Thevet, the Jesuits Manoel de Nóbrega and José de Anchieta, the early chronicler Pero de Magalhães Gândavo, and the country's first governor general, Mem de Sá.) Pereira dos Santos recognized that all the sources are individual interpretations of the period when they were written. In the film he uses them to help reconstruct a bygone era, but he also constructs his own interpretation. As Pereira dos Santos has stated, "The reality portrayed had disappeared. I had to reconstruct the long-ago past, which implied a personal interpretation of History. I respected all the data available about the Tupinambá culture. As for the relations between the Indians and the French, they were evidently subjected to what I always felt about the question."[9] In other words, *How Tasty Was My Little Frenchman* offers not so much a denunciation of history as a new reading of historic sources, adapted in the form of a quasidocumentary narrative about the encounter between cultures.

As I have already indicated, the film's primary source is Hans Staden's *Brazil*, which recounts two separate voyages made by the German adventurer, the first in 1547 and the second in 1549. During the second expedition Staden became friends with Portuguese settlers and their Tupiniquim allies, helping them fortify their coastal enclave against attacks by roving French troops and their allies, the Tupinambá.

While aiding the Portuguese, Staden was captured by the Tupinambá, who believed he was Portuguese. According to Staden, his faith in God and good luck enabled him to endure his months of captivity. They also helped delay and ultimately postpone indefinitely his execution and consumption by the Indians, who came to believe he possessed magical powers when he correctly predicted an enemy attack and later "cured" an ailing tribal chief. Held in captivity for nearly a year, he escaped on a French ship in 1554—just months prior to the arrival of Villegaignon in Brazil.

Among several liberties Pereira dos Santos took with Staden was to make the film's captive-protagonist a Frenchman and member of the Villegaignon community. Suspected of conspiring against the French leader, he is the character who appears in the film's opening sequence in ball and chain being pushed off the hillside into the sea. After a lengthy credits sequence, he is shown struggling with ball and chain to reach land, where he is first captured by the Portuguese and Tupiniquim, who are enemies of the French, then by the Tupinambá, who, in events similar to those in the Staden account, mistake him for a Portuguese. Both the Staden account and the film emphasize the issue of mistaken identity, but the former describes at some length Staden's efforts to convince the Tupinambá that he is a German national and a "relative" of the French. By introducing the film with the Villegaignon letter, by incorporating the music of the 1960s French newsreel, and by making his protagonist a Frenchman named "Jean" as opposed to a German named "Hans," Pereira dos Santos is focusing on a nation and culture that, ironically, has constituted a greater influence on the mental life of the nation than the actual colonizing power, Portugal, which ousted the French from Brazil in the mid-sixteenth century. Despite Brazil's status as a Portuguese colony until the early nineteenth century, its cultural and intellectual life after 1822 was far more profoundly influenced by France; indeed French was the primary language used in Brazilian schools until quite late in this century.

When Jean is captured along with the Portuguese, the Tupinambá order him and the others to speak in order to verify their nationality. One by one the Portuguese captives recite recipes from cookbooks—an unexpectedly amusing moment that contributes to the motif of eating while reinforcing a comic Brazilian stereotype of the Portuguese as a people obsessed with food. Jean's words in French are vividly different, and they puzzle the Tupinambá. (His words, "The savage walks naked and we walk unrecognized," echo Montaigne's own sentiments as expressed in his famous essay, "On Cannibals.") Although the natives believe he is Portuguese, they do not kill and eat him because of his demonstrated expertise with the small cannon—an expertise that, later in the film, he uses on behalf of the Tupinambá against the Tupiniquim and that gives him a false sense of security and superiority over his captors.

Like the Staden book, the film introduces an old French trader who is regarded as a friend in the Tupinambá village, and who agrees to speak with Jean to determine his true nationality. In contrast to the Staden book, however, the film is quite cynical in its depiction of this character. The trader in the film immediately knows that Jean is French, but he tells the Tupinambá that their captive is an enemy. Jean is furious when he realizes what the trader has done, but the trader promises to rescue him on a later visit if, in the meantime, he will help to collect native wood and pepper that have commercial value. Jean agrees, but only when the trader leaves him some kegs of gunpowder. On the trader's return to the village, Jean tells him of his discovery of gold coins among the Indians, and he uses the discovery as leverage to ensure his freedom. Unfortunately, in the process of digging up Jean's hidden cache of treasure, the two men begin to quarrel over its ownership. Jean kills the trader with a blow to the back of his head with a shovel, then buries him in the same hole that once contained the gold.

There is nothing like this brutal miniature version of *The Treasure of the Sierra Madre* in the Staden text, in which all violent acts are committed by the Indians. Indeed the purported savagery of the indigenous population is made all the more vivid to readers of Staden because his book contains a series of woodcut illustrations showing Indians in various stages of anthropophagy. Pereira dos Santos presents thirty-two of these xylographic images as the backdrop for the long credit sequence that follows the Villegaignon opening. Particularly striking is a woodcut of legs and arms drying on top of a large rack; another depicts a man's head with eyes open on a platter. Perhaps most unsettling of all is a picture of women and children eating body parts that look like fingers or phalluses. Accompanying the sequence is a soundtrack consisting of steady drumbeats and whoops and cries that most moviegoers would associate with Hollywood's "circle and burn" image of Indians on the warpath. It therefore seems ironic when the most explicitly violent act in *How Tasty Was My Little Frenchman* is Jean's attack on the trader. Compared with this cowardly and desperate killing, scenes involving anthropophagy in the film are presented as a serious and civilized ritual; they, too, involve a blow to the victim's head, but the blow is administered face to face, and the ritual requires the victim to face his executioner and call out, "When I die, my friends will come to avenge me." The emphasis in the anthropophagic act, at least as the film treats it, is on heroism and blood vengeance. Far from being a casual or indiscriminate practice, it is reserved for specific individuals, who are both symbolically and literally ingested. By contrast, the deadly encounter between the two Frenchmen is internecine, based on mutual suspicion and protocapitalist greed.

The Staden text also differs markedly from the film because it is filled with references to Christianity. In *Brazil* Staden frequently prays

Figure 6. Advertisement for the Brazilian release of Nelson Pereira dos Santos's How Tasty Was My Little Frenchman *(1971). Helena Salem collection.*

for his safety and recites verses from the Bible to calm his growing fears of execution. At one point he threatens the Tupinambá warriors with vengeance from his angry God; and almost immediately, as if by a miracle, one of the Indians who has taunted him most vigorously suddenly falls ill and dies. Later Staden is asked to come to the aid of an ailing chief and his family by praying to the European God; seeing an opportunity, he strikes a bargain with the tribe and agrees to pray on the condition that his own safety be guaranteed. Sure enough, the chief survives, and the legend grows that Staden has magical powers. When a cross he has placed outside his hut is stolen and used for firewood, a powerful storm erupts; and when the chief's son erects a new cross in its place, the storm subsides. "Everyone was amazed," Staden writes, "believing that my God did everything that I wanted."[10]

By contrast with this figure, who is both religious and something of a con man, Jean in the film is a relatively emotionless character, and at no times does he demonstrate any religious inclinations. The faith on which Jean relies for his survival rests not in God, but in his belief in the power of commodities (gunpowder and gold), as well as in his technological expertise. Somewhat like Staden, however, Jean plays on the Indians' belief system. He feigns an ability to produce gunpowder out of sand, and he accompanies the Tupinambá into battle, where he fires a cannon against the Tupiniquim. So great is his sense of confidence with respect to his position in the community that at one point he equates himself with Mair, the god who taught the Indians about fire, food, and weapons. But just as Mair was finally rejected by the Tupinambá for his arrogance, so too is Jean, whose every effort to define his individuality and superiority is eventually undercut and punished.

Where the book and film diverge most dramatically is in the representation of women. In Staden's book the protagonist is chaste (so far as we can determine), and women are described in strictly collective terms. Shortly after Staden is captured, he is taken to a village where a group of women lead him by a cord around his neck and perform a dance. Soon afterward the women shave off his eyebrows, beat him, and despite his vigorous protests, cut off his beard with a pair of French scissors. In subsequent episodes of the book, these and other women are mentioned occasionally, but they recede into the background while the narrative concentrates on Staden's relationships with the male leaders of the tribe. The film, on the other hand, portrays the early dance/depilation scene and then goes on to tell quite another story. Shortly after proclaiming that Jean will be killed at the eighth moon, the leader of the tribe announces that Seboipep, the widow of the leader's brother, will serve Jean until he is put to death. From this point on the film pays a great deal of attention to the developing relationship between Jean and Seboipep. Jean initially rejects Seboipep's attempts to sleep with him in a hammock, but eventually she lives with him like a wife, teaching him the ways of her community.

Here in this part of the story we encounter another of the film's sources or intertexts, which in this case lies outside the realm of pure history: the story of *Iracema* (1865), one of Brazil's most cherished nineteenth-century novels about the Indian and the colonization process. Written by the romantic José de Alencar, *Iracema* describes the arrival in Brazil of Martim, the first Portuguese colonizer in northern Ceará; his encounter with the Tabajara tribe; and his attraction to the chief's daughter, Iracema, the "honey-lipped maiden" whose name is an anagram for America. When he arrives in Brazil, Martim is told that Iracema, the designated "virgin of Tupã," guards the secret of her tribe's life or well-being. Later, in one of the most sensuous chapters of the novel, Iracema climbs into Martim's hammock while he is sleeping and makes love to him. As a result of this act, she can no longer function as the protectress of her community, and she abandons her family to go off with Martim. Soon afterward the Tabajara are decimated by an enemy tribe.

Iracema dies of grief, but she leaves behind a son, Moacir, who represents a union between two races.

Alencar's "bon sauvage" creations, including *Iracema* and the equally popular *O Guarani* (1857), a novel that describes the encounter between an Indian warrior and a European maiden, took on mythical importance during a period of nationalistic fervor in Brazil, when the Indian became a symbol of the country's proud heritage. Ironically (but not surprisingly), the Indian population had largely disappeared by the nineteenth century, its numbers having been reduced substantially by colonial wars and diseases brought by the Europeans. Nonetheless, so popular were the writings of Alencar, and so powerful were his characterizations of the noble savage, that Brazilians began to take pride in their indigenous heritage, in many cases adopting Indian names for their children. The modernist movement of the early twentieth century, which was also steeped in nationalism, perpetuated the same romanticized view of the Indian as hero-symbol by playfully insisting that Brazilians adopt a metaphorical anthropophagism—which, in the eyes of one of the movement's chief proponents, Oswald de Andrade, was one way to counter cultural imperialism. Despite the fact that *antropofagismo* was itself an imported model from Europe, Andrade's representation of the Indian as symbolic defender of the nation's culture influenced a number of authors, including Mário de Andrade and Raul Bopp, whose fiction and poetry in the 1920s and 1930s portrayed the Indian in new and often phantasmagoric ways.

How Tasty Was My Little Frenchman appropriates these familiar conventions of Brazilian narratives about the colonial period, but it provides a fascinating counterpart to the romanticized image of the Indian created by Alencar and later by Andrade. Unlike the "romance" between Martim and Iracema, the encounter between Jean and Seboipep is not idealized. Jean shows absolutely no interest in Seboipep, who is not a virgin and whose name in Tupi means "bloodsucker";[11] in fact, he altogether rejects her amorous advances until his conversation with the French trader, who counsels him to follow the customs of the tribe and take advantage of the situation for profit-making purposes. In one of the most sensuous scenes in the film, when the two are playing in the water, the eroticism is cut short by Jean's discovery of a gold coin in Seboipep's navel. Because gold, unlike gunpowder and firearms, has no commercial value to the Tupinambá, Seboipep tells Jean of the location of the gold pieces in a burial ground—which, in turn, leads him to conspire with and then murder the French trader.

Shortly after the killing, Jean nearly makes his escape with the treasure by paddling a canoe toward a passing ship. As he makes his way toward the ship, he sees Seboipep watching him from the shoreline. In what at first seems like a passage out of Alencar, he paddles back to shore to take her with him. But unlike Iracema, who sacrificed her

Darlene J. Sadlier

Figure 7. Arduíno Colasanti and Ana Maria Magalhães as Jean and Seboipep in How Tasty Was My Little Frenchman. *Helena Salem collection.*

people to be with Martim, Seboipep refuses to go off with Jean. When he heads back to the canoe to make his escape, she shoots him in the leg with an arrow. Later, when Jean somewhat plaintively asks her if she intends to make a meal of him, a close-up shows her with a Mona Lisa smile. She calls him her "little neck," which refers to the prize morsel given to her as the captive's wife/keeper; and as the film draws to an end, we see her contentedly gnawing on this very morsel. Unlike Iracema, Seboipep survives her encounter with the colonizer and has no offspring from him. On the contrary, she appears quite pleased when Jean's execution day arrives, as if she were looking forward to his final "integration" into the community.

Pereira dos Santos does not end the film on this comic-satiric note, because to do so would be as much an historical distortion as the sentimental endings in Alencar's fiction. As the camera backs away from Seboipep to show a panoramic view of the community, a final quote appears on the screen. The words are from Mem de Sá, the governor general of Brazil, who wrote in 1557: "There I fought on the sea, so that no Tupiniquim remained alive. The dead stretched rigidly along the shoreline, covering nearly a league." The sudden appearance of the quote is shocking. The film as a whole has made the indigenous world look relatively vibrant, harmless, and healthy; but we are told that Jean's death (like the Portuguese bishop's death in actual history) will eventually be avenged by a mass extermination carried out by the Portuguese. The quote is particularly unsettling given the fact that during the period in which the film is set, the Tupiniquim were the wartime allies of the Portuguese. As Helena Salem points out, all the values of the historical sources are undermined by the film's conclusion, which underlines the sheer brutality of the Europeans:

> The truth (visualized) of the colonized is counterposed by the ethnocentric view of the European colonizer, who is unable (nor tries) to comprehend an unknown and different culture from his own, and who is merely concerned with conquering it. On the one hand, the Indians marvel at the technological superiority of the Europeans (gunpowder, presents) and they bow in the face of that technology. . . . On the other hand, they remain faithful to their own culture, eating the European seen as the enemy, regardless of how good natured he reveals himself to be. The Indians live a natural and free existence, without sin. . . . And if the Indians kill and eat a few whites considered as enemies, the whites exterminate thousands and thousands of Indians, as Mem de Sá attests in the final quote. Who then are *"les barbares"*?[12]

One of the most important functions of the quote from Mem de Sá is to remind Brazilian audiences that their national identity, even down to the present day, has depended on the continued extermination of the "New World's" original inhabitants. At the time *How Tasty Was My Little Frenchman* was made, the Brazilian government was in the midst of a drive to uproot indigenous communities in the interior who were standing in the way of the trans-Amazon highway; these people were being not only physically uprooted, but also violently forced, quite against their inclinations or abilities, to become "modern." For Pereira dos Santos the cultural encounter begun in the 1500s was far from over. If past history were any indication, the chance for the survival of the few remaining Indians looked increasingly bleak.

But to read *How Tasty Was My Little Frenchman* exclusively as an allegory about the demise of indigenous groups in the northeast is to overlook its subtle implications for another kind of cultural imperialism that had begun in the mid-1950s, when President Juscelino Kubitscheck opened the nation's doors to massive foreign investment in an attempt to rapidly transform Brazil into a modern industrial nation. That policy, known as "developmentalism," was in place for more than twenty years and brought with it an influx of foreign capital from multinational corporations, as well as a burgeoning national debt. By the early 1970s the failure of this plan was evident; indeed, the much-touted economic "miracle" turned out to be a disaster, resulting in skyrocketing inflation, unemployment, and general unrest. The situation was akin to that of the colonial period: once the natural resources were exhausted or no longer profitable, foreign companies began moving on to richer lands. In the meantime, the presence of those companies had already wrought vast changes in the culture as a whole. Since Brazil's independence, France had been the single most powerful cultural force in Brazil; but with developmentalism the United States assumed prominence. American television programs and music, along with the ever-popular Hollywood cinema, now became an integral part of the nation's culture, and English replaced French as the most desirable foreign language to learn in schools and universities.

In the early 1920s Oswald de Andrade's "Manifesto Antropófago" had espoused the "ingestion" and adaptation of foreign ideas, which would supposedly function dialectically with the folkloric and popular cultures associated with Indians, thus creating a distinctive national identity. Nearly a half century later, *How Tasty Was My Little Frenchman* takes up the same cannibalist theme; Pereira dos Santos's film, however, is suspicious of European influences and radically different in tone from Andrade's cannibalist manifesto, which had summarized its aims with the famous statement, "Tupy or not Tupy, that is the question." Unlike the "anthropophagous" movement (and unlike Joaquim Pedro de Andrade's 1969 film, *Macunaíma*, a wildly irreverent version of Mário de Andrade's 1928 fantastic novel about cannibalism and Brazilian culture), *How Tasty Was My Little Frenchman* offers a subdued, unromantic portrait of a community that avenges any attack on its sovereignty by killing and devouring the invader. The Tupinambá in the film are neither the noble-savage heroes of the nineteenth-century European imagination nor the fierce mythic symbols of 1920s literary nationalism. They are, however, representatives of the postcolonial nation. What is most compelling about Pereira dos Santos's use of this familiar symbolism is his blending of "otherness" and "ordinariness" in the depiction of the Indians, who live a rather docile, mundane existence while trying to cope with foreign armies.

Pereira dos Santos is not unrealistic about the ability of less technologically advanced countries such as Brazil to keep foreign interests at bay; even so, he suggests by analogy or allegory that the contemporary culture is at risk. Like the Tupinambá, the citizenry must be united in their desire to preserve their identity. The ritual of cannibalism becomes a metaphor for a paradoxical kind of modern consumerism that regards whatever is "devoured" as an alien substance and is careful to resist being utterly transformed by it. The consumption of any foreign element, the film seems to argue, ought to become a discriminating, proactive, even aggressive strategy; a culture should be highly selective about what it takes in, and it should ingest the foreign only in order to strengthen the local community.

In interviews given at the time the film was made, Pereira dos Santos underplayed the themes I have just described, insisting that *How Tasty Was My Little Frenchman* was an "anthropological" as opposed to an "ideological" project. Perhaps he was being disingenuous, concealing his real purpose. And yet there can be no question of his efforts to faithfully replicate the lifestyle and language of a civilization that had suffered foreign invasion and extermination. He used an approximation of Tupi (a lost language) for nearly all the dialogue, and he subtitled the film in Portuguese. (In this regard, he was being consistent with Staden, who describes everyone—including the French who pass through the Tupinambá village—as speaking Tupi.) In an even more daring move, he depicted the actual dress of the Indian community, which, according to Staden and others, consisted of little more than feathers, dye, and beads. (He even insisted that the actors have no surgical marks on their bodies.) Ironically, however, it was the ostensibly "anthropological" aspect of his film that ultimately caused problems with the Brazilian censors. The nakedness of the cast, especially of the white males, was strongly frowned on by the government. Although the film was released abroad, it was initially suppressed nationwide; in fact, even the Cannes Film Festival committee rejected it on the grounds of nudity.

It is important to note that the people in the film seem naked rather than nude. As John Berger and others have pointed out, "nudity" is a form of dress—a fetishized, artfully composed imagery of the human body that has a long history in European art. By contrast, Pereira dos Santos shows us people without clothes, and his practice is especially unorthodox when he allows us to see the frontal nakedness of Jean, the European, who goes through most of the film wearing virtually nothing. Where Jean's particular nakedness is concerned, one of the common distinctions between literature and film as media becomes highly relevant. Because photography is not only iconic or symbolic, but also indexical, Pereira dos Santos is able to provide us with a literal presentation of what Staden wrote about indirectly—and in so doing, he tends to undermine the authority of the European. In Staden, we might say, we have the Phallus (a symbolic expression of European power and adventure, controlled by a male voice), whereas in the film we have the phallus (a body part, placed on view). This may explain why the Brazilian censors were more troubled by the naked Jean than by anything else in the film. In a wry essay, "How to Avoid a Naked Man," written for the *Jornal do Brasil*, the novelist Clarice Lispector, who had seen *How Tasty Was My Little Frenchman* at a private showing and greatly admired it, took issue with the government's decision to compromise on the unclothed Indians but not on the white captive. Responding to the censorship board's racism, which had been hidden under the guise of a kind of *National Geographic* conception of "anthropology," Lispector wrote, "Perhaps it's my innocence, but kindly inform me: what is the difference between the naked body of an Indian male and the naked body of a white man?"[13]

With the appointment of a new head of the censorship bureau in November 1971, the film was finally granted exhibition rights throughout Brazil. Although dos Santos had characterized *How Tasty Was My Little Frenchman* as an "anthropological" and not an "ideological" film, his particular use of historical texts and the images he juxtaposed with them clearly had a political purpose. We might say that he was attempting to reassess what Raymond Williams has called the "selective cultural tradition" by incorporating back into that tradition the lost record of the Tupinambá. As Williams points out, the historical record and the culture as a whole always involve a process of discrimination and omission:

> Within a given society, selection [of whatever is significant] will be governed by many kinds of special interests including class interests. Just as the actual social situation will largely govern *contemporary* selection, so the development of the society, the process of historical change, will largely determine the selective tradition. The traditional culture of society will always tend to correspond to its contemporary system of interests and values, for it is not an absolute body of work but a continual selection and interpretation.[14]

Viewed in these terms, Pereira dos Santos's film is less interested in distorting a canonical text than in revealing what that text omits. Its documentarylike or "anthropological" style directly participates in an effort of reinterpretation by providing the viewer with a simulation of what has been lost, not just in time, but also through the selective cultural process. Pereira dos Santos's solidarity with the Tupinambá can therefore be described as an ideological position in powerful contrast with the interests and values of the dominant class in Brazil, which has always identified with the Europeans, especially with the French. His political statement, however, was indirect, and was not completely apparent to everyone who first saw the film. In fact, despite his reassessment of the colonial encounter and the great attention and detail he gave to representing the Indians, the majority of the original audience in Brazil (including the censors) persisted in identifying with the French protagonist.[15] Pereira dos Santos had nevertheless directed one of the most talked-about pictures in the history of Brazilian cinema—a picture whose politics seem to become more clear with the passing years. After all, no matter what changes modernity has wrought, certain things have remained the same: Brazil's economy is still troubled, and in one sense the film's depiction of a rich local culture under siege is equally true for the colonial period, for the 1970s, and for the present day.

NOTES

1. See Rolli Poppino, *Brazil: The Land and the People* (New York: Oxford University Press, 1968), p. 280.

2. Helena Salem, *Nelson Pereira dos Santos: O Sonho Possível do Cinema Brasileiro* (Rio de Janeiro: Editora Nova Fronteira, 1987), p. 258.

3. Ibid., p. 257.

4. Ibid., p. 259.

5. Richard Peña, *"How Tasty Was My Little Frenchman"* in *Brazilian Cinema*, ed. Randal Johnson and Robert Stam (Austin: University of Texas Press, 1982), p. 193.

6. Randal Johnson, *Cinema Novo x 5* (Austin: University of Texas Press), p. 193.

7. Philip P. Boucher, *Cannibal Encounters: Europeans and Island Caribs, 1492–1763* (Baltimore: The Johns Hopkins University Press, 1992), p. 22.

8. See, for example, "Como Era Gostoso Meu Francês," *O Globo* 1 (July 1972).

9. From an interview in *O Globo*, 29 June 1971, and quoted in Salem, *Nelson Pereira dos Santos*, pp. 266–67. My translation.

10. Hans Staden, *Viagem ao Brasil* (Rio de Janeiro: Coleção Afránio Peixoto, Academia Brasileira de Letras, 1988), p. 133. My translation from the Portuguese version of *Brasilien*.

11. Salem, *Nelson Pereira dos Santos*, p. 259.

12. Ibid., p. 261.

13. Clarice Lispector, "De Como Evitar Um Homem Nu," in *A Descoberta do Mundo*, 3rd ed. (Rio de Janeiro: Livraria Francisco Alves, 1984), p. 413. My translation.

14. Raymond Williams, *Culture and Society* (Harmondsworth, UK: Penguin, 1963), p. 253.

15. In a 1977 interview for the *Folha de São Paulo*, Pereira dos Santos looked back on the film's reception, stating: "The public didn't identify with my ideas. For example, they identified with the Frenchman, the colonizer. Everyone was saddened by the death of the 'hero.' They were so influenced by John Wayne 'bang-bangs' that they didn't understand that the hero was the Indian and not the young fellow." Quoted in Salem, *Nelson Pereira dos Santos*, p. 267. My translation.

Jonathan Rosenbaum

Two Forms of Adaptation:
Housekeeping and *Naked Lunch*

I

*Two or three days and nights went by; I reckon I might
say they swum by, they slid along so quiet and smooth
and lovely.*

—Mark Twain,
The Adventures of Huckleberry Finn

Marilynne Robinson's novel *Housekeeping* is virtually defined by its slow, swirling rhythms, but one of the first things that is apparent about Bill Forsyth's passionate, faithful film adaptation is that, as storytelling, it starts out with a hop, skip, and jump; and although an idea of leisurely pacing is sustained throughout, the movie never dawdles, stalls, or grinds to a halt. Like the magical opening of Terrence Malick's 1973 *Badlands* and the no less incandescent ending of his 1978 *Days of Heaven*—two more films in which the heroine's offscreen narration plays a musical role in the narrative structure—the story unfolds with the combined immediacy and remoteness of a fairy tale. An elliptical stream of details and events spanning three generations flows by in minutes, without imparting any feeling of haste.

For fans of Bill Forsyth, who has become something of a directorial brand name, the effect may be more than a little disconcerting. My own spotty sense of Forsyth's previous work—mainly restricted to having seen *Gregory's Girl* (1980) many years ago—had not led me to expect a film with this sort of ambition or depth. A lowercase filmmaker in the sense that e.e. cummings is a lowercase poet, Forsyth is a master of the small point, the sidelong glance, and the quirky off moment. Perhaps by associating *Gregory's Girl* with the behavioral charm of a François

Truffaut or a Milos Forman, I was misled into assuming that the Scottish filmmaker was not above milking his audience with a related form of humanist hype, effective but rather facile; now I am inclined to suspect that he may be a good deal more subtle than either.

The story is about two sisters, Ruthie (Sara Walker, the narrator) and Lucille (Andrea Burchill) Foster, who, after an early childhood in Seattle and the early departure of their father, are raised in the small town of Fingerbone—a lakeside community in the mountains of the Pacific Northwest—by a succession of women. After their mother, Helen (Margot Pinvidic), drops them at the family homestead before driving off a cliff and drowning in the lake, for mysterious reasons that are never discussed, they are raised first by their grandmother; then, after she dies, by two great-aunts; and finally by Helen's itinerant and eccentric younger sister Sylvie (Christine Lahti), who returns to Fingerbone to assume this job.

Although the sisters are very close and mutually isolated from the community, the weirdness of their even more isolated aunt and her impact on the town eventually drive them apart and Lucille goes to live with her home economics teacher. After Sylvie takes Ruth on an excursion by boat to a frost-covered valley and they wind up staying out all night and returning home by hopping a freight car, the sheriff and various local women begin to question Sylvie's suitability as guardian. When a hearing is scheduled, Sylvie and Ruth burn their house down and set out for a life on the road.

This is more or less the plot of the film, although it omits a major incident in the memory of the family and the town that hovers over the entire action and setting like a gigantic phantom. The girls' grandfather—who grew up in the flat plains of the midwest, dreaming of and painting mountains—married and settled in Fingerbone, working for the railroad. Returning home one night from Spokane, his train derailed on the bridge and sank into the lake without leaving a trace; none of the 200 passengers were ever recovered. As reminders and sole witnesses of this tragedy, the elevated train tracks, mountains, and lake might be said to function in the story as characters equal in importance to the Fosters.

Two hauntingly beautiful shots of these train tracks frame the main body of the narrative, from the grandmother's death to the final departure of Ruth and Sylvie. In the first and briefer of these, the mountains, lake, and an approaching train might be considered the scene's major protagonists, although the tiny figures of the young sisters and their grandmother are also visible at the base of the embankment. In the second only the tracks are visible, glowing luminously at night, and this semiabstract image is held on the screen for an extended length of time.

As fictional material, Robinson's novel is at times closer to reverie and landscape painting than to straight narrative, and part of Forsyth's remarkable achievement is to have captured much of this

Figure 8. Christine Lahti (center) with Andrea Burchill (left) and Sara Walker (right) in the Bill Forsythe adaptation of Marilynne Robinson's Housekeeping (1987). Museum of Modern Art.

mood without impeding the narrative flow. A certain parallel to the book and film can be found in elements from *Huckleberry Finn* and its own reflections on the conditions and meaning of freedom, with orphaned Ruth standing in for Huck, Sylvie as a counterpart to Jim—her onetime marriage and her escape from it give her some of the status of an "escaped slave"—and Lucille's hankering after middle-class acceptance and respectability putting her roughly in Tom Sawyer's camp. Admittedly, these parallels are loose and approximate, but the all-male world of Mark Twain's novel and the all-female world of Robinson's account for some of the differences, whereas the relationship between black struggle and feminist struggle serves to elucidate others.

Film adaptations of literary works can be compared in certain ways to translations from one language to another; both require, I think, a technique that bears a resemblance to Method acting, a manner of working inside rather than outside the material. Although it is often thought that the best translation of a text is literal and word for word, professional translators know that such a model is generally unworkable because of the idioms involved. To take a crude example, the French term *baise anglaise* means literally "English kiss" but signifies the same thing that we and the English mean by *French kiss*; a more complex example would point up the syntactical differences between French and English, such as the fact that all French nouns have masculine or feminine genders.

The syntactical differences between prose and film are a good deal more complex, and it is naive to assume that the best film adaptations of novels can provide precise equivalents to each of the elements in the originals. Although one can plausibly cite Stroheim's *Greed* as a model film adaptation, the common assumption that Stroheim made it by filming Frank Norris's *McTeague* "page by page, never missing a paragraph"—as Kenneth Rexroth puts it in the Signet edition—could not be further from the truth. In fact, Stroheim got so far inside the spirit and texture of the original that, like any good Method actor, he was able to generate his own material out of it: almost the first fifth of the published script of *Greed*, nearly sixty pages, describes incidents invented by Stroheim that occur prior to the action at the beginning of the novel.

Forsyth's adaptation of *Housekeeping* is much closer to Stroheim's method than it is to the more literal—hence reductive—approach taken by adapters ranging from Joseph Strick to John Huston. (It is true that Tony Huston's script for *The Dead* is at least bold enough to add a character to Joyce's story; but on the whole Huston *pere* followed a route of faithful reduction rather than one of empathetic embellishment.) This is not merely a matter of rearranging the exposition—so that, for instance, the account of the train plunging to the bottom of the lake occurs in detail much later in the film than in the novel, figuring as a flashback—or ending the story many years and pages before the novel does, but also of adding new details and lines of dialogue that are improvisations on elements found in the original.

The film's treatment of Helen and her suicide are characteristic of this inventiveness. While driving into downtown Fingerbone with her daughters early in the morning, she stops at a green light, pauses, and then charges ahead when it changes to red. (Forsyth frames this gag in a Tatiesque long shot, and, again like Tati, waits patiently for it to happen—a small addition, but one that deftly anticipates the quirkiness of Sylvie.) Prior to her suicide, she parks her car in a field and gets stuck in the mud. As in the novel, a group of boys offer her a hand and she gives them her purse in return. Forsyth's embellishment is to have her insist that they put her own jacket and overcoat under a rear wheel before they push the car—another small detail that speaks volumes. When, moments later, she sails over a cliff into the lake, Forsyth's depiction of the event, restricted to the boys' viewpoint, is as elliptical as the suicide in Bresson's *Une Femme douce*; we see only the bubbles rising to the lake's surface. And because the account of the train disaster occurs shortly after this, the mysteriousness of the plunge both prepares us for it and subtly suggests—as Robinson does in other ways—that Helen's suicide was probably inspired in part by her father's demise.

A slippery character in book and film alike, Sylvie projects a combined serenity and distractedness that makes her antisocial and emotionally sealed off in a friendly way, and blissfully daffy without ever losing her basic grip on reality. (One of her favorite activities is sitting alone in the dark.) It is alarming to hear that Diane Keaton was originally cast in the role, and backed out of it only at the last moment—not because she lacks the talent to play such a character, but because it is almost impossible to imagine her not doing a star turn with the part. Although Christine Lahti, her inspired replacement, has already been criticized in some quarters for not being more of a show-off as Sylvie, it is clear that any grandstanding could shatter the delicate textures that Forsyth carefully builds around her. One of her loveliest speeches, about the train accident—"The lake must be full of people. I've heard stories all my life. You can bet there were a lot of people on the train nobody knew about"—could be crushed by anything but an offhand delivery, and Lahti makes it sweetly sing.

Indeed, Lahti seems so buried in the character's inwardness that she becomes the perfect instrument for the kind of grace notes that Forsyth's style abounds in. When Fingerbone becomes flooded and the sisters come downstairs one morning to encounter their aunt casually greeting them with a coffee cup while trudging around in several inches of muddy water, Keaton, one imagines, would likely have given the moment a Neil Simon inflection. Lahti's consummate professionalism—

all the more impressive in her seamless interplay with the Vancouver nonprofessionals who play Ruthie and Lucille—is to blend her throaty Paula Prentiss voice, dopey smile, and spiky movements with the film's overall low-key temperature, resulting in some of the best naturalistic acting to be found anywhere at the moment. It is the kind of nonegotistical performance, moreover, that allows her to fit in a period context without any hint of anachronism—a virtue she already displayed as Goldie Hawn's next-door neighbor in *Swing Shift,* and which Keaton conspicuously lacked as Louise Bryant in *Reds.*

It is a sensitivity that Lahti shares with Forsyth and his largely Scottish crew in getting the early 50s just right without trumpeting the fact—although a director friend points out that the film *does* fudge Lahti's makeup in relation to the period on a few occasions. Some of the movie's finer inventions—Sylvie laughing at a hokey refrigerator ad with a smiling couple in a shop window, Lucille and Ruthie softly singing "Oh My Papa" while smoking grapevine on a leafy hillside, and an impeccably imagined red vinyl soda shop where "Sh-boom" is purring on the jukebox—come from this unobtrusive perfection, which extends to its gorgeous use of the local scenery. (The film was shot in Nelson, British Columbia, which was also used in *Roxanne.*) A period song mentioned in the novel, "Irene," is utilized as well, but elaborated on so effectively, in separate scenes with Helen and Sylvie, that the film intensifies its meaning.

Although the early 50s is a period we usually associate with affluence and stolidity (unless we think of *On the Road*), part of the film's mysterious beauty relates to the lives of the wandering and the homeless that we more readily associate with the 30s—the grim yet lyrical world of Nelson Algren's *Somebody in Boots,* which has more than anecdotal relevance to the world of the homeless today. (The hoboes often passed by Sylvie, Ruth, and Lucille near the lake and railroad tracks are mainly ignored by the characters and plot, but their presence is frequently felt and remarked on twice in Ruth's narration.)

The discomfort that some spectators may feel about Sylvie, which may lead some of them to dismiss her as a "bag lady"—a comfortable, reassuring epithet for anyone unwilling to consider too closely her current, real-life counterparts—points to the degree to which non-Americans may be privy to certain insights about this country that we are too shielded to see for ourselves. After a second look at *Housekeeping,* I would not call it a great film, but it comes very close to being a perfect one in everything that it sets out to do. Which is only to say that it may have taken a Scotsman to show us the contemporary importance, the depths and radiance, of Robinson's novel.

II

---

*And some of us are on Different Kicks and that's a thing
out in the open the way I like to see what I eat and vice
versa mutatis mutandis as the case may be. Bill's Naked
Lunch Room. . . . Step right up. Good for young and old,
man and bestial. Nothing like a little snake oil to grease
the wheels and get a show on the track Jack. Which side
are you on? Fro-Zen Hydraulic? Or you want to take a
look around with Honest Bill?"*

—William S. Burroughs,
introduction to Naked Lunch (1962)

The first time I read William S. Burroughs's *Naked Lunch*—or at least
large portions of it—was in 1959, a few months after its first printing, in
a smuggled copy of the seedy Olympia Press edition fresh from Paris. As
I recall, it was missing most or all of the accompanying matter—the introduction ("Deposition: Testimony Concerning a Sickness"), "Atrophied
Preface" ("Wouldn't You?"), and appendix ("Letter From a Master Addict
to Dangerous Drugs")—that gave so much body, flavor, shape, and out-
right usefulness to the Grove Press edition published in the United
States three years later. Without this fancy dressing it read like a simple
parade of fantasy horrors laced with gallows humor and separated by
ellipses, and to my sixteen-year-old mind it was interesting only for its
wild and extravagant obscenities—precisely what had caused it to be
banned in the first place.

When I later came to read and reread the American edition, the
work no longer seemed quite so formless. The introduction provided
biographical, moral, and metaphysical focus—the story of Burroughs's
fifteen-year heroin addiction and what he called the pyramid of junk and
the algebra of need—whereas the "preface" at the end was full of lovely
formal and thematic clues about what Burroughs was up to. Moreover,
both sections were written in a powerfully condensed, poetically precise American vernacular that arguably surpassed everything else in
the book—in fact, they were so pungently written that they placed the
entire work in a fresh perspective. (The prosaic appendix, by contrast,
was useful mainly in my early experiments with peyote and marijuana,
and Burroughs as a reference point on this subject was secondary to the
lyrical effusions of other Beat writers, namely, Jack Green and Jack
Kerouac.)

This second helping of *Naked Lunch* had such an impact on me
that on my first trip to Paris a few years later I snatched up any other
Burroughs books I could find, *The Ticket That Exploded* and *Dead
Fingers Talk* (the second was confiscated by British customs—in those

days such a book could be deemed illegal in England before it was published there). During the remainder of the 60s I continued to keep up with Burroughs: *Nova Express, The Soft Machine,* the American edition of *The Ticket That Exploded* (also superior to its Olympia forerunner), and many pamphlet-size publications from obscure smaller presses.

But even then my enthusiasm for Burroughs was waning. By the 60s Burroughs had come under the influence of painter Brion Gysin and was fully committed to cut-ups—a technique of arbitrarily folding texts by himself and others and grafting the halves together to see what unexpected meanings flashed out of the jumble. To me this sort of Dada throwback, which usually produced meager results, was only a mechanical means of effecting sudden changes of syntax midsentence, a sort of druggy turnaround that Burroughs had already achieved much more forcefully by instinct in his earlier writing.

These "natural" cut-ups allowed some passages to undergo mysterious seachanges of emphasis and focus in the midst of a monotone patter and permitted certain similes and metaphors to sprout independent lives and narratives of their own in the course of seemingly logical arguments. Two examples from *Naked Lunch,* both from the "Atrophied Preface" follow:

> Sooner or later The Vigilante, The Rube, Lee the Agent, A. J., Clem and Jody the Ergot Twins, Hassan O'Leary the After Birth Tycoon, The Sailor, The Exterminator, Andrew Keif, 'Fats' Terminal, Doc Benway, 'Fingers' Schafer are subject to say the same thing in the same words to occupy, at that intersection point, the same position in space-time. Using a common vocal apparatus complete with all metabolic appliances that is to be the same person—a most inaccurate way of expressing *Recognition:* The junky naked in sunlight. . . .

> You can cut into *Naked Lunch* at any intersection point. . . . I have written many prefaces. They atrophy and amputate spontaneous like the little toe amputates in a West African disease confined to the Negro race and the passing blonde shows her brass ankle as a manicured toe bounces across the club terrace, retrieved and laid at her feet by her Afghan Hound. . . .

What seemed natural and funny in *Naked Lunch* began to seem forced and abstruse in some of the later books. Furthermore, the relentless misogyny of Burroughs's writing, coupled with the eventual knowledge that he had killed his own wife, finally got to me, and my ardor for his work went through a distinct cooling-off phase.

Still, I yield to no one in my admiration for the second edition of *Naked Lunch.* It may not be politically correct, but neither is *War and Peace* (as Tolstoy, in his subsequent born-again decrepitude, was the first to admit). Neither, for that matter, is David Cronenberg's highly transgressive and subjective film adaptation of *Naked Lunch,* which may well be the most troubling and ravishing movie since *Eraserhead.* It is also fundamentally a film about writing—even *the* film about writing, the same one that filmmakers as diverse as Wim Wenders (in *Hammett*), Philip Kaufman (in *Henry & June*), and the Coen brothers (in *Barton Fink*) have been trying with less success to make. Part of what makes it politically incorrect is that it posits an intimate interdependence between the act of creation and the act of murder.

> Heads explode. Parasites fly at people's faces. Television sets breathe. A woman grows a spike in her armpit and unleashes a cataclysm on the world. These are the startling images David Cronenberg uses to shock and disturb us as his films travel through a nightmare world where the grotesque and the bizarre make our flesh creep. (Jacket copy, *The Shape of Rage: The Films of David Cronenberg* [1983].)

My acquaintance with Cronenberg is much spottier than my acquaintance with Burroughs, and it was made at a relatively late stage in his career. I was impressed but repelled by *Scanners* when it came out in 1981, but I walked out of a revival of *They Came from Within* (1975) a few years later, more repulsed than enlightened, and felt pretty neutral about *The Dead Zone* (1983) and *The Fly* (1986). It was only three or four years ago, when I caught up with *Videodrome* (1982) on video (I have seen it again at least twice), that I realized just how brilliant Cronenberg is. I did not exactly warm to *Dead Ringers* (1988), but it was such a tour de force that I could not help but think Cronenberg's craft was growing by leaps and bounds. A subsequent look at *The Brood* (1979) further persuaded me that his oeuvre has an overall coherence and complexity unmatched by those of any other contemporary horror film director, including David Lynch and George Romero.

All of Cronenberg's recent works are linked by a style and vision that belong to a particular annex of contemporary art, an annex that might be called biological expressionism. Burroughs is a longtime resident of this annex, and so is his disciple J. G. Ballard; Lynch is the most obvious example of another filmmaker of this persuasion. What all these biological expressionists have in common is a certain deadpan morbidity about the body that borders on comedy—and a tendency to depict paranoia, helplessness, and insect horror in such a way that "inside" and "outside" become indistinguishable.

Dipping into *The Shape of Rage* (a critical collection published in Canada that is unfortunately no longer in print), I discovered that several other critics had arrived at some of these connections before I did. I learned from a lengthy interview in the same book that Cronenberg, born in 1943 in Toronto, grew up hoping to become a writer, and that Burroughs was a seminal influence, along with Henry Miller, Vladimir Nabokov, and Samuel Beckett. The fact that Cronenberg is Canadian also seems to have shaped his work. Piers Handling, the editor of the collection, speculates that Cronenberg's "benign but misguided" father figures, who are usually scientists—Dr. Benway (Roy Scheider) in *Naked Lunch* is a near facsimile—point to a specifically Canadian sensibility, an alienated consciousness that incorporates repression, puritanism, a sense of marginality and victimization, a feeling of entrapment, and perhaps even "a colonized mentality." ("The land has been exploited but not for the profit of the people who live there.") Moreover, Handling argues that the fear of external horrors in the first films has been replaced by the fear of internal horrors in all the films subsequent to *The Brood* and that the "internalization of this dread achieves its apotheosis in *Videodrome.*" It is back again with a vengeance in *Naked Lunch.*

I was forced to the appalling conclusion that I would never have become a writer but for Joan's death, and to a realization of the extent to which this event has motivated and formulated my writing. I live with the constant threat of possession, and a constant need to escape from possession, from Control. So the death of Joan brought me in contact with the invader, the Ugly Spirit, and maneuvered me into a lifelong struggle, in which I have no choice except to write my way out. (Burroughs, introduction to *Queer* [1985].)

Perhaps the most transgressive aspect of Cronenberg's adaptation of *Naked Lunch* is that it follows the general approach of some of the very worst movie versions of literary classics—for example, *Hemingway's Adventures of a Young Man* and *Mishima*—by turning what was once fiction into ersatz biography of the author. The vulgar presumption of this approach is that the artist's life counts for more than the art itself, which is regarded as little more than a symptom. In effect, whatever the artist has done to transform and transcend the banality of his or her own experience is undone by the filmmakers, who turn it back into raw material; by assuming that biography and art are coextensive and virtually interchangeable, they produce works that lack the integrity of either.

On the face of it, this is what Cronenberg has done. He has reduced the many protagonists of the book to one, William Lee (Peter Weller), who is clearly meant to be Burroughs himself; indeed, Weller's fine performance is often little more than an uncanny impersonation. The film opens in New York in 1953, where Lee is working as an exterminator who hangs out with two writers easily recognizable as Allen Ginsberg and Jack Kerouac (Michael Zelniker and Nicholas Campbell),

Figure 9. Peter Weller (left) with Robert A. Silverman in the David Cronenberg adaptation of William S. Burroughs's Naked Lunch *(1991). Museum of Modern Art.*

neither of whom appears in recognizable form in the narrative sections of Burroughs's book. Cronenberg also supplies a drug-addicted wife, Joan (Judy Davis), plainly modeled after Burroughs's wife Joan Vollmer, who also is not in the book. There is even a fanciful restaging of Burroughs's shooting his wife by playing a game of William Tell with her, getting her to balance a drinking glass on her head, firing at it, and missing.

In fact, Burroughs shot his wife in Mexico City in 1951. In 1953 he was not even in New York, but was traveling about South America looking for the hallucinogenic drug *yage;* his only stint as an exterminator was in Chicago in 1942, a year or so before he first met Ginsberg and Kerouac in New York. In other words, although the movie is full of references to Burroughs's life, it is not really biography at all, and in fairness to Cronenberg it should be added that this is perfectly evident almost from the start—when a gigantic insect starts talking to Lee, enlisting him as an "agent" and giving him orders. It is rather as if Cronenberg has taken snippets from *Naked Lunch,* various Burroughs autobiographical texts (chiefly "Exterminator!" and the 1985 introduction to *Queer*), a few details of Burroughs's biography, and assorted Burroughs-inspired fancies of his own and placed them all inside a kaleidoscope—or, to switch metaphors, performed an elaborate cut-up with them. Even the film's haunting and lovely score, which juxtaposes classical themes by Howard Shore with wailing free-form alto-sax solos by Ornette Coleman backed by Coleman's trio, creates an ambience that is not so much Burroughs as commentary on Burroughs.

What emerges is recognizable but fully transformed Burroughs material. In the film, Lee gets into trouble when he discovers that someone has been stealing his roach powder. His boss, A. J. Cohen, is livid: "You vant I should spit right in your face!? You vant!? You vant!?" This line and Cohen both appear in "Exterminator!" but the missing bug powder is Cronenberg's addition. When Lee applies to a Chinaman in the office for more powder he gets a curt reply: "No glot . . . C'lom Fliday." This line comes from the final words of *Naked Lunch*, a passage that is glossed ninety pages earlier: "In 1920s a lot of Chinese pushers around found The West so unreliable, dishonest and wrong, they all packed in, so when an Occidental junky came to score, they say: 'No glot . . . C'lom Fliday.'"

Shortly after Lee discovers that his wife has been shooting the missing bug powder and is now addicted, two cops arrest him, take him to a decaying office with vomit-green walls, and leave him alone with a gigantic bug who actually gets off on the very substance that is supposed to exterminate it ("Say Bill," it says, "do you think you could rub some of this powder on my lips?"). The bug orders him to kill his wife, insisting that she is an "Interzone" agent and not even human. Later, after Joan asks Lee to rub some bug powder on her own lips and they make love, he procures another drug called "black meat" from the sinister Dr. Benway—a drug made from dried "aquatic Brazilian centipedes" that is supposed to get Joan off her habit. But at this point Lee winds up "accidentally" killing her.

Significantly, Lee trades his gun for a portable typewriter at a pawnshop; he then travels to Interzone, a North African city like Tangier where most of the remainder of the film is set. Lee's "ticket" to Interzone, however, which he shows to one of his writer friends, is the drug-filled syringe procured from Benway, so it is highly questionable whether Lee or the film ever really leaves New York. (Enslaved by his addiction, he may not even leave his flat.) If one looks closely at certain scenes in Interzone, fragments of New York are plainly visible—a patch of Central Park seen from a window, even an Eighth Avenue subway entrance seen from a car—and at one point Lee remarks that a certain living room reminds him of a New York restaurant. Lee's flats in New York and Interzone are nearly identical, and he even encounters Kiki (Joseph Scorsiani), who becomes his lover in Interzone, initially in a New York waterfront bar.

Bearing all this in mind, the extreme distortions of Paul and Jane Bowles, fictionalized as Tom and Joan Frost (Ian Holm and Judy Davis) in the Interzone sections, have to be seen as projections of Lee—and beyond that, projections of Cronenberg—rather than as tenable figures having anything to do with literary history or with Burroughs himself. Tom Frost is an older and more overt Lee who acts openly on his desires; Joan is an alternate version of his wife, "addicted" to lesbianism as the other Joan was addicted to bug powder. These characters, as well as Yves Cloquet (Julian Sands), Hans (Robert A. Silverman), and Kiki, show that Cronenberg has taken considerable license in fashioning this world, which clearly has more relationship to his own universe than to Burroughs's.

Cronenberg's method for "adapting" *Naked Lunch* is roughly analogous to Burroughs's device of "natural" cut-ups, a process of hallucinatory transformation: roach powder becomes hallucinogenic drug, drug taking becomes sex, roach becomes paranoiac operative, wife becomes insect, and Interzone becomes New York experienced in a drugged state. Later, when Lee becomes a writer in Interzone, the transformations become even more dense and metaphorical: typewriters, for example, become talking cockroaches or Mugwumps (a Burroughs beastie that the film works wonders with, in New York and Interzone alike), functioning variously as Ugly Spirits, muses, prophets, psychiatrists, lovers, friends, bosses, and drug dispensers, so that writing, sex, and drugs become virtually interchangeable. The moment of each transformation, moreover, becomes impossible to pinpoint, because the identities do not strictly mutate but overlap or interface—rather like the colored geometric shapes that traverse the screen in the film's beautiful opening credits.

Some of these principles of transformation operate formally in a series of short experimental films made in England in the 60s by the late Antony Balch, now available on video, all of them involving Burroughs as writer or actor/performer. (The best are *Towers Open Fire* and *The Cut-Ups.*) The transformations here often involve one character's assuming the identity of another. A more mainstream, thematic approach to such transformations can be found in two later shorts by Gus Van Sant that are fairly literal adaptations of Burroughs texts: *The Discipline of DE* (1978) develops from a how-to essay with Zenlike behavioral tips (mainly on housework shortcuts) into a specific fictional illustration, a shoot-out between a Wyatt Earp protege and Two Gun McGee; *Thanksgiving Prayer* (1991) quickly turns from a counting of American blessings into a parade of all-American horrors. (These shorts are not available on video, but they should be.)

Cronenberg's approach is neither a strict application of Burroughs's cut-up principles (as in Balch) nor a straightforward adaptation of his texts (as in Van Sant), but an *absorption* of certain principles and texts from Burroughs into the filmmaker's particular cosmology and style. The resulting portrait—and it should be stressed that Cronenberg's

Naked Lunch, unlike Burroughs's, *is* a portrait of a single character—is not of Burroughs or Cronenberg, but of some mysterious composite, an overlap and/or interface of these two personalities.

———

[The biographer did not] share Burroughs's misogyny, which at the bottom was probably an attempt to smother his own contemptible femininity. Born in his hatred of the secret, covered-up part of himself that was maudlin and sentimental and womanly, misogyny was his form of self-loathing. (Ted Morgan, *Literary Outlaw: The Life and Times of William S. Burroughs* [1988].)

The philosophical parallels between Lynch's *Eraserhead* and this film are striking. Both movies are often creepy comedies generated by lurid puritanical imaginations infected by guilt and a will toward censorship, echo chambers of projections and disavowals. When William Lee is "enlisted" as an agent in Interzone, the reports he types up turn out to be *Naked Lunch* itself, a book he has no recollection of writing. (In his introduction Burroughs said, "I have no precise memory of writing the notes which have now been published under the title *Naked Lunch.*") Lee's homosexuality and his drug taking provoke comparable disavowals, as he projects his desires onto others. Whether he is engaged in sex, drugs, or writing, Lee can be seen simultaneously as a voyeur and as an active participant in the diverse intrigues and activities of Interzone, which corresponds to the inner zone of his head. Like "innocent" Henry in *Eraserhead,* he ultimately figures as both progenitor and victim of the diverse horrors surrounding him.

But a key difference between Lynch and Cronenberg corresponds to an equally key difference between Cronenberg and Burroughs. Though Lynch's vision depends on darkness and cruelty and Burroughs's more pessimistic and mature vision is tinged with feelings of great loss and sorrow, neither artist can be said to have a tragic vision—as Ballard does, at least in *Empire of the Sun.* Cronenberg has such a vision, and his *Naked Lunch,* like *Dead Ringers,* is suffused with it.

The central tenet in *Naked Lunch* is that Lee needs his wife in order to live and needs to kill her in order to write, and all the film's transactions and transformations derive from this appalling fact. He literally has to kill his wife again and again in order to keep on writing, and this condemns him to perpetual psychic imprisonment. (It is no wonder that by the end of the film Benway, Lee's bisexual father figure, has enlisted him in the CIA as a secret agent posing as an American journalist and sent him off to an old-style totalitarian state: Annexia, a Cronenberg invention.) Given Lee's tragic dilemma, the matching aphorisms that appear at the beginning of the movie resound with irrevocable finality. The first comes from Hassan-e Sabbah, an eleventh-century Persian religious agitator much admired by Burroughs: "Nothing is true, everything is permitted." And the second comes from Burroughs himself: "Hustlers of the world, there is one Mark you cannot beat. The Mark inside. . . ."

Lesley Stern

Emma in Los Angeles:
Remaking the Book
and the City

Cher Horovitz, handsome, clever, and rich, had lived nearly sixteen years in Los Angeles with very little to distress or vex her—just like Emma Woodhouse, who, "with a comfortable home and happy disposition, seemed to unite some of the best blessings of existence." Emma, it is true, is a little older—nearly twenty-one—at the beginning of Jane Austen's novel than is Cher at the beginning of Amy Heckerling's movie; and Emma, so we are told, lives not in LA but "in the world." These minor differences aside, there is something uncanny in the way Cher reprises the role that Emma Woodhouse vacated in 1816. We are told that Cher has an ancient and glorious lineage, although not in the novelistic tradition: both she and her best friend Dionne are named after "great singers of the past who now do infomercials." Cher generously acknowledges Cindy Crawford as a role model,[1] but her uncredited model, and the true—albeit truly transmogrified—inspiration for *Clueless* is undoubtedly Emma/*Emma*.

Kids in America

The movie begins with a spinning overhead shot of a group of girls having fun in a white Jeep, which careens all over, as does the hand-held camera, as do the colors. This shot initiates a montage of Cher and her friends having fun—shopping, driving, kidding about by the pool. The colors are garishly bright, every frame is crowded and energetic, and music pumps out. The song is "Kids in America" by the Muffs, who are covering an early 80s hit by Kym Wilde.[2] Before too long one of the girls in the opening emerges as "heroine" both on the image track and in a narrating voice-over: "So OK, you're probably thinking, 'Is this, like, a Noxema commercial, or what?!' But seriously, I actually have a way-normal life for a teenage girl. I mean, I get up, I brush my teeth, and I pick out my school clothes." Having picked out her faux–haute-couture school clothes with the aid of a mix-and-match computer program, to the accompaniment of David Bowie's "Fashion Girl," Cher begins her day. We are introduced to her father, a wealthy litigation lawyer, and are given a bumpy tour of the neighborhood as we set off for school with her, driving past the Beverly Hills mansions, with "Just a Girl" on the soundtrack. "Did I show you the lumped-out Jeep Daddy got me?" she asks. (She does not have a licence yet, but, as she says, "I need something to learn on.") We pick up her friend Dionne, sporting an extravagantly exotic hat, and proceed to school, the girls exchanging greetings and trading insults en route: "Shopping with Dr. Seuss?" Cher asks. "Well, at least I wouldn't skin a Collie to make my backpack," responds Dionne.

This account might seem to render the links between this teen movie set in LA and a novel of manners set in a nineteenth-century English village tenuous. But let us backtrack to the first paragraph of the novel: "Emma Woodhouse had lived nearly twenty-one years in the world with very little to distress or vex her."[3] A few pages on we find that "the world" is in fact Highbury, a "large and populous village almost amounting to a town" (p. 29). It is this conflation between the world and the village that gives to *Emma* much of its distinctive flavor—the parochialism derived from the characters' conception of the world and their misconception of their place in it provides a source of satire and simultaneously a stage for the enactment of a certain ethnographic impulse (focusing on the day-to-day lives of ordinary middle-class people) that heralded a modernity in the novel. And it is precisely this conflation (between world and village), along with the dual impulse to satirize and to elaborate a kind of fictional ethnography, that provides a key to *Clueless* and its central conceit: Los Angeles as a village, a village peopled moreover by teenagers who think that Beverly Hills is the center of the world.

From certain critical perspectives, we might note, Jane Austen's satire has been dubiously regarded. As Edward Said has pointed out,[4] her preoccupation with the local served not as the basis of satire, but rather as a means to consolidate and advance the interests of the Empire, by figuring a little patch of England as universal—as center, home, norm.[5] However, feminist critics have drawn attention to the particularity of Austen's modernist impulse, pointing out that her novels brought onto center stage a world that had not previously been deemed suitable for literary treatment. She conjured up a new world of women, and although she certainly subjected this world to satire, she also delineated its quotidian contours meticulously and celebrated its denizens with wry affection. These different approaches to Austen indicate, I think, dual impulses in her work. They are worth noting, not only because film critics tend to reproduce these approaches in their appraisals of *Clueless*,[6] but also because the genius of the film derives from its deployment of what we might call the Austenian dual impulse, a deployment that indicates a careful and imaginative reading of the novel *Emma.*

The film opens with a declaration that these are "Kids in America," but the image gives us a very particular kind of America and a particular kind of kids. To a certain extent, of course, these images are 'way normal'; even if we live on the wrong side of the tracks or in Australia, we recognize this LA as metonymic of movie-made America, we are familiar with all the jokes about West Coast culture, and we recognize Beverly Hills as a very privileged, albeit often tacky, enclave of LA (normalized if not by the movies, then by television, by shows such as *Beverly Hills 90210*). Cher is truly a child of Hollywood, her mother having died in "a fluke accident during a routine liposuction," and her conception of the Beverly Center as *the* center of the world serves as an index of Hollywood's imperialism—its promulgation of a universalizing insularity, its relentless celebration of consumer culture and ready-to-go false consciousness.

Luckily for the critics of the culture-and-imperialism nexus, however, this parochialism is satirized. Cher thinks that Bosnia is in the Middle East and hazards a guess that Kuwait is in the Valley. The Valley itself, as far as these kids are concerned, is literally off the map; they get lost going to a party there, since the only place they can find on the Thomas street map is Bel Air. Cher cannot figure out why Lucy, the maid, who comes from El Salvador, is angered when Cher assumes that "Mexican" is her language, and she is duly rebuked by Josh, the Mr. Knightley figure: "You get upset if someone thinks you live below Sunset." But for some, this satire is not quite enough; too gentle, it is overshadowed by the uncritical and affectionate treatment accorded the characters: "This version of 90s Californian materialism has a tang of conservatism that is both intriguing and repellent."[7]

My feeling is that, just as Jane Austen gave the novel a newly modernist inflection through stretching generic boundaries, so Amy Heckerling has renovated old rhetorical devices in the service of new insights and pleasures. By reading *Emma* through the lens of a contemporary genre—the teen movie—and by rendering this teen world through a predominantly feminine consciousness, she has exercised the sort of fictionally ethnographic exploration epitomized by Austen. Like Austen, she asks, What are the preoccupations, language, courting and/or dating rituals, fashion, and mores of a wealthy and privileged group of young people? And, like Austen, she transforms a documentary rendering of the quotidian into an imaginative and lively delight in fictionality. Via a quite distinctive rhetorical modality, she creates a space in which we can both identify the unrelenting banality and callow foolishness of these characters and also delight in their engagement in witty wordplay and visual jokes, their hyperbolic sense of style, their strings of quotations

Figure 10. Alicia Silverstone (center) with Stacey Dash (left) and Brittany Murphy (right) in Amy Heckerling's Clueless *(1995). Museum of Modern Art.*

and misquotations, the way in which they generate a new female topology and language: Baldwins and Bettys, "cruising the crimson wave" (having your period), "hymenally challenged" (being a virgin), "boink-fest" (lots of sex), "shame spiral," "calorie fest," and "full-on Monet" ("It's like a painting, see? From far away, it's OK, but up close, it's a big old mess"). In short, *Clueless* is characterized by an utterly engaging impulse—an impulse at once utopian and comic—to remake or refashion the world.

Refashioning the World, or "I Remember Mel Gibson Accurately"

HEATHER: It's just like Hamlet said, "To thy own self, be true."

CHER: Ah, no, uh, Hamlet didn't say that.

HEATHER: I think that I remember Hamlet accurately.

CHER: Well, I remember Mel Gibson accurately, and he didn't say that. That Polonius guy did.

In this chapter I posit that *Clueless* is a remake. Through certain remaking strategies—a consciousness of intertextuality if you like—LA materializes in the film as a particularly interesting configuration of spatial and cultural tropes. Just as Cher and her friends take particular delight in the personal makeover, so the film exercises a makeover on both the city and the book, throwing the place itself into relief as a patterning of repetition and difference.

If we describe the film as a remake, a question inevitably arises: Is it necessary to have read *Emma* in order to make sense of and truly enjoy *Clueless?* Well, if you are familiar with *Emma* you can have a lot of fun entering into a kind of guessing game—identifying the parallels and deviations or transformations. Then again, if you are the sort of person who has read *Emma*, you might not in fact get a lot of the other more contemporary allusions. Clearly *Clueless* appeals to different audiences who bring to the movie different knowledge and expectations, but what makes it particularly fascinating is that it actually assumes, through the heterogeneity of its references and allusions, that quotidian knowledge is informed by and woven out of a diversity of cultural practices—not distinguishable according to "high" and "low" markers. In this context Los Angeles is figured not simply as an imitation of or deviation from Highbury, but rather as an intertextual site spun by the movies, television series, MTV, and a variety of remakes and adaptations. Although it is certainly not necessary to be familiar with *Emma* in order to enjoy *Clueless*, my argument is that it is the spirit and operation of remaking

that serves to generate and sustain the movie's intricate network of relations—between different texts, different media, different cultural signs
and temporalities.

A remake is generally considered a remake of an earlier film.
Adaptations are not, strictly speaking, remakes, although if a property
has previously been adapted, the more recent film is almost by default a
remake, and particularly in a case in which the source is not a classic
text, the reference point will be the earlier film. But the reference point
is also generic, because remakes tend to update and modernize earlier
texts in terms of their generic possibility. This generic quality indicates
a paradox: remakes reflect the conservative nature of the industry; they
are motivated by an economic imperative to repeat proven successes.
But in order to maintain economic viability, in the very process of repetition remakes are also compelled to register variation and difference
(from the originals), to incorporate generic developments. They are often,
then, through the patterning of repetition and difference, a way of test-
ing and also flexing generic boundaries. Also, over time they provide an
index of changes in social and cultural values.

Clueless is not, strictly speaking, a remake, but neither is it a
straightforward adaptation, in which the aim is generally to reduce difference, to find the correlative of one medium (literature) in another
(film). The fidelity that is so imperative here—insofar as there is a motivation to preserve a classic text—is primarily conservative, even nostal-
gic. In terms of the taxonomy of remakes sketched out by Thomas
Leitch,[8] *Clueless* is closest to the update, in which a precursor text is
translated into a contemporary idiom. The modernity of *Clueless* derives
from the generic choices that Heckerling has made. Most simply, her
choice was to turn an early nineteenth-century comedy of manners into
a late twentieth-century teen movie.

Before discussing this generic reframing of *Emma*, I am going to
pause and take a moment to outline some of the main structural features
of both texts and gesture toward the imitations, reverberations, and
transformations.

Matchmaking and Boinkfesting

The parallels and echoes occur both on a structural level—having
to do with plot and the way it is articulated through the figuring of characters and the combinations they enter into—and on a more incidental
level, through the representation of quotidian practices and passions.
Clueless is remarkably faithful as a structural repetition, and it is inven-
tively divergent in terms of incidentals. In fact, it is the tension between
these two that generates pleasure. In outlining the structural echoes, perhaps the more incidental details will come into focus, rather like a view

of Los Angeles taking shape on the computer monitor—dots and digital doodles eventually cohering into an image.

Emma is both a comedy of manners and a cautionary tale. It takes a simple moral precept that is dramatized through a largely episodic structure. It centers on a young woman, wealthy, endowed with "the power of having rather too much her own way and a disposition to think a little too well of herself" (p. 27). Assuming the role of a kind of female Svengali, she adopts and undertakes the transformation of Harriet, a young woman new to the village. While orchestrating her protege's social elevation, Emma arranges a series of romances for Harriet, but as the matchmaking goes repeatedly wrong our heroine is revealed as supremely clueless when it comes to sex and romance. Eventually she realizes her own snobbishness and blindness not only to others' desires, but also to her own. With self-revelation (and a touch of remorse) comes reformation, romantic fulfillment, and a happy ending—that is to say, marriage.

Emma is motherless; her father is a "kind-hearted polite old man" (p. 259) whose habit of eating watery gruel and whose hypochondria she indulges good-naturedly. At the beginning of the novel she is friendless, having lost her governess, who was also her companion, to marriage. This loss, however, was orchestrated by Emma herself, or at least she takes the credit for arranging the match and thus saving Miss Taylor from a penurious and loveless existence. Mr. Knightley is the old family friend who is also her brother-in-law and is the only person who dares criticize Emma. Eventually she realizes that he is the one she loves. But before this she falls for Frank Churchill, who, like Harriet, is an outsider. In her flirtation she fails to discern Frank's secret—that he is in love with Jane Fairfax (although indeed this knowledge is largely withheld from the reader as well). This capacity for misreading the signs of attraction, sometimes willfully, sometimes ignorantly, leads Emma into lots of trouble. Dismissing the object of Harriet's affection, Mr. Martin the farmer, she becomes convinced that Mr. Elton (whom she deems more socially suitable) is enamored of Harriet, failing to see what is obvious to the reader and some other characters—that it is Emma whom he loves.

Cher is also motherless, but her father is a high-powered, wealthy, and far-from-polite litigation lawyer. His gruff manner, however, hides a kind heart as far as his daughter is concerned, and she indulges him and carefully watches his low-cholesterol, high-vitamin diet. Instead of a governess Cher has a teacher who cannot be talked out of giving her low grades. Her solution to the dilemma—"I have tried everything to convince him of my scholastic aptitude, but I was brutally rebuffed"—is to make him sublimely happy by arranging a "boinkfest" for him with another teacher, Miss Geist, herself most amenable to the prerequisite makeover. Mr. Knightley becomes Josh, a student of environmental law and the son of one of her father's previous wives, therefore a sort of step-brother. The two outsiders are Tai (the Harriet figure), who arrives from the East Coast with a broad Bronx accent, and Christian (the Frank Churchill figure), who arrives from Chicago and is gay. Mr. Elton, the snobbish vicar, becomes the snobbish Jaguar-driving college boy, Elton, and Mr. Martin, the farmer, becomes the dope-smoking, skateboarding Travis, who takes the bus to school. Jane Fairfax disappears from the film, but there is a new figure—Dionne, a rich black girl who is Cher's best friend.

Emma, who is wealthy enough not to have to work, spends most of her time socializing, refining her accomplishments (which are those of her age, class, and gender), such as painting, playing the piano, reading, composing and deciphering riddles, cultivating the art of conversation, doing occasional good deeds, thinking about sex and romance, talking obliquely but at great length about sex and romance, and enjoying sex and romance via matchmaking and flirting. The plot progresses episodically, configuring and reconfiguring character clusters via a series of social events such as dinner parties, afternoon teas, picnics, very occasional excursions out of the village—to Box Hill, for instance—and dances. The topology of Highbury and its environs is mapped out in the same movement by which social relations are charted—through detailed descriptions of travel and modes of communication. The sending of notes is one way the characters communicate, but mostly physical and psychic distance is conquered through interminable traipsing around the village, on foot or by carriage.

Cher, who is wealthy (and smart) enough not have to try too hard at school, spends most of her time hanging out with her girl-friends, learning to drive, shopping, flaneusing in Rodeo Drive, dieting, exercising to *Buns of Steel*, watching *Ren and Stimpy* and *Beavis and Butthead* on television, refining her dress sense, cultivating the art of the argot, eventually doing some good deeds, thinking about sex and romance, talking ostentatiously and at great length about sex and romance, and enjoying sex and romance via matchmaking and flirting. The plot progresses episodically, configuring and reconfiguring character clusters via a series of social events such as dinners, calorie fests and Christian Slater movies at the mall, excursions into the distant deep and dark environs of Sun Valley, take-out picnics at home, and dances. The topology of Los Angeles and its environs is mapped out in the same movement by which social relations are charted—through detailed descriptions of travel and modes of communication. The cellular phone is the primary means of communication (heralded by the swelling theme music of *2001* and imagistically invoked as a version of the plinth), but mostly physical and psychic distance is conquered through interminable traipsing around the mall or driving around town.

"Isn't My House Classic?"

In this minimal account of the "updating" of *Emma* a couple of things become apparent. The modernization is manifested in a process of Los Angelesization and teenification. Los Angeles and the teenage phenomenon are not unrelated and in fact are connected through the motif of modernity, of updating, of contemporaneity. Configured by the generic imperatives of a teen movie, LA comes itself to signify the "modern," the contemporary, the new, the stylish, the fashionable. Simultaneously, however, the consciousness of modernity is satirized, and it is satirized precisely by invoking the spurious sense of originality that provides a basis for updating—witness Cher's notion of the classic: "Isn't my house classic? The columns date all the way back to 1972."

The kind of image of LA that is summonsed up here is framed by the postmodern, but *Clueless* gives us a very different postmodern LA than that evoked by a film such as *Blade Runner,* in which the family romance, photography, and memory are in the service of a metaphysical thematic dedicated to loss and nostalgia. The fatigued irony of *Blade Runner*'s "I think Sebastian; therefore, I am" is replaced by the tongue-in-cheek "I shop; therefore, I am" of *Clueless.* The concept of teenager is of course itself very modern and did not exist in Austen's time; moreover, the teen movie is a genre often concerned with what is hip and of the moment. By setting the film in Beverly Hills and by concentrating on a group that is obsessed with style, fashion, and being up to date and that talks in an arcane and localized argot, Heckerling undertakes a potentially hazardous project, runs the risk of creating a film that is precariously of the moment: like everything that is "in," it is doomed to go "out"; what is fashionable one moment is out of fashion the next. As one of the reviewers of the film says, not without appreciation, "It's genuinely exciting to find a film that reminds you of the pleasures of disposable trash."[9]

But *Clueless* actually performs a complex maneuver whereby the cliché of LA as postmodern city supreme, city without memory, surface pastiche, a giant shopping mall, is simultaneously invoked and undercut. Before settling too easily for the slightly superior sense of satisfaction that always attends satire, let us note that Cher's short-term memory actually takes her a long way—Mel Gibson is a mnemonic with legs, taking us back not just to one prior text, but through a circuit or network of signifiers. The teen movie might be very modern (coming into prominence in the 80s), but it has a prehistory, both in the movies and in other forms, such as the novel. *Clueless* not only remakes and comments on *Emma,* but remakes the teen movies that preceded it and also the twentieth-century apparatus of modernity that provides the preconditions of the genre—not just Hollywood, but, most spectacularly, the proliferation of popular consumer culture, manifested particularly in the music and television industries. Another way of saying this is that the film is alert to and permeated by the myriad influences that shape the very experience and notion of contemporaneity.

What Did You Do in the War, Daddy?
"I Broke in My Purple Clogs"

There are three aspects to *Clueless* as teen movie that I want to note here: first, it belongs to a subgenre of girls' movies; second, it belongs to a strand that inflects the genre toward clean-cut and utopian comedy; and third, it strongly exploits a tendency that combines an ethnographic impulse with a highly rhetorical narrative modality. These three aspects are of course all interrelated, but I shall try, for purposes of exposition, to tease them apart.

Clueless has a fine lineage; it belongs not only to a group of films that feature girls coming of age, but more specifically to a group of such films set in LA: *Valley Girl, Earth Girls Are Easy,* and *Buffy the Vampire Slayer.* Almost all these films involve the conceit of a bimbo or ditz with a credit card who turns out to be (or turns into via various trials and tribulations) a sassy, smart-talking, inventive young woman who takes control of her destiny through the conquering of space and time (the space of LA and the time of antiquated values, particularly as regards gender). The conquering of time entails a utopian rather than nostalgic and dystopic vision, and the conquering of space (and this is where LA becomes a crucial location) involves taking control of the freeways and of that cinematically revered masculine object, the car. In the mall it is OK to sit and stroll, and at school of course you have to walk a little. When someone asks Cher, "What did you do at school today?" she indicates a day well spent: "I broke in my purple clogs." She is at once dead serious and in on the joke. The conceit of the smart bimbo is of course a staple of Hollywood comedy going back to the 30s at least; but the incarnation of this figure as a Los Angeles bat-out-of-hell is more recent and in many respects is conceivable only as a remaking of modern classics such as *American Graffiti.*

Cher and Dionne do not love their cars in the way that Paul Newman in *Hud,* say, loved his pink Cadillac; they love driving and the control that driving promises. The big joke here is that in fact they are not able to drive; they are learning, and none too successfully, but to great comic effect. Interestingly, in transforming *Emma* into *Clueless* the conversion of carriages to cars and the replacement of endless walking by continuous driving both indicates a very neat series of substitutions and also suggests that the process of updating does more than simply find contemporary signifiers for old-fashioned modes of communication. The process actually effects certain transformations, so we get a sense of what it is like to be young and female today. Where *Clueless* differs not only from *Emma* but from the boys-and-cars-and-sex genre of movies is that it links the car not primarily with sex (or women), but with fashion. There is no simple inversion here; for these girls the car is not a substitute for a man, but rather a means of autonomy and a link in the great chain of fashion. For many women I have talked to about this movie, one of the most exhilarating and hilarious moments is when Cher is driving in platforms; it is an emblematic and enduring moment in the feminization of the movies and the feminization of the movie image of Los Angeles. The first great trauma of Cher's life is her failure of her driving test—and what distresses her so much is not that she does not pass, but that she cannot talk her way out of it: "I felt impotent and out of control, which I really hate. I needed to find sanctuary in a place where I could gather my thoughts and regain my strength"—and where do we find her, but in the mall.

Shopping and driving go together like a horse and carriage. This is Cher's response to her father's injunction that she can only go out with a licensed driver: "A licensed driver with nothing to do? Where would I find such a loser?" It does not take her long, however, to locate Josh by the pool. "Daddy says I can't take the Jeep out without a licensed driver, and since you're not doing anything and all, you know?" Josh is in fact reading Nietzsche—although this is read by Cher as doing nothing. It is not that Cher does not read; the joke here has to do with the clichéd reading of boys and girls. Christian reads William Burroughs's *Junky* (remember, he is from the East Coast), and Cher and Tai (as part of their makeover program for improving their minds as well as their bodies) read *Fit or Fat?* and *Men Are from Mars, Women Are from Venus*. This is more than Emma manages: "Her views of improving her little friend's mind by a great deal of useful reading and conversation had never yet led to more than a few first chapters and the intention of going on tomorrow" (p. 79). When necessary, however, Cher can play hidden cards, revealing her knowledge of the classics: "It's like that book I read in ninth grade that said, ''tis a far, far better thing doing stuff for other people."

The reason we take such delight in all the driving and fashion and shopping jokes is because of the payoff when the bimbo bounces back, when the space cadet suddenly does a Katherine Hepburn or Rosalind Russell. For instance, when Josh, finding Cher uncharacteristically at home, says, "Hey, who's watching the Galleria?" Cher quips straight back: "So, the flannel shirt deal. Is that a nod to the crispy Seattle weather, or are you just trying to stay warm in front of the refrigerator?"

Who's Minding the Galleria?

Much of the humor of *Clueless* is played out on and around fashion. But the humor is not at the expense of style. Certainly the moral precept of *Emma* is narratively played out in *Clueless;* matchmaking as the central plotting device is also a mechanism for the moral improvement of the heroine. Cher learns that the Beverly Center is not the center of the world, and that there are people less fortunate than herself, through doing good work for Pismo Beach Relief. But she does not give up on style. And although she is made fun of, there is a degree to which, as already indicated, she is in on the joke. In terms of the feminizing of the genre and of the image of LA, this can best be understood through the makeover motif. In terms of the movie as remake, this is a particularly bold and, as it turns out, fairly intricate move.

On one level Cher's adoption and makeover of Tai faithfully follows Emma's adoption and makeover of Harriet, but in terms of Hollywood the model is more complicated. The Svengali story is of course not exclusive to Hollywood, but it has prospered there: *Gigi, My Fair Lady,* and *Pretty Woman,* to mention just a few films, have all gotten a lot of mileage out of the trope of the ugly duckling (read lower-class woman) turned into a swan.[10] Almost by definition, the Svengali figure is male; this is because the narrative is concerned with feminization, with educating a woman to take up her proper womanly place. Cher Horovitz is the first woman I can think of who occupies this position. What is remarkable about this is not that it is a first for women—like the first woman engineer, say—but that structurally a simple inversion is impossible. Cher gets her comeuppance much more severely than the slimy Gaston or Professor Henry Higgins or the horrible Richard Gere (who all emerge triumphant in their projects), but it is not at the expense of women, nor at the expense of fashion. *Clueless* is every bit as stylish as the other films, and the somewhat more outlandish fashions are infinitely more integrated into the wild mise-en-scène. This emphasis on fashion certainly comes from Hollywood, but the feminist twist comes from Jane Austen. Heckerling, however, updates the incidental details in interesting ways.

Where Harriet tends to be in awe of Emma, Tai goes along with the project because of the absolute novelty of having straight (read rich Californian) friends. Harriet never turns against her patroness, but Tai's fight with Cher is in fact anticipated in the novel. After the announcement of Emma and Mr. Knightley's romance, the two women communicate only by letter: "Harriet expressed herself very much, as might be supposed, without reproaches or apparent sense of ill usage; and yet Emma fancied there was a something of resentment, a something bordering on it in her style, which increased the desirableness of their being separate. It might be only her own consciousness, but it seemed as if an angel only could have been quite without resentment under such a stroke" (p. 385).

Tai, however, is no angel. She turns on Cher the harshest insult one can imagine being turned on a Beverly Hills mall princess: "You're a virgin who can't drive!" This outburst provides a narrative opportunity for a sisterly reconciliation later, for developing the scenario of female friendship further than Jane Austen was able to—and in much more spicy terms than those provided by many "sisterhood" films (such as *Steel Magnolias*): "I'm the tart here," "I've been in a spiral of remorse," and so on.

"You're a Virgin Who Can't Drive!"

Tom Doherty, in an intelligent review entitled "Clueless Kids," describes a new type of teen pic characterized by "loopy humor and chaste decorum" (as opposed to *Porky's* and *Fast Times at Ridgemont High*). *Clueless*, he claims, "fits the model like a spandex gym suit."[11] Now it might be true that there is not much explicit and old-fashioned actual sex in *Clueless*, but to describe the film as chaste seems to me to be quite wrong. It is all about sex. But perhaps to understand the modality of this apparently clean-cut and utopian comedy I need to address, simultaneously, its tendency to combine an ethnographic impulse with a highly rhetorical narrative modality.

Jane Austen identifies at least two habits pertaining to the youth of her day, in a sense providing the preconditions for the fiction—flirting and dancing:

> It may be possible to do without dancing entirely. Instances have been known of young people passing many, many months successively without being at any ball of any description, and no material injury accrue either to body or mind; but when a beginning is made—when the felicities of rapid motion have once been, though slightly, felt—it must be a very heavy set that does not ask for more. (p. 221)

And later:

> In the judgment of most people looking on it must have had such an appearance as no English word but flirtation could very well describe. "Mr. Frank Churchill and Miss Woodhouse flirted together excessively." They were laying themselves open to that very phrase—and to having it sent off in a letter to Maple Grove by one lady, to Ireland by another. (p. 318)

Clueless, too, presents a subculture in which dancing and flirting figure as major pleasures and preoccupations. Cher is saving herself for Luke Perry—the star, incidentally, of *Beverly Hills 90210* and *Buffy the Vampire Slayer*. However, when Christian (a James Dean look-alike) appears, she changes her mind and sets out to snare him. Much flirting ensues, facilitated by Cher's failing to register the signs of Christian's gayness (even though he has a thing about Tony Curtis and Billie Holiday). Although of course Jane Austen does not have an explicitly gay figure in *Emma*, we can read her symptomatically:

> Emma's very good opinion of Frank Churchill was a little shaken the following day, by hearing that he was gone off to London, merely to have his hair cut. A sudden freak seemed to have seized him at breakfast, and he had sent for a chaise and set off, intending to return to dinner, but with no more important view that appeared than having his hair cut. There was certainly no harm in his travelling sixteen miles twice over on such an errand; but there was an air of foppery and nonsense in it which she could not approve. (p. 188)

And later:

> He came back, had his hair cut, and laughed at himself with a very good grace, but without seeming really at all ashamed of what he had done. He had no reason to wish his hair longer, to conceal any confusion of face; no reason to wish the money unspent, to improve his spirits. He was quite as undaunted and as lively as ever. (p. 194)

Just as Emma's infatuation with Frank Churchill evolves into friendship, so Cher comes to recognize Christian's virtues as a playmate; and in each case the deferral of conventional heterosexual sex serves the narrative well in generating lots of talk *about* sex. Heckerling's script plunders youth culture, but also invents an ingenious new language (which is presented in guides on MTV, the Internet, and so on), much of which serves to spin a complicated web of proliferating intrigue around sex. In this movie actual depictions of sex are sparse and allusive; talk about sex, however, is abundant and intriguing. It is a very talkative movie. We might say that this has partly to do with its timing as a teen movie in the era of AIDS, but the rhythm and timing of dialogue delivery, the repartee, the complex and shifting mode of address, and the interweaving of different registers of address are all inspired by Jane Austen.[12]

"Wow! You Guys Talk Like Grown-ups."

Let us return to the beginning. The first words of the movie address the audience directly as "You," and this assumed intimacy is elaborated via a series of shared insights and revelations about Cher's world. But the tone is not invariably intimate; sometimes the voice-over assumes a much more omniscient tone, and sometimes the mode of direct address actually serves to invoke not intimacy, but distance—such as when Cher tries to give her viewers advice: "Anything you can do to draw attention to your mouth is good. Also, sometimes you have to show a little skin. This reminds guys of you naked, and then they think of sex." This is just after Christian has appeared on the scene, when she is trying to get him, but because the signs of Christian's gayness have been ostentatiously elaborated for the audience, this address serves to rebound on the narrator, underlining her cluelessness about sex.

These fluctuations in tone and person, between narration and drama, between direct and indirect speech, are echoed in the fluctuations in register of speech that are prone to occur within dramatized exchanges as in the juxtapositions "buyer's remorse" and "brutally rebuffed":

> DIONNE: Dude, what's wrong? Are you suffering from buyer's remorse or something?
>
> CHER: God, no! Nothing like that. It's just that, we've been shopping all day and I still don't know what to do about Mr. Hall. I have tried everything to convince him of my scholastic aptitude, but I was brutally rebuffed.

This kind of rhetorical playfulness is surely derived from *Emma*, in which the narrative voice shifts between that of Jane Austen's persona and Emma's subjective voice, the latter often guiding the novel even though it is in the third person. Thus even though it is, in both the novel and film, a very circumscribed, parochial, and remarkably homogeneous world that is being depicted, it is sketched out in a highly rhetorical manner and through a heterogeneous variety of discursive means that allow space for satiric reflection.

Rhetorical felicity and delight in verbal play are not restricted to the narrative or the narrator. The characters themselves evidence a wry knowingness about the various discursive registers that define and shape their world: discourses, for instance, about California, teenagers, black language. When Dionne asks her boyfriend Murray not to call her woman, he responds: "OK, but street slang is an increasingly valid form of expression. Most of the feminine pronouns do have mocking overtones, but not necessarily in a misogynistic undertone." Which elicits from Tai an awed "Wow! You guys talk like grown-ups."

If *Clueless* can be considered a remake of *Emma* and, in the process, a remaking of Los Angeles, it is surely the rhetorical felicity of the movie and its delight in playing both with images and words that is most persuasive. In concluding I am tempted to let the film and the book speak for themselves by juxtaposing a few passages. In the novel Emma senses and is mortified by Mr. Knightley's disapproval of her rudeness toward Miss Bates at the picnic:

While they talked, they were advancing towards the carriage. It was ready; and, before she could speak again, he had handed her in. He had misinterpreted the feelings which had kept her face averted, and her tongue motionless. They were combined only of anger against herself, mortification, and deep concern. (p. 325)

In the film this is rendered as Josh's disapproval of Cher's rudeness to the maid:

> I had an overwhelming sense of ickyness. Even though I apologized to Lucy, something was still plaguing me. Like Josh thinking I was mean was making me postal.

But it is the "revelation" scene, the discovery of true love, that is the pièce de résistance of *Clueless*. The moment when Cher discovers her true self is also the moment when the nineteenth-century comedy of manners set in an English village is most succinctly translated into a twentieth-century teen pic set in LA. In the novel it is Harriet's confession of her love for Mr. Knightley and her belief that her feelings are returned that sets Emma off:

> Emma's eyes were instantly withdrawn; and she sat silently meditating, in a fixed attitude, for a few minutes. A few minutes were sufficient for making her acquainted with her own heart. A mind like hers, once opening to suspicion, made rapid progress; she touched, she admitted, she acknowledged, the whole truth. Why was it so much worse that Harriet should be in love with Mr. Knightley, than with Frank Churchill? Why was the evil so dreadfully increased by Harriet's having some hope of a return? It darted through her, with the speed of an arrow, that Mr. Knightley must marry no one but herself! (pp. 350–51)

Restlessly she paces, moving from her own room to the shrubbery where she reflects:

> With insufferable vanity had she believed herself in the secret of everybody's feelings; with unpardonable arrogance proposed to arrange everybody's destiny. She was proved to have been universally mistaken; and she had not quite done nothing—for she had done mischief. (p. 355)

Following Tai's confession, Cher goes flaneusing in Rodeo Drive. We see her wandering past the luxury shops while in voice-over (functioning here as a kind of inner speech) she says:

> Everything I think and everything I do is wrong. I was wrong about Elton, I was wrong about Christian, and now Josh hated me. It all boiled down to one inevitable conclusion, I was just totally clueless. Oh, and this Josh and Tai thing was wigging me more than anything. I mean, what was my problem? Tai is my pal, I don't begrudge her a boyfriend, I really . . . . Ooh, I wonder if they have that in my size. What does she

want with Josh, anyway? He dresses funny, he listens to complaint rock, he's not even cute . . . in a conventional way. I mean, he's just like this slug who hangs around the house all the time. And he's a hideous dancer, I couldn't take him anywhere. Wait a second, what am I stressing about? This is like, Josh! OK, OK, so he's kind of a Baldwin, but what would he want with Tai? She couldn't make him happy. Josh needed someone with imagination, someone to take care of him, someone to laugh at his jokes . . . in case he ever makes any. Then suddenly . . .

In direct speech Cher interrupts her own inner thoughts:

Oh, my God. I love Josh!

And in voice-over again:

I am majorly, totally, butt-crazy in love with Josh.

It is true, as Jocelyn Harris writes, "In an age when the visual is said to have superseded the verbal, the movie *Clueless* provides extraordinary pleasures to people who still read books."[13] But it is also true that *Clueless* is a movie about movies, about the place where movies and dreams are manufactured, and about what it is like to be young and female in today's multimedia world.

NOTES

1. Cher does not drink coffee because it might stunt her growth and she says, "I wanna be five-foot ten like Cindy Crawford." She exercises to Cindy Crawford's videos, *Aerobicise* and *Buns of Steel.*

2. Gemma Connolly drew this fact to my attention. My thanks to both her and Nicholas During—wise and entertaining informants. Jodi Brooks also gave me some invaluable references.

3. Jane Austen, *Emma*, intro. by Margaret Drabble (New York: Penguin Books [Signet Classic], 1996), p. 27. Hereafter page references will be given in the body of the text.

4. Edward Said, *Culture and Imperialism* (New York: Random House, 1993).

5. This tendency is perhaps epitomized in Emma's reflections on the view from Boxhill: "It was a sweet view—sweet to the eye and the mind. English verdure, English culture, English comfort, seen under a sun bright, without being oppressive" (p. 312).

6. See, for instance, Amanda Lipman's review of *Clueless, Sight and Sound* 5:10 (October 1995), p. 46.

7. Ibid.

8. Thomas Leitch, "Twice-Told Tales: The Rhetoric of the Remake," *Literature/Film Quarterly* 18:3, pp. 138–49.

9. Jonathan Romney, *New Statesman and Society* (20 October 1995), p. 35.

10. There is an explicit reference to *Gigi* when Cher, on her first date with Christian and watched by Josh, makes an entry descending the stairs in her little white Calvin Klein dress. The scene is "accompanied by the music from *Gigi,* from the scene in which Gaston suddenly realizes that Gigi is no longer a gawky girl but a beautiful young woman to whom he is much attracted." I picked up this allusion from Karen P in "Some Reactions from Janeites: *Clueless* and Jane Austen's *Emma,*" at the web site URL:http://uts.cc.utexas.edu/~churchh/clueless.html, 16 August 1996.

11. Tom Doherty, "Clueless Kids," *Cineaste* 21:4 (1995), p. 14.

12. According to a statistical analysis, Emma Woodhouse talks more than any other character (42,800 words); Fanny Price is the next most vocal, but she speaks less than half as much as Emma. See Eric Johnson, "How Jane Austen's Characters Talk," *TEXT Technology* 4:4 (Winter 1994), pp. 263–67. A version of this article has been reproduced on the Internet.

13. Jocelyn Harris, a review of three Austen adaptations, *Eighteenth Century Fiction* 8:3 (April 1996), p. 430.

Annotated Bibliography

This bibliography is highly selective and is limited almost exclusively to books or essays about film and prose fiction. A few entries on film and theater are also included. For important items having to do with narrative theory and other related issues, see the notes to the individual chapters collected in the anthology.

Astruc, Alexandre. "The Birth of the New Avant-Garde: La Camera-Stylo," in *The New Wave*, ed. Peter Graham (London: Secker and Warburg, 1968), pp. 17–23.
> A 1948 essay that was greatly admired by members of the French New Wave, written by a talented novelist and film director who compared film with language, the camera with a writing instrument, and the director with an author.

Bazin, André. *What Is Cinema?*, ed. and trans. Hugh Gray. Berkeley: University of California Press, 1967.
> The distinguished editor of *Les Cahiers du Cinéma*, Bazin is generally acknowledged to have been one of the world's most influential theorists of film. Several of his essays in the American edition of *What Is Cinema?* are important to the study of adaptation, especially "In Defense of Mixed Cinema," "Theater and Cinema," "*Le Journal d'un Curé de Campagne* and the Stylistics of Robert Bresson," and "Painting and Cinema."

Beja, Morris. *Film and Literature*. New York: Longman, 1979.
> A university textbook on film adaptation centered on adaptations of canonical novels.

Bluestone, George. *Novels into Film: The Metamorphosis of Fiction into Cinema*. Baltimore: Johns Hopkins University Press, 1957.
> The first full-scale academic analysis of film adaptation in American cinema.

Boose, Lynda E., and Richard Burt, eds. *Shakespeare, The Movie: Popularizing the Plays on Film, TV, and Video*. New York: Routledge, 1997.
> An anthology of essays on Shakespeare in the modern and postmodern media.

Braudy, Leo. "Zola on Film: The Ambiguities of Naturalism," in *Native Informant: Essays on Film, Fiction, and Popular Culture*. New York: Oxford University Press, 1991, pp. 95–106.

As of 1969, when this essay was written, sixty or more films had been based on the work of novelist Emile Zola. In a brief, subtle discussion, Braudy argues that these movies are not only important to the history of film, but also "a key to its essential epistemological and aesthetic nature."

Burgess, Anthony. "Signs on Paper," in *Joysprik: An Introduction to the Language of James Joyce.* London: Andre Deutsch Limited, 1973, pp. 13–26.

Burgess makes an interesting contrast with Cohen and Spiegel, two writers on literary modernism who are listed elsewhere in this bibliography. He begins by rewriting the first chapter of *Ulysses* in the form of mainstream realist fiction (or in what he calls "the manner of one of the American Irvings, say: Stone or Wallace"). He argues that such work, which constitutes most of the "drugstore bestsellers," is "closer to film than to poetry, and it invariably films better than it reads." Indeed it can only be properly fulfilled "when the narrated action is transformed into represented action: content being more important than style, the referents ache to be free of their words and to be presented directly as sense-data."

Cartmell, Deborah, and Imelda Whelehan, eds. *Adaptations: From Text to Screen, Screen to Text.* New York: Routledge, 1999.

An intelligent anthology of writings about the transformation of written texts into movies and vice versa. Contains several essays on contemporary Hollywood.

Chatman, Seymour. "What Novels Can Do That Film Can't (and Vice Versa)," in *On Narrative*, ed. W. T. J. Mitchell. Chicago: University of Chicago Press, 1980, pp. 117–36. Originally published in *Critical Inquiry* 7:1 (Autumn 1980), pp. 121–40.

Argues that "narrative is a deep structure independent of its medium." Compares Jean Renoir's *A Day in the Country* with its source, a story by Guy de Maupassant.

———. *Coming to Terms: The Rhetoric of Narrative in Fiction and Film.* Ithaca: Cornell University Press, 1990.

An elaboration of Chatman's theories of narratology, with detailed arguments about how description and narration function in film versus prose fiction.

Cohen, Keith. *Film and Fiction: The Dynamics of Exchange.* New Haven: Yale University Press, 1979.

Emphasizes a "convergence" between film and the modern novel on the grounds of "showing" rather than "telling." Argues that writers such as Proust and Woolf employ the techniques of montage.

Corrigan, Timothy. *Film and Literature: An Introduction and Reader.* Upper Saddle River, N. J.: Prentice Hall, 1999.

A useful and intelligent textbook for undergraduates, containing an historical overview of the industry, a commentary on narrative strategies, and an anthology of writings on film adaptations. Has a good bibliography.

Durgnat, Raymond. "The Mongrel Muse," in *Films and Feelings.* London, Faber and Faber, 1967, pp. 19–30.

An early and still-important essay on the mixed or "mongrel" nature of cinema, especially good in its attack on Anglo-American literary attitudes.

Eisenstein, Sergi. "Dickens, Griffith, and the Film Today," in *Film Form*, trans. Jay Leyda. New York: Harcourt, Brace and World, 1949, pp. 195–255.
The standard English translation of one of the most influential essays ever written about film and literature.

———. "Literature and Cinema: Reply to a Questionnaire (1928)," and "Cinema and the Classics (1933)," in *Eisenstein: Writings, 1922–1934*, ed. and trans. Richard Taylor. London and Bloomington: BFI Publishing and Indiana University Press, 1988, pp. 95–99, 276.
Eisenstein argues that "work on the classics must not be organized along the lines of superficial borrowing but as a matter of studying all the elements that constitute their specificity. We must interpret their signs and observe how a particular element should develop into a new one, passing through different stages in time and class."

Ellis, John. "The Literary Adaptation: An Introduction," *Screen* 23:1 (May–June 1982), pp. 3–5.
Offers a brief theoretical discussion of the "compulsion to repeat."

Fell, John. *Film and the Narrative Tradition*. Norman: University of Oklahoma Press, 1974.
An intelligent discussion of film in relation to nineteenth-century narrative.

Geduld, Harry M., ed. *Authors on Film*. Bloomington: Indiana University Press, 1972.
An interesting compilation of writings on film by famous literary figures.

Goodwin, James. "Literature and Film: A Review of Criticism." *Quarterly Review of Film Studies* 6:2 (Spring 1979), pp. 227–46.
A survey and summary of important issues.

Hamilton, Ian. *Writers in Hollywood, 1915–1951*. New York: Carroll and Graf, 1991.
A readable if somewhat breezy account of celebrated authors who worked in classic Hollywood.

Henderson, Brian. "Tense, Mood, and Voice in Film (Notes after Genette)," *Film Quarterly* 36:4 (Summer 1983), pp. 4–17.
An application of narrative theorist Gérard Genette's ideas about prose fiction to the medium of film.

Jorgens, Jack. *Shakespeare and Film*. Bloomington: Indiana University Press, 1977.
One of the best of many books about Shakespeare adaptations in film.

Kawin, Bruce. *Faulkner and Film*. New York: Unger, 1977.
Contains intelligent observations about Faulkner as both novelist and screenwriter.

Klein, Michael, and Gillian Parker, eds. *The English Novel and the Movies*. New York: Ungar, 1981.
A large anthology of essays about film adaptations of canonical British literature.

Literature/Film Quarterly. 1979– .
> Since 1979 this journal has been published at Salisbury State College. It is one of the world's primary sources of academic writing about literary adaptation in film.

Marcus, Millicent. *Filmmaking by the Book: Italian Cinema and Literary Adaptation.* Baltimore: Johns Hopkins University Press, 1993.
> A theoretically informed and lucid discussion of adaptations by major Italian directors.

McFarlane, Brian. *Novel to Film: An Introduction to the Theory of Adaptation.* New York: Oxford, 1996.
> A neoformalist discussion of adaptation centered on complex analysis of six case studies from Hollywood and England. Displays McFarlane's high level of awareness of current theoretical debates over intertextuality and his knowledge about both film and literary history. Has a fine bibliography.

Morse, Margaret. "Paradoxes of Realism: The Rise of Film in the Train of the Novel." *Cine-Tracts* 13 (Spring 1981), pp. 27–37.
> An interesting discussion of Ian Watt's *The Rise of the Novel* in relation to film study.

Naremore, James. "Modernism and Blood Melodrama," in *More than Night: Film Noir in Its Contexts.* Berkeley: University of California Press, 1998, pp. 40–95.
> A discussion of the symbiotic but often conflicted relationship between literary high modernism and the movie industry in the 1940s, with particular emphasis on noir novels and films by Dashiell Hammett, Graham Greene, James M. Cain, and Raymond Chandler.

Orr, Christopher. "The Discourse on Adaptation." *Wide Angle* 6:2 (1984), pp. 72–76.
> A useful thematizing of adaptation study.

Peary, Gerald, and Roger Schatzkin, eds. *The Modern American Novel and the Movies.* New York: Ungar, 1978.
> A large anthology of writings about movies based on famous American novels.

Rentschler, Eric, ed. *German Film and Literature: Adaptations and Transformations.* New York: Methuen, 1986.
> A good collection of essays on German film adaptations.

Spiegel, Alan. *Fiction and the Camera Eye: Visual Consciousness in the Film and the Modern Novel.* Charlottesville: University of Virginia Press, 1976.
> An urbane and intelligent discussion of "camera-eye" techniques in high-modernist literature.

Tibbetts, John C., and James M. Welsh. *Encyclopedia of Novels into Film.* New York: Facts on File, Inc., 1998.
> A useful encyclopedic reference to more than 300 film adaptations from America and abroad. Discusses an impressive variety of movies. Has a good bibliography and historical appendixes.

Toles, George E., ed. *Film/Literature.* Winnipeg: University of Manitoba Press, 1983.

A fine anthology of writings on film and literature, edited by an important screenwriter-critic.

Truffaut, François. *Hitchcock*. New York: Simon and Schuster, 1983.
A revised edition of the famous Hitchcock-Truffaut interview, containing many interesting observations about the relations among film, prose fiction, and theater.

Vardac, A. Nicholas. *Stage to Screen: Theatrical Method from Garrick to Griffith*. Cambridge, Mass.: Harvard University Press, 1949.
An important book on theater history describing Griffith's indebtedness to the nineteenth-century stage.

Welch, Geoffrey Eagan. *Literature and Film: An Annotated Bibliography, 1909–1977*. London: Garland, 1981.
A useful listing of early writings on the topic.

Contributors

MICHAEL ANDEREGG is Professor of English at the University of North Dakota. He is the editor of *Inventing Vietnam: The War in Film and Television* and the author of *David Lean, William Wyler*, and *Orson Welles, Shakespeare, and Popular Culture.*

DUDLEY ANDREW is the Angelo Bertocci Professor of Critical Studies at the University of Iowa, where he directs the Institute for Cinema and Culture. He has published several books on film theory and French cinema, including *Mists of Regret: Culture and Sensibility in Classic French Film.* He is currently writing on world cinema issues.

ANDRÉ BAZIN was the editor of *Cahiers du Cinéma* during its most influential period. His more than sixty essays collected in *Qu'est-ce-que le Cinéma?* are among the most important theoretical statements in the history of the medium.

MATTHEW BERNSTEIN is Associate Professor of Film Studies at Emory University and the author of *Walter Wanger, Hollywood Independent.* He is the editor of *Controlling Hollywood: Censorship and Regulation in the Studio Era* and the coeditor (with Gaylyn Studlar) of *Visions of the East: Orientalism in Film.*

GUERRIC DEBONA is a Benedictine monk of Saint Meinrad Archabbey. A Ph.D. in English, he teaches homiletics and communication at Saint Meinrad School of Theology. He has published an essay in *Cinema Journal* on Orson Welles's screenplay for *Heart of Darkness* and is currently writing a book about Hollywood adaptations of canonical novels.

RICHARD MALTBY is Professor of Screen Studies and head of the School of Humanities at Flinders University, South Australia. He is the author of *Harmless Entertainment: Hollywood and the Ideology of Consensus, Dreams for Sale: Popular Culture in the Twentieth Century,* and *Hollywood Cinema: An Introduction.* With Melvyn Stokes, he has edited *American Movie Audiences from the Turn of the Century to the Early Sound Era* and *Identifying Hollywood's Audiences: Cultural Identity and the Movies.*

JAMES NAREMORE is Chancellors' Professor of Communication and Culture and English at Indiana University. He is the author of several books on modern literature and film, including, most recently, *More than Night: Film Noir in Its Contexts.*

GILBERTO PEREZ is Professor of Film Studies at Sarah Lawrence College and film critic for *The Yale Review*. His essays have appeared in *Artforum, The Nation, Raritan,* and *Sight and Sound.* He is the author of *The Material Ghost: Films and Their Medium.*

ROBERT B. RAY is Professor of English and Director of Film Studies at the University of Florida. He is the author of *A Certain Tendency of the Hollywood Cinema: 1930–1980* and of *The Avant-Garde Finds Andy Hardy.* He is currently working on a theoretical book about a series of classic American films.

JONATHAN ROSENBAUM is the film critic for the *Chicago Reader.* His writings appear regularly in such journals as *Film Comment, Film Quarterly,* and *Trafic.* A former Guggenheim Fellow, he is the author of several books on film, including *Moving Places, Placing Movies,* and *Movies as Politics.*

DARLENE J. SADLIER is Professor and Chair of the Department of Spanish and Portuguese at Indiana University. Her books include *The Question of How: Women Writers and New Portuguese Literature* and *An Introduction to Fernando Pessoa: Modernism and the Paradoxes of Authorship.* She is also the editor and translator of *One Hundred Years after Tomorrow,* a collection of fiction by Brazilian women authors. Currently she is writing a book about Brazilian film adaptations of literature.

ROBERT STAM is Professor of Cinema Studies at New York University. He is the author of several books on cinema and culture, including *Reflexivity in Film and Literature: From Don Quixote to Jean-Luc Godard, Subversive Pleasures: Bakhtin, Cultural Criticim and Film,* and (with Ella Shohat) *Unthinking Ethnocentrism: Multiculturalism and the Media.* His most recent book is *Film Theory: An Introduction.*

LESLEY STERN teaches in the School of Theatre, Film and Dance at the University of New South Wales, Sydney. She is the author of *The Scorsese Connection* and *The Smoking Book.* She is also the coeditor of *Falling for You: Essays in Cinema and Performance.*

Index

Dickens, Charles (*continued*)
106–28; *Dombey and Son*, 108;
Oliver Twist, 4, 70; *Tale of Two
Cities, A*, 107, 109, 113
"Dickens, Griffith, and the Film
Today" (Eisenstein), 108
Dieterle, William, 156
digests, 19–27
Dinner at Eight (1933), 120
Discipline of DE (1978), 218
discourse of fidelity, 48
Disprezzo, Il (Moravia), 62
Doherty, Tom, 233
Dolce Vita, La (1960), 38
Dombey and Son (Dickens), 108
Donaldson, Peter S., 164, 165, 169
Don Quixote (Cervantes), 11, 30
Dorrance, Ethel Smith, 85, 102n
Dos Passos, John, 4, 5
Dostoyevsky, Fyodor, 178; *Brothers
Karamazov, The*, 25; *Crime and
Punishment*, 7; *Idiot, The*, 21, 22, 25;
Notes from the Underground, 56
Dovzhenko, Aleksandr, 150–1
Down There (Goodis), 173
Dr. Strangelove (1964), 60
Dragnet (television program), 174
Dramatists' Guild, 89
Dreiser, Theodore, 79, 88–92, 93, 95,
99, 100, 102n, 103n, 104n, 112; *see
also American Tragedy, An*
Dressler, Marie, 120
Dubbers, 61, 62
Duhamel, Georges, 27n
Dumas, Alexandre, 35
DuMaurier, Daphne, 7, 12, 80
Duras, Marguerite, 75
Duvivier, Julien, 66
Dyer, Frank, 112

Earth (1930), 150–1
Earth Girls Are Easy (1989), 230
Eckert, Charles, 121
Edinburgh Festival, 154
Effi Brest (1974), 12
Eikhenbaum, Boris, 48–9, 52n
Eisenstein, Sergei, 5, 44, 74, 88, 93,
108, 114, 115, 119, 137
Eliot, T. S., 2, 38, 45
Ellroy, James, 10
Elmer Gantry (Lewis), 83
embourgeoisement, 43, 51n
Emma (Austen), 65, 221, 222–3,

225–8, 229, 230–1, 232–4, 235–6,
237n, 238n
Empire of the Sun (1987), 219
Empson, William, 147
Eraserhead (1978), 214, 219
esoterism, 22
essence, 58–62
Estabrook, Howard, 111
evaluative authority, 80
"Exterminator!" (Burroughs), 216, 217

Farrow, Mia, 69
Fassbinder, Rainer Werner, 12
Fast Times at Ridgemont High (1982),
233
Faulkner, William, 4, 5, 86
Fauré, Elie, 62
Fechter, Charles, 164
Feldman, Charles K., 168
Fellini, Federico, 38, 168
Femme et le Pantin, La (Loüys), 66
F for Fake (1973), 154
fidelity, 8–9, 11–12, 28, 29, 31–2, 64;
censorship and, 80; chimera of,
54–8; discourse of, 48
Fielding, Henry, 67–8, 74
Fields, W. C., 119, 123
*Film and Fiction, The Dynamics of
Exchange* (Cohen), 33–4
Film Art (Bordwell and Thompson), 3
Film Daily's Ten Best, 110
filmic mode, 157–8
Films of Akira Kurosawa, The
(Richie), 173
Fine, Richard, 89
Finnegans Wake (Joyce), 8
Finney, Albert, 68
Fitzgerald, F. Scott, 4
Flaming Youth (1923), 85
Flaubert, Gustave, 5, 14, 23, 40, 55,
71, 74–5; *see also Madame Bovary*
Fly, The (1986), 214
focalization, 72
Forbidden Christ (1950), 26–7n
Ford, John, 5, 7, 20, 55–6, 71, 73, 190
Forester, C. S., 11
form, 20, 22–3, 25
Forman, Milos, 207
Formula, The, 85, 87, 94
Forster, E. M., 11, 13
Forsyth, Bill, 206–11
For Whom the Bell Tolls (1943), 21
Foucault, Michel, 58, 116